T0360533

The World of
Negotiation
Theories, Perceptions and Practice

The World of
Negotiation
Theories, Perceptions and Practice

Amira Galin
Tel Aviv University, Israel

World Scientific

NEW JERSEY · LONDON · SINGAPORE · BEIJING · SHANGHAI · HONG KONG · TAIPEI · CHENNAI · TOKYO

Published by

World Scientific Publishing Co. Pte. Ltd.

5 Toh Tuck Link, Singapore 596224

USA office: 27 Warren Street, Suite 401-402, Hackensack, NJ 07601

UK office: 57 Shelton Street, Covent Garden, London WC2H 9HE

Library of Congress Cataloging-in-Publication Data
Galin, Amira.
  The world of negotiation : theories, perceptions and practice / Amira Galin (Tel Aviv University, Israel).
    pages cm
  ISBN 978-9814619325
  1. Negotiation in business. 2. Negotiation. I. Title.
  HD58.6.G355 2015
  302.3--dc23
                            2015017667

British Library Cataloguing-in-Publication Data
A catalogue record for this book is available from the British Library.

ISBN 978-981-4740-67-8 (pbk)

Desk Editors: Dr. Sree Meenakshi Sajani/Philly Lim

Typeset by Stallion Press
Email: enquiries@stallionpress.com

Printed in Singapore

To my loved ones

Danny, Michal, Yoav, Guy and Maayan

Contents

Chapter 5: Negotiators' Interests and Objectives   85

Chapter 6: Common Power Sources and the Balance of Power   107

Preface

While negotiation, as a way of resolving conflicts is as old as human history, over the last several decades, especially where authority, obedience and the urge to fight have declined, the search for alternative ways to manage and resolve conflicts and disputes has become essential. Workers and managers, students and university authorities, businessmen and their suppliers, minority groups and governments, and even rival groups and nations have gradually chosen to confront their conflicts through negotiation. Negotiation is perceived by many as the ultimate way to solve conflicts, whereas by others it is perceived as only one of several alternatives with which to confront a conflict. Determining the best alternative in terms of conflict resolution, and whether or not the answer is negotiation, have become serious topics of discussion and study for both practitioners and researchers alike. The thirst for knowledge on negotiation has run high, as well as the expectation that negotiation is indeed the best way to confront and resolve conflicts. This probably explains why the number of research projects and teaching programs in the field of negotiation is constantly increasing.

Persistence in attempts to use negotiation, and the ongoing search for more appropriate forms of negotiation, raise a number of questions. For example, why, in spite of the hopes that negotiation will solve conflicts are there still doubts about its prospects? What lies behind the differences of opinion regarding the most desirable character and form of negotiation? Why do so many negotiations fail to fulfill disputants' expectations? And finally: Why and when is it reasonable to let others negotiate on the disputant's behalf? Such questions, as well as additional interesting questions have intrigued, occupied and, at times, disturbed me over the past years.

My interest in negotiation began with my first research study on Collective Bargaining. While conducting this study, I observed and analyzed over 100 collective bargaining processes at all negotiation levels (the firm, local, and national level). In addition, I interviewed numerous union and management negotiators. The findings of this study and the reactions of the negotiators fascinated me, opening a window to a new world — the world of negotiation. In a way, I felt somewhat like *Alice in Wonderland*. For the first time, I began to notice the delicate nuances of the negotiation process and the various factors that affect the negotiation outcome — whether it ended in an agreement or an impasse. I also observed many other complex features of negotiation, which I had not known existed. At that time, I understood that collective bargaining was only one window onto the whole wide world of negotiation. In order to satisfy my curiosity about this world I expanded my studies and observations, and began examining a wide range of negotiations, which still continues to intrigue me today. It is my greatest hope that I will be able to spark the interest of my readers and pass on to them my acquired body of knowledge in the pages of this book.

This book is a product of many years of intensive work in the fields of negotiation, mediation and judicial issues. These years were spent intensively researching, consulting and working as a negotiator, mediator and lay-judge at the Israeli National Labor Court. I also participated in many public and private committees and boards of directors; negotiations were an essential part of these activities. Apart from my practical, research, and academic experience I have also watched, and closely and carefully analyzed, many negotiations in which I did not directly participate. Some were successful and others less so; I tried to analyze why. I discovered that many negotiators tend to believe that intuition or what some call natural talent is the main cause for successful negotiations. As a result, they simply conclude that "studying negotiation is a waste of time" because "either you *have it* or you don't". Such beliefs, as I found out, explain why so many intuitive and "naturally gifted" negotiators end their negotiations in an impasse or experience rather poor outcomes. I also learned that these intuitive negotiators often conclude their negotiations with feelings, such as: "I could have achieved a much better deal" or "I just had bad luck". Such typical feelings often lead to frustrated and disappointed negotiators. Of course, intuition is effortless, and does not require much time in terms of preparation and analyzing the situation. In contrast, systematic analysis and inquiry are slower processes, which involve both efforts and knowledge. Without a systematic analysis, a negotiation impasse and feelings of failure are almost guaranteed.

Intuition and amateurism in negotiation is often disastrous. In the fields of finance and economics, negotiation failures could be critical for commercial companies, and could even lead to bankruptcy. In the diplomatic arena, negotiation deadlocks can bring about the discontinuation of diplomatic relationships and, in some cases, may even result in war. In the extreme example of a hostage crisis, the failure to negotiate well may mean death for the hostages. Even between loving couples, a negotiation breakdown might lead to a shaky relationship, and may even end in divorce. Obviously, sometimes *something* is simply missing during the negotiation process. This *something* is systematic knowledge and a thorough understanding of the negotiation process.

Studying negotiation has proved to yield striking results in the real world of negotiation. Deepak Malhotra, a Professor in the Negotiations, Organizations and Markets Unit at the Harvard Business School, reported on students' negotiation performance after studying negotiation. When negotiating something of value for themselves, students gained a total of one million dollars; in contrast, when negotiating on behalf of their employer, they gained 42 million dollars. Most of these gains were accredited to the knowledge and skills they acquired during their negotiation studies. An even more surprising finding of this study is that many of the students felt that the non-monetary benefits they gained as a result of their post-academic negotiation experience were more valuable than their monetary gains.[1] Therefore, it is essential that practicing negotiation should be based on knowledge and expertise, rather than some vague rule of thumb or intuition. Of course, good luck is always important and helpful as well.

Thus, readers of this book are presented with a systematic approach to all aspects of the negotiation process. They are exposed to the most crucial factors influencing negotiation outcomes, such as the impact of information, the influence of the global world, the utilization of power sources, and the various possible results of honesty and trust, as well as the impact of subjective perceptions. The book interweaves real-life negotiation scenarios from various fields, including: Industrial relations, political commerce, and day-to-day negotiation.

Many individuals have contributed to this book. Among them, I would like to especially thank Dr. Daniel Galin, Sharon Erez, Roberto Spindel, Philly Lim and Dr. Sree Meenakshi Sajani — without them the writing of this

---

[1] Malhotra, D.K. (2003), Approaching Negotiation as Art: Some Striking Results of Students Negotiating in the Real World, *SSRN Working Paper Series*, February, 2003.

book would not have been possible. Last but not least, I would like to thank all my colleagues and students who contributed to the book. Special thanks go to the many practitioners and managers among my colleagues and students, who further enriched my wide and diversified knowledge and experiences from the world of negotiation.

Amira Galin

"If you would work any man
you must either know his nature and fashions, and so lead him,
or his ends, and so persuade him,
or his weakness and disadvantages, and so awe him,
or those that have interest in him, and so govern him....
In all negotiations of difficulty
a man may not look to sow and reap at once,
but must prepare business,
And so ripen it by degrees".

Francis Bacon (1561–1626) — "Of Negotiating"

Introduction — About the Book's Content

Let me take you on a short tour through the world of negotiation by reading a book, which will give you a systematic understanding of a wide array of negotiation topics. **Potential readers of this book include**: Graduate and undergraduate students studying negotiation, along with other academic scholars with an interest in the field, or those who use negotiation in their profession, such as jurists, lawyers, physicians, diplomats and accountants. In addition, practitioners such as managers, sellers and buyers for large or small companies, along with senior-level executives, will certainly find this book useful. My aim is that this book will serve as a source of knowledge for students and scholars, and a general 'road map' for practitioners.

The book includes a total of 14 chapters; here is a chapter-by-chapter glimpse of their contents. It is noteworthy that each chapter ends with a Practical Applications section, based on the specific chapter's contents. The Practical Applications section provides readers with an opportunity to implement what they have learned from the chapter, and make better decisions in real negotiation situations. Please join me now for a short review of the book's chapters.

Part one: Conflict — Confrontations and Negotiation: Theories and Perceptions

Chapter 1 — Alternatives to Resolving Conflict

Sometimes the question is not *how* to negotiate, but *whether* to negotiate at all. It is of great importance to know when it is advisable NOT to negotiate. Chapter 1 presents negotiation as only one of several ways to confront a conflict, and not always the most effective way. There are various alternatives for settling a conflict, which are at times more effective than negotiation.

Even during the negotiation process, if one or all of the disputants realize that negotiation is not the most effective way to resolve their conflict, they can find other alternatives, such as coercing, deferring or opting out of the process entirely. Therefore, the first decision people should make when confronting their conflict is to examine all available alternatives. Choosing the best alternative is influenced by time and expected utility, among other considerations. In this chapter, readers can learn about the various main alternatives to confronting a conflict, and the kinds of considerations that are relevant to choosing the best alternative.

Chapter 2 — Main Negotiation Theories

Several theories can be used to explain the negotiation process and, at times, its consequences. The traditional outlook includes both *rational* and *behavioral* theories. Rational theories, for the most part, involve competitive and Win–Lose types of approaches. Behavioral theories are mainly comprised of cooperative (integrative), and Win–Win types of approaches. Finally, there are the *hybrid* theories of negotiation, which are a product of both rational and behavioral theories. Apparently, there is more to negotiation than simply Win–Win or Win–Lose approaches. Readers of this chapter will learn about the various theories describing the negotiation process, and may discover that the famous saying: "There is nothing more practical than a good theory" is entirely justifiable.

Chapter 3 — A Matter of Perception: Subjective Rationality and Its Effects

Some theories perceive some negotiation behaviors (as a result of emotional involvement, the similarity effect or the Endowment Effect, etc.) as biases or irrational negotiation behavior. However, these behaviors are not always irrational. At most, they are based on the *subjective rationality* embedded in the negotiators' perception of their interests and objectives — on the negotiators' perceptions of what is good for them. For example, the effects of similarities, and the Endowment Effect are not irrational. Yet, they often trigger typical negotiation behaviors, which have a great influence on negotiation processes and outcomes. Readers of this chapter will obtain insights into the differences between 'objective rationality' and 'subjective rationality', as well as the various causes and effects of subjective rationality on the negotiation process and outcome. Readers will gain particular insight into the effects of emotions, similarities and the Endowment Effect.

Part two: Becoming Acquainted with the Negotiation Process

Chapter 4 — Preparing for Negotiation

It is impossible to exaggerate the role and importance of preparing in advance for the negotiation process. Despite the fact that this process is both time-consuming and requires resource expenditure, it is an integral and essential part of negotiation, and not to be neglected. Readers will gain insight into the various activities of preparation, such as: Information gathering, and especially the difficulties related to analyzing the available data; decisions regarding face-to-face negotiation versus the use of emails instead of, and in addition to, face-to-face negotiations; initiating and obtaining support, including the support of other groups or lobbies; and e-negotiation support systems.

Chapter 5 — Negotiators' Interests and Objectives

The different parties' various interests obviously have a significant effect on the negotiation process and outcome, as do the often-diverse negotiation objectives. Readers will learn about the various types of interests, such as short- and long-term interests, practical and social interests, overt and covert interests and the interests of "unseen" parties. Readers may also receive some replies to frequently asked questions, regarding the impact of setting objectives during the negotiation. For example, how do highly ambitious negotiation objectives presented as initial proposals affect the negotiation and its outcomes? What is the difference between "intention point" and "resistance point"? Should negotiators be the first ones to put their objectives (initial proposals) on the negotiation "table"? What are the limitations of making the first move? And finally, what is the best way to manipulate the objectives in order to reach a better outcome?

Chapter 6 — Common Power Sources and the Balance of Power

Unfortunately, most negotiators are not aware of the many power sources available to them during the negotiation process. The use of power sources has the potential to influence the opponents, as well as change the negotiation's balance of power. In order to exercise power effectively, negotiators have to be familiar with their own various sources of power, as well as those of their opponents. In this chapter, readers will become familiar with various sources of power, and the ways in which to neutralize or reduce their opponents' power, thus shifting the negotiation's fundamental balance of power in their favor.

Chapter 7 — Choosing the Appropriate Strategies and Tactics

Strategies involve long-term planning and decisions aimed at achieving the most efficient negotiators' outcomes. *Tactics* are the means by which strategies are carried out through short-term actions aimed at achieving specific ends. The main strategies discussed in this chapter are classified into several general categories: Cooperative, competitive, disengagement, reciprocating, pretending and "beating around the bush" strategies.

The most common tactics can be divided into several categories: *Agenda tactics* (such as deciding about the order of the negotiation issues); *hard tactics* (such as threats, expressions of anger, ultimatums, and opting out); *soft tactics* (such as consulting the other party, concession-making gestures, and active listening); *time-related tactics* (such as time delays, time pressures and deadlines); *tension-relief tactics* (such as humor and small talk).

Problems regarding the use of each strategy and tactic, and their consequences, are presented in this chapter. Readers of this chapter will learn about the advantages and shortcomings of typical strategies and tactics, and about their possible results.

Chapter 8 — Negotiating a Hostage Crisis with a Terrorist Group

Negotiating a hostage crisis with a terrorist group is an extreme type of negotiation because it often means the life or death of the hostages. There is a critical dilemma about whether or not to negotiate with terrorists in the first place. Such a decision can be made within the framework of the best and the worst possible alternatives. If negotiation seems to be the best alternative, additional intelligence regarding the hostage-takers is of the highest importance and should be gathered before and during the negotiation. There are various terrorist groups that are inclined to take hostages, including national domestic terrorist groups, as well as transnational terrorist groups. There are also criminal, ideological and the very dangerous transnational religious terrorist groups. Chapter 8 discusses the various negotiation strategies and tactics that are relevant to each group, including their advantages and shortcomings in achieving a hostage release. Readers of this chapter will learn about the problems related to possible ways of negotiating hostage crises with various terrorist groups, especially the extremely fanatic transnational religious hostage-takers.

Part three: Values and Perceptions — How they Influence the Negotiation Process

Chapter 9 — *Globalization and Culture: Their Impact on Negotiation*

Globalization enables the easy and rapid transference of diverse resources such as money, goods, labor, ideas, information, and so on. Global communication devices enable negotiators to communicate "on the spot", with remote parts of the world, thus saving significant expenditures when negotiating with distant counterparts. However, the globalization process has not done away with cultural differences and cultural identities. On the contrary globalization has brought about a significant increase in cultural negotiations. In many cases, negotiators' behaviors are highly influenced by their culture — before, during and at the end of the negotiation process. Cultural values and rules of conduct make cross-cultural negotiation problematic. Barriers, such as differences in communication perceptions (both in face-to-face and on-line negotiation); interpersonal relations; "face" and honor considerations; time perceptions; and differences regarding the importance of the final agreement all arise as a result of cultural differences. Understanding the other parties' behaviors and perceptions becomes extremely challenging when negotiating with other cultures. Readers of Chapter 9 will learn about major cultural classifications and their impact on negotiation styles. Readers will also obtain knowledge about communication barriers as well as other barriers related to cross-cultural negotiation. Furthermore, readers will gain some insight into the advantages and disadvantages of the different kinds of technology being used today to bridge the gap between different cultures.

Chapter 10 — *Ethical Behavior*

Ethics is a somewhat vague concept, which relates to norms of conduct based on perceptions about what is good or bad, right or wrong. Determining what constitutes "ethical behavior" in negotiation is somewhat ambiguous and depends on the negotiators' perceptions, beliefs and moral codes. However, despite this difficulty, it is essential to understand how various negotiators perceive ethical behavior, as this may determine the negotiation process and outcome. Readers of this chapter will learn about the many faces of ethical behavior. Moreover, readers will learn about the incentives behind unethical behavior in negotiation, including information imbalances, power struggles, the desire for benefits and the ability (or inability) to avoid sanctions. Readers may obtain some additional knowledge regarding the possible benefits of unethical behavior and the relation between ethical behavior and trust during and after the negotiation.

Chapter 11 — Trust, Suspicion and Distrust

Trust, suspicion and distrust result from various expectations about the opponents' intentions and behavior. Most negotiators believe that trust is the most important element in successful negotiation. This belief is not too far off the mark, provided that negotiators know that trusting one's opponents means making oneself vulnerable to the opponents' possible negative behavior. At times, trust may be risky, whereas suspicion and distrust may create defense mechanism to protect negotiators from the opponents' exploitation of their vulnerability. In order to better understand the meaning of trust, suspicion, and distrust, Chapter 11 discusses their positive and negative perceptions. Readers of this chapter will acquire some ideas regarding the meaning of trust, the risks of trust, as well as the positive contribution of suspicion and distrust in negotiations. Moreover, they will gain insight about the incentives to engage in a violation of trust, as well as when and how trust can be rehabilitated after it has been violated.

Part four: Third-Party Intervention in the Negotiation Process

Chapter 12 — Voluntary, Compulsory and International Mediation

The history of mediation is as old as negotiation. Throughout the history of mankind, when disputants wished to prevent a conflict or reached an impasse during negotiation, the help of third parties — usually in the form of mediators — was engaged. The two main forms of mediation are *voluntary* and *compulsory*. In voluntary mediation, the parties choose the mediators and retain complete control over the mediation process and its outcomes. In compulsory mediation, the mediation is mandatory and the parties do not choose their own mediators. They must accept the ones that are chosen for them, but usually can reject the mediators' final suggestions for resolving the conflict. As regards these forms of mediation, there are the questions of when and why, if at all, they are desirable to the disputants involved in a conflict. Additional questions are: What are their advantages and disadvantages? When and how might they help the disputants in solving their conflict?

It is also important to distinguish between *domestic* mediation (which deals with conflicts within one area or country) and *international* mediation (which often deals with complex, and sometimes bitter, conflicts between international entities or countries). International mediation shares some similar characteristics with domestic mediation (voluntary or compulsory), but the two methods also have their own unique characteristics. International mediation is more complicated and risky than domestic mediation, as it usually deals with international rivals, which are more powerful than domestic disputants. In addition, international mediators' attempts to resolve conflicts usually involve more risks. Readers of this chapter will learn about the different behaviors of disputants and mediators in voluntary and compulsory mediation, as well as the unique characteristics of international mediation.

Chapter 13 — Negotiating Representatives

Representatives are individuals or delegations appointed by principals in order to negotiate on their behalf in exchange for remuneration. Theoretically, representatives are always loyal to their principals and negotiate to the best of their ability to achieve an agreement that will satisfy their principals. However, in practice both principals and representatives confront various problems. For example, principals' expectations of their representatives — to protect their interests during the negotiation — are sometimes betrayed by their representatives. Ambiguous instructions given by the principals may confuse their representatives, leaving a lot of room for the representatives' erroneous, as well as self-serving, decisions. However, in many cases, there are significant advantages to employing representatives instead of negotiating directly with one's opponents. Readers of this chapter will learn about the problems, advantages and value of employing representatives to negotiate on the principals' behalf. They will also learn about the difficulties of representing organizations, whether business companies, labor organizations or even nations.

Chapter 14 — Concluding Remarks

At the end of our tour of the World of Negotiation, certain lessons are emphasized. These lessons are concentrated into the five fundamental stages of negotiation: The pre-negotiation stage, the preparation stage, the initial offers (objectives) presentation stage, the haggling stage, and the conclusion stage — reaching an impasse or an agreement.

About the Author

I was born in Israel into a family that had been living in the area for several generations. As a daughter of such a "distinguished" family, I was sent, with high expectations, to the best school of classic ballet. However, soon enough my ballet teacher made it clear to me that I would never be a prima ballerina and that unfortunately, the only thing that I might have the potential for was to be a university Professor. Not to be a ballerina is bad enough, but a university Professor — what kind of a future is that? Unfortunately, having no alternative, I graduated from one of the best high schools in the country, received my B.A. Degree from the Hebrew University in Jerusalem and my MSc. from the Technion — the Israel Institute of Technology. Not many years later I found myself on the stage — wearing a black "toga" and receiving my DSC, also from the Technion. My doctoral thesis on Collective Bargaining brought me my first research prize, allowing me to buy the audio player I had been wanting for years. Well, in light of the prize, a future as a university Professor no longer seemed so intimidating. Also, that is how I became a "researchaholic". Some years later, I became a university Professor — as my ballet teacher had so sadly predicted many years ago. At that time I realized that in order to better understand the impact of culture on negotiation and other phenomena I must travel the world. As a researcher and scholar, I was invited to visit several universities, such as Monash and Melbourne Universities in Australia, Berkeley and Florida International University in the USA, and the University of British Columbia in Canada. I must admit — I learned a lot during my visits around our global village. Based on my own experience and research findings, as well as the findings of many other researchers, I wrote several books, among them "The Dynamic of Negotiating — From Theory to practice" (in Hebrew), which again won me a distinguished prize, and "Negotiation — The Hidden Dimension" (also in Hebrew). In addition, I wrote too many papers, both in Hebrew and English, and I continue to do so. I believe that my father lost most of his assets because he did not read my books and articles. But of course they were written some years after he passed away. However, I find some comfort in the thought that you, my dear readers, having read this book will be extremely successful in all your negotiations. Enjoy the book and please don't be sad about my lost career as a prima ballerina. . . . . .

Amira Galin
Tel Aviv University
Israel

PART ONE

Conflict-Confrontation and Negotiation: Theories and Perceptions

Chapter 1

Alternatives to Resolving Conflict

"One might as well try to ride two horses moving in different directions, as to try to maintain in equal force two opposing or contradictory sets of desires".

Robert Collier

Ask yourselves the question: When do you negotiate? Some people, when asked this question, reply: "All the time", while others say "on many occasions". The fact is that no one negotiates all the time; we negotiate only on particular occasions; that is, only when we experience *conflict* with others. Negotiation is a way to confront conflict. In the absence of conflict, there is no reason to negotiate. However, the extent of success in resolving the conflict through negotiation depends, among other things, on the nature of the conflict and the available alternatives for actually finding a solution.

So, what do we know about the nature of conflict, the sources of conflict and the alternatives available to us when confronting a conflict? Is negotiation always the best alternative when confronting a conflict? How can we decide when negotiation is the optimal alternative for confronting a conflict or whether some other alternative should be considered? In the following chapter, all these issues and their implications are discussed.

1. On the Nature of Conflict

What is conflict and how can we define it?[1] A *conflict* usually emerges when there is a change in the *status quo*, which also changes the existing balance

---

[1] A great deal of the literature has dealt with conflict over the last decades. Most of the classic literature developed in the 80s and the 90s of the 20th century. We shall only refer here to a few important contributions to the knowledge of conflict and conflict confrontation: Coombs, C.H. and Avrunin, G.S. (1988), *The Structure of Conflict*, Lawrence Eribaum Associates, Inc.; De Drew, C.W.K. and Van De Vliert, E. (1997), *Using conflict in Organizations*,

of control over resources or values. As long as the *status quo* is maintained, the probability of conflict is low because people usually prefer to maintain the current state of affairs, rather than change it. However, the world has become a "small village", which is constantly experiencing rapid changes in politics, values and resources. The *status quo* is also changing rapidly in all areas of life, stimulating conflicts between individuals, groups and nations. As a result, conflict has become an integral part of people's daily lives.

The nature of conflict is studied in many disciplines, among them Decision-Making, Game Theory, Economics, Political Science, Sociology and Psychology. Each discipline perceives conflict from a different point of view. Some emphasize the negative aspects of conflict, while others observe the positive aspects. Nevertheless, conflicts prevail everywhere, in personal relations, among groups and among national entities; and a high proportion of human interaction and effort is invested in trying to resolve conflicts. Therefore, the question is not whether conflict is "good" or "bad", but rather what are the causes of conflict and how can we best confront it.

1.1. *Defining Conflict*

There are many definitions of the term *conflict*, but the most prevailing definition relates to *opposing interests* (objective or conceptual) between and among individuals, groups or nations, involving scarce resources and values such as religion and ideology.[2]

Conflict can occur as a result of an objective situation or a *subjective perception*. When conflict results from what seems to be an objective change in the *status quo*, it is referred to as a "external" or "objective" conflict. However, the same conflict may exist only in the minds of the parties or individuals, in which case it can be referred to as a "concealed" or "subjectively perceived conflict.[3] In other words, conflict also exists in situations

Sage Publications; Pruitt, D.G. (1998). Social Conflict, Chapter 27, in Gilbert, D. Fiske, S.T. and Lindzey, G. (eds.), *Handbook of Social Psychology* (4th Edition, Vol. 2, pp. 470–503), McGraw-Hill; Rubin, G. Pruitt, D.G. and Kim, S.T. (1994), *Social Conflict: Escalation, Stalemate and Settlement*, 2nd Edition. McGraw-Hill.

[2]Wade-Benzoni, K.A. Hoffman, A.J. Thompson, L.L. Moore, D.A. Gillespie, J.J. and Bazerman, M.H. (2002), Barriers to Resolution in Ideologically Based Negotiation: The Role of Values and Institutions, *Academy of Management Review*, Vol. 27(1), pp. 41–57.

[3]Pruitt, D.G. (2001), *Conflict and Conflict Resolution*, International Encyclopedia of the Social and Behavioral Sciences, Elsevier Science Ltd.

where people only perceive opposing interests. In a situation where there is an objective change in the *status quo*, but people do not perceive opposing interests, there is no conflict. In a situation where there is no change at all, but people perceive opposing interests, there is conflict. Perceiving conflict may be influenced, on a case-by-case basis, by many features relating to the involved parties, such as their emotions, fear, stereotypes, cultural values and their perceived power balance. Nevertheless, regardless of whether the conflicts are objectively or subjectively perceived; their consequences can be severe, often damaging relationships between close friends and even between married couples, or triggering on a larger scale, struggles, strikes and even terror and wars.

It is noteworthy that the traditional literature discusses either "*conflict resolution*" or "*conflict management*". "Conflict resolution" refers to the termination of a conflict, whereas, "conflict management" refers to minimizing the negative aspects of a conflict. However, conflicts are not always easy to resolve or manage. Therefore, the main issue is neither "conflict management" nor "conflict resolution", but rather "conflict confrontation". Obviously, the causes of the conflict should be taken into account when calculating the best way to confront it. While it is not possible to discuss all the causes of all conflicts here, we can still give some examples of the most typical causes of conflicts.

1.2. *What are the Main Causes of Conflicts?*

Scarce resources as the cause of conflict: The access and control of scarce resources[4] has been a source of conflict for centuries. It is worth noting that scarce resources can be either tangible or sociological/psychological. Some examples of tangible scarce resources are: Land, as in a conflict between neighbors over a property dispute, at the individual level, or at the national level, in regard to water, which has long been the cause of bitter conflicts in many regions and countries, as Mark Twain said: "Whiskey is for drinking — water is for fighting over". Disagreements over oil and natural gas have also been a serious source of conflict in many regions throughout the world. Some examples of the sociological/psychological causes of conflict

---

[4]An interesting review of the literature regarding scarce resources as a cause of conflict can be found in Struver, G., (2010): Too Many Resources or Too Few? What Drives International Conflicts? *SSRN Working paper Series*, October 2010.

are: The perception of group deprivation, sometimes as a result of vertically differentiated group; competition over an important (scarce) civil service office, which is a source of power and other rewards. Other examples are: Population density (objective or conceptual), which leads to demands for non-available food or space, as well as a desire for territorial control, and regime survival, are all causes of conflicts.

Values as a source of conflict: Religion has for centuries been a cause of brutal, ongoing conflicts. It was already an important cause of conflict in early ages,[5] and also in so-called "modern times". Conflicts over religious domination exist between and within various religious sectors, as well as between religious and secular populations. Religion, one of the main causes of conflict, has been and remains the source of countless wars and acts of terrorism.

Ideology has also been responsible for many painful conflicts throughout human history. Thus, religion and ideology are similar in respect to being major sources of conflict; they are also the most difficult conflicts to confront.

The "traditional" perception attributed to conflicts is that they trigger competition and struggles between the different interests of individuals, groups and nations. According to this conception, a system without conflicts or even with a few minor conflicts is the most desirable one; the assumption being that conflicts should be prevented at all costs.

Later perceptions of conflict considered it a natural phenomenon, typical to every social system. Conflicts are inevitable when people live and work together.[6] Since conflicts are unavoidable, people should learn to live with them, resolve them, and if possible, even reap some benefits from them.

While traditional conceptions are interested in preventing conflicts, and other conceptions focus on resolving conflicts, it is also important to mention some positive attributes of conflicts. Conflicts sometimes serve as a trigger for social change and innovation, According to this conception, a social system without conflicts may degenerate in the absence of triggers that lead to change. Moreover, considering our subject matter, conflicts are important because they are the reason and the trigger behind negotiation.

---

[5] See, for example, Brams, S.J. (2003) *Biblical Games: Game Theory and the Hebrew Bible*, 2nd revised Edition, Cambridge, MA and London: MIT Press.

[6] De Drew. C.W.K. (2006), When Too Much and Too Little Hearts: Evidence for Curvilinear Relationship between Task Conflict and Innovation, *Journal of Management*, Vol. 32(1), pp. 83–107.

National, international and diplomatic conflicts are good examples of conflict confrontation. While in this chapter only day-to-day examples are presented, it is noteworthy that the type of considerations and methods used to choose the best confrontation resolution alternative are the same, regardless of whether we are facing day-to-day conflicts, national, labor relations or any other type of conflict.

2. Considerations in Conflict Confrontation

2.1. *What do People Consider When Confronting a Conflict?*

As a rule, people take into consideration their expected gains versus their expected losses in each decision during conflict confrontation. Since losses are more painful than gains, it is reasonable to assume that the parties involved in a conflict will not consider a decision in which the expected gain is slightly higher than their expected losses. They also would not, rationally, consider a decision in which they believe that their losses would outweigh their gains.

Imagine, for example, a scenario in which graduate students are studying towards their Master's degree. Their curriculum includes a fixed number of elective courses and two seminars, which the students must complete in order to qualify for their Master's degree. It is important to note that a seminar is considered the most demanding type of a course, especially in terms of the students' remaining leisure time. Now imagine that the university authorities wish to make a change in the curriculum by adding an additional (third) seminar — to the students' curriculum. The students, however, oppose the university authorities' intentions, by refusing to accept an additional seminar. The conflict is obvious. The interest of university authorities is to optimize the quality of teaching, which they believe will promote the university's image, as well as increase the number of highly qualified students that enroll in the Master's program. The student representatives' interest is to preserve the students' leisure time, which they believe is very limited, due to the current curriculum. Another interest of the students is to prevent any additional initiatives on the part of the university that may harm them. What should university authorities consider when deciding on how to confront this conflict with their own students? In order to optimize their gain, should they require a third seminar if, by doing so, they risk a students' strike, bad publicity, as well as a possible reduction in the number of students enrolling the graduate program? It seems that in order to optimize their own interests, university authorities should take into consideration the possible consequences of requiring students to take on a third seminar. Another alternative is that university authorities will consider some kind of cooperation from their students. Then again, the authorities may consider giving up the third seminar requirement, thereby endangering the university's image as a leading university and perhaps bringing about further student demands. University authorities might come to the conclusion that in making such a decision, their losses would outweigh their gains.

Imagine another scenario: A firm's management has a great demand for a senior professional employee with unique and rare knowledge. The human resources manager has invested a lot of time trying to find a suitable candidate. When an appropriate candidate is finally found, the management is ready to offer him generous work conditions and a good salary. However, soon enough the management discovers that the candidate's demands far exceed what the management believes is a fair and generous offer.

What should the management consider when deciding how to confront the conflict with the desirable candidate? Trying to force the candidate to accept the management's original offer with a sort of "take it or leave it" attitude may be the best alternative to maximize management gain. However, since the candidate may reject the offer, such a decision may backfire, ending with the company losing a rare and desirable employee, resulting in added expenditures and time spent looking for another suitable candidate. Should the management consider conceding to the candidate's demands, since it has already invested so much time trying to find a suitable employee? How would such concessions affect its other employees' demands? Alternatively, should the management try to negotiate, at the risk of failing to satisfy the candidate? Might a new offer simply serve as an incentive for the candidate's increased demands? What kind of decision, on the part of the management, would ensure that the gains outweigh the losses.

2.2. *Cooperation as the Preferred Alternative to Confront a Conflict*

Perhaps the most famous theory that refers to conflict confrontation is the *Dual Concern Model*. The Model assumes that the combination of the first party's concerns to both itself and the other party's concerns provide some insight into the parties' considerations when confronting a conflict. This combination of concerns yields four alternatives for confronting a conflict:

Contending, Yielding, Problem Solving and Inaction.[7] It seems that the concept of *Problem Solving* is very close to that of *Negotiation.*

In recent decades, various theories have maintained that choosing the cooperation of all parties' interests should be the main consideration when confronting a conflict. In the dual concern theory, for example, Problem Solving is the preferable consideration. The assumption is that if all involved parties are concerned about one another and motivated to mutually confront the conflict, there is a high probability of finding a resolution that satisfies everyone. In other words, a competitive alternative, if chosen as a way to confront a conflict, can bring about a non-optimal outcome. This is a debatable assumption because in some situations there are some better alternatives than cooperation, in terms of gains and losses. In other situations, both competitive and cooperative approaches to a conflict could yield the best result.

3. Alternatives to Confronting Conflict

It is possible to divide the alternatives to confronting a conflict into five broad categories[8]:

3.1. *Coercion*

One (or both) parties wishes to end the conflict by dominating the other party, in order to achieve its own interests. At the individual level, for example, in a divorce conflict, one party wishes to end the conflict by forcing the other party to give up custody of the children, taking over all property gained by the couple over the years or both.

3.2. *Surrender*

Yielding completely to the other party. Many conflicts have ended by one party (usually the weaker one) giving up everything to the other. In business, one firm may completely yield to another firm that wishes to control it. In many cases, one of the parties has no choice, but to yield. However,

---

[7] Pruitt, D.G. and Rubin, G. (1986), *Social Conflict*, McGraw-Hill.

[8] Kleiman and Hassin, who examined unconscious conflicts in individuals, argue that this type of conflict increases the likelihood of multiple thinking, rather than narrowing alternative options . See Kleiman, T, and Hassin, R.R. (2013), When Conflicts are Good: Unconscious Goal Conflicts Reduce Confirmatory Thinking, *Journal of Personality and Social Psychology*, Vol. 105(3), pp. 374–387.

sometimes yielding is voluntary. For example, in a conflict between loving couples one party voluntary yields to the other party in order to preserve good relations.

3.3. *Withdrawal*

One or both parties can escape the conflict by maintaining that no conflict exists. In the face of conflict, parties may simply ignore one another's demands, convincing themselves and others, that the situation is not actually a conflict, but a normal situation. "It's not that you're spitting on me, it's just raining": This old saying is an analogy for withdrawal from a conflict. If there is no conflict, no response is needed, and the parties can easily maintain their normal lives. For example, in a relationship between a couple, one or both can leave the relationship, still maintaining good relationships, as if there were never any conflicts between them.

3.4. *Deferral*[9]

Deferred conflict is time-related. One or both parties can defer the conflict for a certain time, maintaining the *status quo*, with the hope that in time the conflict will become irrelevant. It is possible to believe that, "if time cures all", it should be able to end a conflict as well. Deference also allows a party to receive more information, to further consider a suitable decision, and also to amend conceptions or misconceptions regarding the conflict. However, if over time the conflict still exists, at least one party or both will have to deal with it.

3.5. *Negotiation*

In order to deal with a conflict, both parties must engage in an exchange process. During this process, each party offers the other objects that the other party needs, while receiving in return objects that they need, with the hopes of reaching an agreement. The main difference between negotiation and the other alternatives to confront a conflict is that all of the other (above-mentioned) alternatives can be accomplished by one party, whereas

---

[9]An interesting discussion of deferred conflict can be found in Tversky, A. and Shafir, E. (1992), Choice under Conflict: The Dynamic of Deferred Decision, *Psychological Science*, Vol. 3(6), pp. 358–361.

in negotiation both (or all) parties must be involved (willingly, and at times, even unwillingly) in the process.

Choosing negotiation as a preferable alternative, when attempting to resolve a conflict, is typically culture-dependent. Due to cooperative socialization, mainly in the so-called "Western" countries, many people believe that negotiation is the preferable alternative when confronting conflict. However, negotiation is only one of several alternatives when trying to deal with a conflict and it is not always the most effective one. Moreover, it could be expensive, both in terms of financial resources and in terms of emotional investment. Even during the negotiation process, if one or both of the parties discover that negotiation is not the most effective alternative to their conflict, they should walk away from the process and decide to deal with their disagreements by using other available alternatives.

Therefore, the first decision people should make in order to confront a conflict is to examine all available alternatives and systematically choose that which they consider to be the most effective alternative. Among other considerations, they should look also at the alternative which is the least risky and costly. In recent discussions of conflict resolution, there has been too much emphasis placed on negotiation in which seemingly joint decisions are made.

4. Choosing from Among the Alternatives

Choosing from among the earlier alternatives is complicated in the face of uncertainty, regarding their consequences. Therefore, in order to choose between the available alternatives, it is essential to assemble and evaluate information regarding each party's interests, goals and points of reservation. In the following section, three methods are presented for choosing the best alternative when confronting a conflict.

4.1. *The Intuitive Choice*

Intuition ("rules of thumb" or Heuristics) is one way to choose from among the alternatives. Individuals and parties confronting conflict, use such "rules of thumb" in order to avoid complicated decisions, by filtering information to fit in with their past experience and previous conceptions. Therefore, intuition is frequently adopted by many, because it is quick and simplifies the complicated matter of choosing among alternatives. Of course, it is not a systematic choice and, in many cases, leads to errors and ends with regrets and/or cognitive dissonance. One example of an intuitive decision is when the management decides to force its initial offer (which the management believes is fair and generous) on the desirable candidate, in the face of the uncertainty regarding the candidate's response to the offer. Such a decision may result in losing the candidate and the need to search for another. Assuming that there is a shortage of high-quality employees, the management might regret its decision, or justify it in order to avoid cognitive dissonance.

4.2. *The Subjective Importance Choice*

The subjective importance attributed by a party to each alternative, taking into consideration its advantages and disadvantages as well as its risk and cost.

4.3. *Choosing According to Each Alternative's Expected Utility*

A more systematic approach when choosing among the available alternatives involves the listing of all of the relevant party's alternatives and a consistent analysis of their feasible outcomes. This type of analysis is based on evaluating the advantages and disadvantages of each alternative, taking into account not only the consequences of a party's own choice, but also the consequences of the other party's possible responses to each alternative. Accordingly, the party can give each relevant alternative a subjective value (which could range, for instance, between one and ten) and then select the alternative with the highest subjective value. For example, we return to the conflict between the management and the candidate: The Forced alternative value could receive a value of 5, as the management predicts a 50% chance that the candidate will decide to accept the offer. The Surrender alternative — yielding to the candidate's demands — could be valued at 3, as the candidate's high demands may influence the requirements of many other employees in the firm. Withdrawal from the conflict is an irrelevant option in this case, and thus does not receive any value. The Deferring alternative gives the management another chance to inspect the labor market, hopefully without losing the candidate; therefore, its value could be an 8. Negotiation could lead to a compromise, but it may take time and effort, and may also be costly in regard to both time and effort (as we will later discuss); therefore, it receives a value of 6. Considering the relative highest subjective given value, the management should choose the Defer alternative as its best choice. It is worth mentioning that when the chosen alternative's value is higher than the other alternatives, the choice is easy. However, when some alternatives receive close or identical subjective values, choosing the "best" alternative becomes more complicated. Therefore, a more comprehensive and refined method for choosing among the alternatives is described as the third method, chosing according to each alternative's expected utility.

4.3.1. *Choosing according to each alternative's expected utility: An example*

Imagine the Braun family who has lived in the suburbs for many years. During all these years, the family has enjoyed a quiet neighborhood, clear air and tranquility. One day, a loud noise is heard from the neighbor's yard. The Braun family believes that this is only an isolated incident. However, the noise continues day after day, from early morning until late at night. The family members soon discover that their new neighbor has set up a little workshop in his yard and intends to carry on certain activities on a daily basis. That is the end of the quiet neighborhood, clean air and tranquility for the Brauns. How should the Braun family confront the conflict with its new neighbor? How should the family choose systematically between the relevant available alternatives? The expected utility approach may enable a more sophisticated systematic choice among the relevant alternatives, by taking into account a few possible scenarios for each possible alternative. The family may ascribe a subjective value to each possible scenario, and consider as far as is possible a realistic probability of each scenario actually taking place. The following is an example of the expected utility calculated for each alternative that might be chosen by the Braun family.

4.3.2. *The coercion alternative*

Solidarity: The family can organize the majority of the suffering neighbors to demonstrate and picket every day in front of the neighbor's workshop.

Scenario 1 — The subjective value (ascribed by the family) to this scenario is 6, while the probability of the evaluated effect of the demonstrations on the new neighbor is 0.5. In other words, there is a 0.5 chance that, in the end, the new neighbor will move his workshop.

Scenario 2 — Another possibility is that, as a result of the demonstrations, the neighbor will agree to substantially reduce the noise level caused by his workshop. The value ascribed by the family to this scenario is 4 (after all, they will still have to deal with some level of noise), while the probability of the neighbor's reducing the noise is evaluated at 0.5. Thus, the expected utility of the Coercion alternative is 5 ($6 \times 0.5 + 4 \times 0.5 = 5.0$).

4.3.3. *The surrender alternative*

The family does not want to quarrel with its new neighbor and decides to keep on living in the house, believing that, in time they will get used to the noise and pollution.

Scenario 1 — The value ascribed by the family to getting used to the noise and pollution under the present conditions is 4, while the probability that the family will actually get used to it is 0.2.

Scenario 2 — The family will stay inside the house as much as possible, as they cannot get used to the noise and pollution. Inside the house, they will suffer less from the noise, but the family knowingly "sentences itself to 'house arrest'" for an undefined time period. The family is not very happy with the idea of being "imprisoned" within their own home. Therefore, the value ascribed by the family to this scenario is 2, but the probability of managing under such conditions is 0.8.

Thus, the expected utility of the surrender alternative is 2.4 ($4 \times 0.2 + 2 \times 0.8 = 2.4$).

4.3.4. *The withdrawal alternative*

The family will sell their house in order to move to a better neighborhood.

Scenario 1 — In the case of success in selling the house for a reasonable price, the subjective value ascribed by the family would be 7, but the evaluated probability of success (as regards selling the house for a reasonable price) is 0.2.

Scenario 2 — The family will sell the house at a low price (a loss), due to the noise and pollution. The subjective value ascribed by the family to such a loss is 3, while the probability to actually sell the house at a very low price is 0.8.

Thus, the expected utility for the withdrawal alternative is 3.8 ($7 \times 0.2 + 3 \times 0.8 = 3.8$).

4.3.5. *The deferral alternative*

The family will "silently" collect information about the neighbor (past problems with neighbors, the law, etc.) and consult a lawyer and a private investigator regarding the neighbor and his workshop's noise and pollution. This will be time-consuming.

Scenario 1 — In the end, the family will be better prepared to confront the conflict and decide upon the desirable measures. However, meanwhile the family will suffer the noise and pay for the information. The subjective value ascribed by the family in this scenario is 6, while the probability of future success is 0.8.

Scenario 2 — The family finds that the collected information yields very little (if any) support for taking real, practical measures against the neighbor. In this case, the ascribed value is 0. Furthermore, since the evaluation of no success in confronting the conflict is very limited; the family estimates its probability at 0.2.

Thus, the expected utility for the Defer alternative is 4.8 ($6 \times 0.8 + 0 \times 0.2 = 4.8$).

4.3.6. *The negotiation alternative*

At the beginning of the negotiations, the family will demand that the neighbor move the workshop to another location.

Scenario 1 — The neighbor may be ready to move the workshop, but will demand that the family fully compensate him for moving expenses. The family evaluates that during the negotiation, the neighbor will lower his initial demands, but the family will still have to pay some of the moving costs. The family estimates the prospects of such a result to be 0.4, while its subjective value is valued at 4. Scenario 2 — The family evaluates that during the negotiations they will not be successful in getting the neighbor to move his workshop, but can reduce its activities from 50 hours a week to 20 hours a week, (4 days, from 8:00 am to 1:00 pm), hours during which the family members are usually away from home. Accordingly, the noise and pollution suffering would be minimized, but the value of the family's property would drop substantially. The family ascribes this type of scenario a value of 3, while the probability of minimizing the trouble as a result of negotiation is evaluated as 0.6. Thus, the expected utility for the negotiation alternative is 3.4 ($4 \times 0.4 + 3 \times 0.6 = 3.4$).

A systematic analysis, in accordance with the expected utility method, enables a better comparison of all the alternatives than Intuition, and even the Subjective Importance as described earlier. According to the Expected Utility method, it is clear that the preferred alternative for the Braun family, at

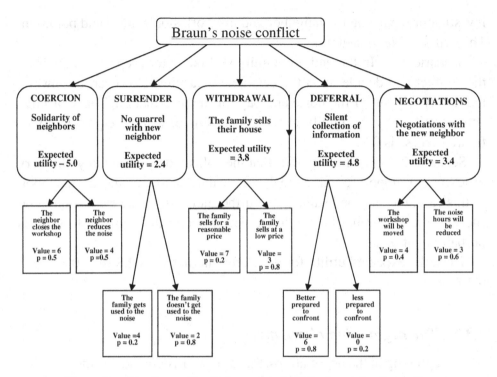

Figure 1:   The Braun family's expected utility for each alternative

least at the first stage of conflict confrontation, is Coercion with an expected utility of 5.0, and definitely not Negotiation, with an expected utility of 3.4.

Figure 1 depicts the Braun family's expected utility for each alternative.

It is possible that the best alternative — Coercion — according to the results of the *expected utility* analysis, will fail to bring about the desired pre-evaluated results, and the noise and pollution will continue. Therefore, due to the continued suffering of the Brauns, as a result of the workshop, the Braun family should try another alternative. However, in the second stage, the family should also base its decision regarding the best alternative on systematic analysis and once more calculate the expected utility of all the remaining relevant alternatives. It should be noted that in the second stage the subjective value and probability evaluations may change, due to new information and a change in circumstances.

When the classical term *BATNA*, "Best Alternative to Negotiated Agreement", is applied to the earlier example, we find that Coercion is the *BATNA* — the alternative with the highest expected utility (5.0); while the Surrender alternative is the *WATNA* — the "Worst Alternative to Negotiated Agreement", having the lowest expected utility (2.4). Of course, when

Fisher and Ury first introduced the classical term, *BATNA*,[10] they referred to the negotiation process, in which the negotiation fails and the involved parties turn to their next-best alternatives. However, it is more reasonable to use the best (*BATNA*) and worst (*WATNA*) alternatives in a previous stage — the stage of choosing the alternatives to confront a conflict. Why choose negotiation, which can reach an impasse and then turn to a better alternative, if it is possible to avoid such (a common) mistake and choose another alternative beforehand?

Finally, sometimes it is much more effective to confront a conflict using two or more alternatives together, rather than one alternative. For example, using a combination of coercion and negotiation might produce a better outcome than using coercion or negotiation individually or any other individual alternative in isolation.[11] In addition, it is also possible to choose another alternative, if the first alternative does not help resolve the conflict. It is most important to systematically calculate your best and worst alternatives each time. Unfortunately, a systematic method of choice is not always applied by the parties who confront conflict.

Practical Applications

- Try to avoid intuition ("rules of thumb") when deciding which alternative is best or worst when confronting a conflict. While intuition might "work" for you by chance, there is a high probability that it will lead you to make wrong decisions.
- You will do better if you choose the preferred alternative by systematically analyzing available alternatives, rather than by using intuition.
- Do not assume that the best alternative when confronting a conflict is always negotiation. At times, it might be the worst alternative.
- Consider alternatives that optimize your expected gains and minimize your expected losses.
- If it is problematic to ascribe value or probability to each alternative in a certain situation, you might as well choose the "Deferral" option. Deferral might not be your best alternative in the end, but it may give

---

[10]See the revised edition — Fisher, R. Ury, W. and Patton, B. (2011), *Getting to Yes: Negotiating Agreement without Giving In*, Penguin Books.

[11]Van De Vliert, E. Nauta, A. Giebels, E. and Janssen, O. (1999), Constructive Conflict at Work, *Journal of Organizational Behavior*, Vol. 20(4), pp. 475–491.

you more time to consider the consequences of each choice, and allow you to collect more and better information. Time and information may be crucial in identifying/detecting the available alternatives and choosing the best one. However, take care since by deferring your decision you might lose the "objects" you wished to gain, such as a house or other important acquisition.

- Your best alternative in the first stage may not be the best alternative as time progresses.
- Be flexible. Do not simply stick to one alternative from the beginning to the end of the confronting conflict process. Switching from the first chosen alternative to another is both possible and legitimate. For example, if Withdrawal does not work for you, switch to Coercion or Negotiation. If neither Coercion nor Negotiation is the best alternatives at the current stage, consider switching to Deferring, and so on. However, before each switch, try to systematically calculate your best and worst alternatives at that time.
- It is sometimes best to choose more than one alternative, such as coercion and negotiation, at the same time, rather than one individual alternative.
- When choosing an alternative, or a combination of alternatives, try to avoid the influence of stress, fatigue or other distractions, which may cause you to choose erroneously.

Chapter 2

Main Negotiation Theories

"Let us never negotiate out of fear. But let us never fear to negotiate".

John F. Kennedy

Negotiation is only one out of several ways to confront a conflict, and not necessarily the most effective one. Consequently, there is always the dilemma of when to choose the negotiation alternative and when not to choose this alternative. When choosing to negotiate, people should take into consideration their expected gains versus their expected losses. Thus, they may consider negotiating when the potential negotiation benefits outweigh, at least, their invested time, emotions and material expenses.

Despite the fact that not everything has to be negotiated, negotiations occur daily in a wide variety of fields: In relations between individuals, as well as in domestic, communal and national situations. Negotiation is also a typical approach to resolving industrial relations, as well as political, business and economic conflicts. Practically, negotiation has become an integral part of most people's lives as it is often chosen, justifiably or unjustifiably, as the best alternative when confronting conflicts. Therefore, it is essential to inquire into what we know about the nature of negotiation and what kinds of insights can be drawn from the foremost negotiation theories. The following chapter is aimed at reviewing some theories that explain the fundamental nature of negotiation.

1. Negotiation Characteristics

In order to understand negotiation and its main characteristics, it is necessary to define its nature. There are several definitions of negotiation, depending on various points of view. Just a few examples: The most optimistic approach defines negotiation as a process which combines opposing interests into a mutual harmony.[1] The emphasis here is on the negotiation outcome, which is always a happy ending to a conflict. In a similar, but not identical, manner, it is possible to define negotiation as a process through which the parties involved in a conflict reach a joint agreement which they believe will better serve their interests than choosing another unilateral alternative.[2] In this case, the emphasis is on the joint agreement, which is the best solution among all of the available alternatives. Another perception of negotiation is as a sort of decision-making process in which the parties to a conflict willingly decide to communicate with each other in order to resolve their opposing interests.[3] Here, the emphasis is on the negotiator as a decision-maker, who willingly makes the "right" decisions. However, describing negotiation purely as a rational decision-making process is problematic, since certain decisional "*heuristics*" (rules of the thumb)" exist amongst negotiators.[4] In this case, here, the emphasis is on heuristics and the impact of these heuristics on the negotiation process and outcome. Finally, negotiation is also defined as a means through which the parties to a dispute arrive at a specific settlement under conditions of strategic interaction and interdependence.[5] In this case, the emphasis is on the parties' strategies and tactics and their possible interdependence during the negotiation process.

While each of the earlier definitions contribute to the understanding of the nature of negotiation, it is important to define negotiation in a more comprehensive way. Such a definition includes several key elements:

- The Conflict: As has already been discussed, there is a conflict which the parties confront.
- The Involved Parties: At least two parties are involved; at times, more than two parties are involved.

---

[1] Kissinger, H.A. (1969), *Nuclear Weapons and Foreign Policy*, W.W. Norton.

[2] See Zartman, L.W. (1977), Negotiation as a Joint Decision Process, *Journal of Conflict Resolution*, Vol. 21, pp. 619–638.

[3] See Lewicki, R.J. Saunders, D.M. and Barry, B. (2011), *Essential of Negotiation*, McGraw-Hill, 5th Edition.

[4] See Bazerman, M.H. and Neale, M.A. (1986) Heuristics in Negotiation: Limitation to Effective Dispute Resolution, in Akers, H.R. and Hammond, K.R. (eds.), *Judgment and Decision Making*, pp. 311–321, Cambridge University Press.

[5] See Lim, L.-H. and Benbasat, I. (1992–1993), A Theoretical Perspective of Negotiation Support Systems, *Journal of Management and Information Systems,* Vol. 9(3), pp. 27–44.

- Making a Choice: The involved parties make a mutual choice to talk about their opposing interests, voluntarily or involuntarily (for example, they may be forced to negotiate and seek a solution by a third entity, such as a court decision or by a dominant nation).
- Preparation: The involved parties prepare for the forthcoming process (by gathering information, choosing an appropriate location, etc.).
- Communication: A communication exchange takes place. The communication process may involve what has been termed "*exchanging concessions*" or, in other words, a "give-and-take" process.
- Strategies and Tactics: The "exchanging concessions" (give-and-take) process is performed by employing strategies and tactics.
- The Outcome: In most cases, the preferable outcome is, of course, an agreement with which both parties are satisfied. However, this is not the only possible outcome. The process may yield various other outcomes, such as an agreement which does not satisfy one of the parties, an impasse or even an escalation of the conflict. Another possible outcome is a decision, accepted by all of the involved parties, to not resolve the conflict at that time, but to carry on living with it peacefully; in other words, a decision wherein both parties "agree to disagree".

It is noteworthy that parties sometimes choose to negotiate not in order to reach an agreement, but with the intention of fulfilling another purpose, such as satisfying a court order to negotiate, in order to gain information or in an attempt to gain time.

1.1. *Negotiation Possible Outcomes*

As has already been mentioned, negotiation is always initiated by a conflict. If there is no conflict, there is no need to negotiate. However, the negotiation results are not always positive in terms of a mutually satisfactory agreement. The opposite may occur. The process may lead to conflict escalation and even rivalry, terror or war. Thus, it is most important to analyze the situation and decide whether negotiation is, at least at the current time, the optimal alternative for the involved parties. Of course, there is always the possibility of walking away from the negotiation "table", being aware that the process may lead to an undesirable outcome. Such an act might be costly — in terms of the lost time, emotions, reputation and, in many cases, also money, which have already been invested in the negotiation process. It is therefore better to foresee the coming problems by evaluating (calculating), in advance, the possible negotiation scenarios, as suggested in Chapter 1 or, in other words, choosing your Best Alternative to a Negotiated Agreement (*BATNA*) in advance **before** you start negotiating. It is just as important to take your Worst Alternative to a Negotiated Agreement (*WATNA*) into account in advance.

Considering the above key elements of negotiation, it is easy to understand that the negotiation process is a complicated interaction between parties involved in a conflict. Therefore, there is unfortunately no one, single best option for achieving the best outcome for any party. The outcome depends on various factors, such as the power balance, negotiation style, and behavior of all parties in any given situation, along with the available outcomes. Consequently, in order to succeed in negotiation, it is essential to understand the nature of the specific negotiation and to be prepared, as far as is possible, for any situation. Figure 1 depicts the key elements of the negotiation process and its possible outcomes.

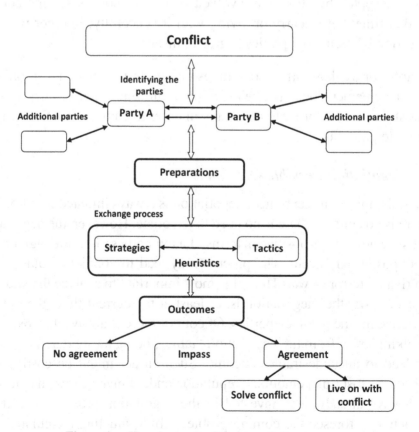

Figure 1:   Key elements of the negotiation process

1.2. *"Bargaining" and "Negotiation"*

It is noteworthy that people are often confused when it comes to understanding the difference between "bargaining" and "negotiation". This confusion is the result of differences in the description of the negotiation process. According to one approach, the term "bargaining" describes a process in which the parties "push" one another, resulting in one party's gains and the other's losses, such as in a Win–Lose type of process. According to the same approach, the term "negotiation" describes a process in which both parties make an effort to reach an agreement that will satisfy both, such as in a Win–Win type of process. However, in many ways this is an artificial differentiation. For example, in Industrial Relations the term "collective bargaining" implies a Win–Win process as well as a Win–Lose process. In most negotiation literature, the terms "bargaining" and "negotiation" are used interchangeably, and rightly so. In this book as well, the terms "bargaining" and "negotiation" are synonymous.

2. On Negotiation Theories

Negotiation theories are derived from many disciplines. Many theories integrate concepts of various disciplines in order to have more comprehensive insight into the nature of negotiations. Different theorists describe the nature of negotiation from various standpoints. Theories such as Game theory, Economics, Psychology, Sociology or Organizational Behavior all emphasize different aspects of negotiation. Yet, other theories analyze negotiations according to their subjects, such as international relations and collective bargaining.

Other theories focus on negotiators' characteristics: Their minds, experience, power and motivations. It is noteworthy that the various classifications of negotiation theories are not mutually exclusive. It is very common that theorists and researchers from one discipline adopt a negotiation analysis viewpoint from a different discipline, at times even attempting to combine several approaches. For example, Professor Daniel Kahneman, whose work in Psychology is most relevant to negotiation, received his Nobel Prize in Economics. As a result, the question of how to classify the main theories regarding the nature of negotiation remains debatable.[6] In the following

---

[6]Alfredson, T. and Cungu, A. (2008), *Negotiation Theory and Practice: A Review of the Literature*, Easypol, On-Line Resource Materials for Policy Making. www.fao.org/easypol/550/4-5_negotiation_background_paper_179en.

chapter, the main negotiation theories are classified according to three main disciplines: The Rational, Behavioral and Hybrid disciplines.

3. Main Traditional Theories

Three main traditional theories, which are briefly described here, are the Rational theories, sometimes referred to as *"prescriptive" theories*; the Behavioral theories, often referred to as *"descriptive" theories* and the Hybrid theories, comprised of both Rational and Behavioral theories.

3.1. *The Rational Theories*

The origins of the Rational theories are mainly: Game theory, Decision-Making theory, Operation Research and Economics.

According to the Rational theories, negotiators perceive the process as a "game", in which they "play" at the "negotiation table", as rational "players" with known alternatives, but in the face of an uncertain outcome. As rational players, their aim in the negotiation "game" is to maximize their gains (or "Payoffs"). Thus, in order to maximize their final gains, the negotiators attribute a subjective value to each alternative and calculate the probability of its achieving maximum gains. Recall that by multiplying the value of the alternative by its probability, negotiators can obtain their expected utility for each alternative. In this way, negotiators can compare the available alternatives and choose the one that received the maximum expected utility. By choosing the alternative with the maximum expected utility, negotiators attempt to maximize their gains, even at the expense of the other players. This "game" is metaphorically described as a competition between rational parties over who gets a bigger slice of a fixed amount of pie, referred to as the *"Magical Fixed Pie"*. Such competition over the larger slice of the *"Pie"* is depicted in Figure 2.

In Figure 2, Party A achieved the bigger "slice" of the "fixed Pie" during the negotiation process at the expense of Party B.

If an equal outcome is desirable, the negotiation "game' should be played according to a different rule, such as Party A slices the pie, while Party B chooses which slice it desires. It is easy to notice that Party A's calculations during the "game" should be based on the estimated behavior of Party B. Claiming a bigger slice of the "pie" often results in focusing on only one party's estimations and calculations, while ignoring those of the

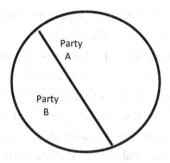

Figure 2:   The fixed pie

other involved parties. However, the other parties may do the same. As each party struggles to get the bigger "slice", the competition intensifies, and the negotiation process may reach an impasse. In this situation, each party will make concessions only if an impasse is more costly than the concession. For example, management negotiating with desirable candidates will concede to candidates' demands if a negotiation impasse means heavy losses, i.e. losing the candidates, having to initiate an expensive search for new candidates, time considerations, and the loss of essential work that is not performed in the meantime. However, in order to concede to the candidates' demands, management should estimate not only the value of its own losses as a result of an impasse, but also the estimated values of the candidates' losses. By taking into account the estimated candidates' calculations as well, management may arrive at a rational decision. According to the Rational theories, each party involved in the negotiation (be it in our example of the management on one side or the candidates on the other) should evaluate the expected utility of both sides, whenever any kind of decision-making is required.

When the number of negotiating individuals exceeds two, coalitions can be formed and the competition over the "Pie" becomes more complicated. One of the theoretical solutions is to conceive of each coalition as one party, provided that no member in the coalition opposes another member in the same coalition, and that the rules of how to split the gains or losses among members of the same coalition are agreed upon. It is noteworthy that participants involved in negotiations may establish coalitions in order to assure winning.

To conclude, Rational theories depict how reasonable negotiators should make decisions during the negotiation process or how they should behave if they strive to achieve their own interests and goals — in other words, how negotiators should "claim value" (claiming the negotiator's share of the "fixed pie", at the expense of the other party).[7]

It is important to emphasize that a basic assumption of the Rational theories is that all negotiating parties are rational, and that the negotiation process is often competitive. A common practice of negotiators is to place high initial demands in the expectation that higher initial demands will yield a greater "slice" of the "fixed pie". In order to maintain their position, these negotiators are inflexible, and express an inability to reduce their demands, supplemented by threats and other harsh behavior. Such a *competitive* or *"distributive"* proccss correlates in many cases with several possible outcomes. The most desirable one for the negotiators is to achieve high gains, even at the expense of the other negotiators. In this sense, competitive "distributive" negotiation often results in a "Win-Lose" outcome.[8] Other possible outcomes of such negotiations are an impasse and, more seldom, a compromise, where each party receives an agreed-upon part of the "pie".

3.2. *Behavioral Theories*

The Behavioral theories mainly come from the fields of Sociology, Psychology, Organizational Behavior, Political Science and Industrial Relations.

The term "cooperative" or "integrative" negotiation is typical to the Behavioral theories, just as the term "competitive" or "distributive" negotiation is typical to the Rational theories.[9] Cooperative negotiation refers to the disclosure of information, the readiness of all parties to consult and explore a variety of available options, and make mutual concessions during the negotiation process. Behavioral theories mainly concentrate on expanding the "fixed pie", i.e. "Creating Value" for all parties participating in the negotiation. Another characteristic of cooperative negotiation is justice. Justice is perceived as a result of the negotiators' expanded "pie", as well as parties'

---

[7]"Claiming Value" and "Creating Value" are terms portrayed by Lax, D.A. and Sebenius, J.K. (1986), in their book *The Manager as Negotiator*, The Free Press.

[8]See Raiffa, H. (1982), *The Art and Science of Negotiation*, Belknap Press of Harvard University Press. See also, Snyder, G.H. and Diesing, P. (1977), *Conflict Among Nations. Bargaining: Decision Making and System Structure in International Crises*, Princeton University Press.

[9]The terms "Cooperative Bargaining" and "Distributive Bargaining" were first developed in the field of Labor Relations by Walton, R.E. and McKersie, R.B. (1965), *A Behavioral theory of Labour Negotiations: An Analysis of Social Interaction System*, McGraw-Hill.

open access to information, and a fair opportunity to "be heard" during the negotiation process.[10] Such a negotiation process may lead to an outcome that satisfies all involved parties. For example, a fire destroyed a high rise office building that belonged to a few businessmen. The insurance company refused to compensate the businessmen for a great part of their losses, since some sections of the contract (usually written in very small print) were disclaimers. The businessmen sent their lawyers to negotiate with the insurance company representatives. The negotiation took the form of a "competitive" or "Zero Sum Game" type of negotiation, where each side tried to "Claim Value" or, in other words, to "push" the other side as hard as possible in order to gain more. It was clear to both sides that the gains of one party would be at the expense of the others. At a certain point in the negotiation, the businessmen's representatives came up with a creative idea, which they suggested to the insurance company. They suggested shifting the insurance of those who were insured by other insurance companies — to *this* insurance company in return for full compensation for the office building fire damages. This was a good deal for both sides, as the businessmen (the building owners) received all of their expected compensation, while the insurance company profited from the new insured subsidiaries. In Behavioral theory "language", the "Pie" was expanded, as can be seen in Figure 3.

When the "Pie" is expanded, each party involved in the negotiation can receive its gains from the surplus without harming the other sides' gains. Such an "integrative" outcome may lead to mutual satisfaction and, hopefully, to

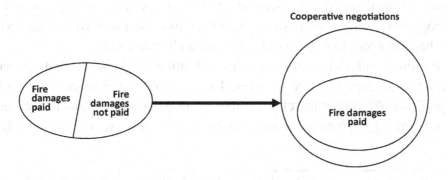

Figure 3: The expanded "Pie"

---

[10]See Wagner, L. and Druckman, D. (2012), The Role of Justice in Historical Negotiations, *Negotiation and Conflict Management* Vol. 5(1), pp. 49–71.

a better relationship among the negotiating parties. In this sense, "Cooperative" negotiation often results in a "Win–Win" outcome, which satisfies all negotiators.

However, there is no guarantee that once the "Pie" has been "expanded", the involved parties would not immediately inaugurate a new "competitive" negotiation regarding the additional section of the "Pie". In this case, all involved parties try to grab as much as possible from the resulting surplus. In our example, the businessmen may demand a substantive reduction in the cost of the subsidiaries' insurance, whereas the insurance company may demand the full rate in order to recover the losses incurred by compensating the fire damages.

As a matter of fact, "Cooperative" negotiation is widely accepted as the type of negotiation that reduces antagonism, restores justice and minimizes rigidity. Some scholars even argue that a "Cooperative" agreement has the potential to remain stable for a long time. However, not all scholars accept these assumptions, especially when they refer to negotiations in countries other than the USA. Thus, for example, empirical findings indicate that Mexican negotiators, compared to North American negotiators, achieved higher gains when they negotiated in a competitive manner, in contrast to the North American way, which is more cooperative.[11] Negotiation, as has already been emphasized, is a complicated process based among others on relative utility calculations, the balance of power between the involved parties, and their degree of interdependence.[12] However, the most fashionable and influential theories are those emphasizing cooperative (integrative) versus competitive (distributive) negotiation styles. The assumption that a "Cooperative" negotiation style guarantees that the involved parties "will live happily ever after" has not been empirically supported.

Rational and Behavioral theories are often, at least at first glance, perceived as contradictory theories. The Rational theories seem to guide negotiators about how to "claim value" or, in other words, how to seek out maximum achievements for themselves, even at the expense of the other

---

[11]Graham, J.L. Mintu, A.T. and Rodgers, W. (1994), Exploration of Negotiation Behaviors in Ten Foreign Countries Using a Model Developed in the United States, *Management Science*, Vol. 40(1), pp. 72–95.

[12]Lewicki, R.L. Weiss, S.E. and Lewin, D. (1992), Models of Conflict, Negotiation and Third Party Intervention: A Review and Synthesis, *Journal of Organizational Behavior*, Vol. 13(3), pp. 209–252.

party. Behavioral theories guide all negotiating parties to "create value", that is, to jointly seek out a solution that is satisfactory for all, even if the different parties have opposing interests. Of course, these contradictions only emphasize extreme negotiating styles and do not reflect the many other possible behaviors that may emerge during the negotiation process. For example, negotiators can "create value" at a certain point in the negotiation and "claim value" at another. They can be competitive at the beginning of the negotiation, and cooperative at the end or *vice versa*. However, the contradicting perception of the Rational and Behavioral theories overlooks some important aspects, which are shared by both.

Both Rational ("competitive") and Behavioral ("cooperative") theories are similar regarding a variety of negotiation behaviors. Mainly, they are both basically beneficial theories. Both assume that all negotiating parties are motivated to incur as many benefits as possible from the negotiation outcome. Each of the theories, in its own way, focuses on giving the best guidance to negotiators about how to gain achievements at the bargaining "table". The Rational theories attempt to do this through competition, whereas the Behavioral theories operate through cooperation.

Finally, ask yourself — are you a cooperative or competitive negotiator? Probably you are both — a "Hybrid" negotiator.

4. The Hybrid Theories

The "Hybrid" theories developed out of both Rational and Behavioral theories. These theories present negotiators' behavior as a kind of mixed-motives behavior. On the one hand, negotiators wish to maximize their gains, even at the expense of their opponents, leading to competitive behavior. On the other hand, both negotiators and their opponents are assumed to be interdependent; hence, they must anticipate and take into account their counterparts' likely reactions and behavior styles. Thus, in addition to competition, engaging in a certain amount of cooperative behavior is unavoidable, if negotiators wish to achieve some kind of an agreement. According to Hybrid theories, during the negotiation process, negotiators move back and forth –from a more competitive type of behavior to more cooperative behavior, and *vice versa*.[13] The Hybrid theories introduce new aspects to the decision-making discussion,

---

[13]Adair, W.L. and Brett, J.M. (2005), The Negotiation Dance: Time, Culture and Behavioral Sequences in Negotiation, *Organization Sciences*, Vol. 16(1), pp. 33–51.

such as: The issues under consideration, the role of incomplete information, the impact of subjective rationality, and the meaning of interdependence between the negotiating parties. The following discussion briefly describes a few examples of The Hybrid theories, bringing the study of negotiators' decision-making to the forefront of Hybrid theories.

4.1. *The Issues on the Negotiation "Table"*

One example of the Hybrid theories is the influence of the negotiation issues. It is intriguing to know what impact, if any, the type of issues on the negotiation "table" have on the negotiation process and outcome. For example, do interests-related issues, such as negotiating over scarce resources or personal benefits, impact the negotiation in a different way than intangible issues, such as values, ideology or religion? On the surface, negotiations about issues of interests may be compatible with the competitive "fixed pie" perception. On the other hand, negotiations about values are about the negotiators' perceptions of justice or about "being right", and thus may seem to be more suited to cooperative perceptions. However, due to the Hybrid theories, this is not always the case.

While Hybrid theories accept the notion that interests-related issues are in line with low cooperative motivation and a "fixed pie" Perception, they also argue that when negotiating about interests, negotiators are also willing to trade concessions; as a result, they may reach an integrative joint outcome. In contrast when negotiating over values, there is no room for trading concessions because negotiators cannot compromise about what they consider to be just or ideologically right. Therefore, when negotiating over values, negotiators tend to be inflexible, competitive, and even aggressive. It takes negotiators who strongly believe that they are "right" and their opponents are "wrong" to end up with a "Win–Lose" outcome or a negotiation impasse.[14]

4.2. *The Role of Information*

Other Hybrid theories address the role of information in negotiations. The Hybrid theories do not assume that negotiators have almost complete information, as the Rational theories do. They assume that negotiators often arrive at the negotiation "table" with incomplete and/or inaccurate

---

[14]Fieke, H. De Dreu, C.K.W, and Van Vianen, A.E.M. (2000), The Impact of Conflict Issues on Fixed Pie Perceptions, Problem Solving and Integrative Outcomes in Negotiation, *Organization Behavior and Human Decision Processes*, Vol. 81(2), pp. 329–358.

information regarding the positions of the other side, and sometimes even regarding their own positions. However, unlike the Behavioral theories, in which such incomplete information may yield the motivation to acquire more information, which may be low-quality information, by cooperating with the other side, the Hybrid theories assume that low-quality information may generate misconceptions. Similar to the Rational theories, it is assumed that low-quality information may cause disadvantages for the negotiating parties, as it distorts their decision-making judgment by creating misunderstandings.[15]

4.3. *Negotiators' Errors*

"Hybrid" theories also address decision-making errors during the negotiation process. It is noteworthy that the failure to make sound decisions during negotiations could be very costly.[16] This is why the Hybrid theories examine potential errors — which often occur far away from the negotiating "table", but which nevertheless impair negotiators' decision-making. Most probably, the origin of errors related to negotiation decision-making is rooted in *intuition*, *heuristics* and *stereotypes* — all of which are not relevant to the negotiation itself. All kinds of negotiations — competitive, cooperative or both — include various errors which affect the negotiation process and outcome.

Most of the times decision-making errors are made by negotiators, who are influenced by problems that are not directly related to the negotiation process. Predispositions regarding women may be an example of this type. Attitude towards women is predominantly generated at home, in school, and within the surrounding environment. These attitudes may have nothing to do with the negotiation. However, during the negotiation process displaying negative attitudes towards a female opponent, based on such predispositions, may be perceived as insulting and humiliating. Such attitudes may even trigger inflexibility and the use of hard tactics by the female negotiator, causing the entire negotiation to end in an impasse.[17]

---

[15]Dunning, D. Griffin, D. Milojkovic, J. and Ross, L. (1990), The Overconfidence Effect in Social Prediction, *Journal of Personality and Social Psychology*, Vol. 58(4), pp. 568–581.

[16]Milkman, K.L. Chigh, D. and Bazerman, M.H. (2009), How Can Decision Making Be Improved, *Perspective on Psychological Science*, Vol. 4(4), pp. 379–383.

[17]Pradel, D.W. Riley Bowles, H. and McGinn, K.L. (2006), When Does Gender Matter in Negotiations? *Contract Management*, Vol. 46(5), pp. 6–10.

4.4. *The Impact of Interdependence*

Hybrid theories address potential problems embedded in the negotiators' decision-making, such as problems which may arise out of the parties' levels of interdependence. It is assumed, both by the Rational and Behavioral theories, that every negotiation process creates interdependence between the parties to some degree.

According to both Behavioral and Rational theories, a negotiation's positive outcome is expected, due to the parties' interdependence. The main assumption is that interdependent parties develop cooperation, which may in turn help to reach a mutual agreement. However, there is no clear empirical support for the assumed cooperation between the negotiating parties, due to their voluntary or involuntary (in the case of forced negotiation) interdependency. The possible effect of interdependency is best described by the famous fable of the frog and the scorpion. The scorpion asks the frog to help him cross the river. The frog refuses, as she fears the scorpion's sting. The scorpion tells the frog to have no fear and reassures her: "A sting would cause both of us to drown in the river and die". The frog is convinced and crosses the river with the scorpion on her back. While swimming across the river the scorpion stings the frog. "What have you done?" cries the frog. "Now we shall both die". "I could not help it," replies the scorpion, "it is my nature".

Thus, interdependence during negotiations does not guarantee cooperation between the involved parties. Negotiators often take advantage of their counterparts, at times at the expense of both parties, obtaining a Lose–Lose situation as their end result.[18]

Moreover, cooperation as a result of interdependence usually requires negotiators to either suppress their own interests or equate them with those of their opponents. These are painful actions. Therefore, in negotiations interdependency may lead to behavior which, in the end, yields a good outcome for one (usually the powerful) party, while hurting the other. The Actor–Partner Independence Model (APIM)[19] can be applied here, in order to better understand the impact of interdependence on the negotiating parties and on

---

[18]Volkema, R. and Rivers, C. (2012), Beyond Frogs and Scorpions: A Risk-Based Framework for Understanding Negotiating Counterparts' Ethical Motivations, *Negotiation Journal*, Vol. 28(4), pp. 379–405.

[19]See Krasikova, D.V. and LeBreton, J.M. (2012), Just the Two of Us: Misalignment of Theory and Methods in Examining Dyadic Phenomena, *Journal of Applied Psychology*, Vol. 97(4), pp. 739–757.

the negotiation outcome. According to the APIM model, although interdependence between the parties can generate cooperation, the parties may be reluctant to cooperate, unless they believe that the other parties will reciprocate and not take advantage of their cooperation. Uncertainty regarding the other side's reciprocation may cause "stinging" behavior. Actually, there are numerous mediating factors that explain the interdependence effect on the different parties' behavior and on the negotiation outcome; for example, the intensive level of conflict on which the negotiation is based may also affect the parties' willingness or unwillingness to cooperate, despite their interdependence. The more intensive the conflict, the less cooperative the parties are — and the greater their temptation to harm one another. The less intensive the conflict, the more cooperative the negotiating parties may become. In addition, the parties' moods and the balance of power may also impact their willingness to cooperate. One party's mood and power is enough to affect all of the other parties' behavior and the negotiation outcome. Take the above-mentioned example of anger, displayed by a high-power negotiator. According to the APIM model, such anger will affect the other, less powerful, negotiator, and improve the high-power negotiator's outcome. In contrast, anger displayed by low-power negotiators will yield them a poor outcome.

To conclude, the Hybrid theories address both rational and behavioral aspects of negotiation. The following chapters in this book are based on Hybrid theories, their assumptions, and their subsequent research findings.

Practical Applications

- Negotiation is not always voluntary. Do not disqualify negotiation because it is forced on you (by a court or other entity). Even involuntary negotiation may help you to successfully confront a conflict — just give it a chance. If it does not work, you can walk away from the negotiation "table", even if you have been forced to negotiate.
- Remember that there is nothing wrong with Win–Lose negotiations, as long as you are on the winning side. One of the most experienced negotiators I have ever known once told me: "Cooperation is great, as long as I get the bigger piece of the pie".
- Cooperation during the negotiation process is indeed great; both you and the other party can reach a Win–Win outcome. Just make sure that the other side is not taking advantage of your cooperation during

the negotiation process. In this case, you will end up with a Lose–Win outcome: You lose, the other side wins.

- There is nothing wrong with not reaching an agreement. An impasse or withdrawal from the negotiation is better than a bad agreement.

- Be aware of the type of issues you present on the negotiation "table". The chances are that interest issues (such as scarce resources issues) will yield a more convenient negotiation for you. Despite the hard-line attitude usually employed when negotiating over interest issues, you will probably end up by trading what is less important to you and more important to the other side, and *vice versa*. Such trading concessions may lead to a potentially integrative Win–Win outcome.

- If you deeply feel that you are "right" and the other side is "wrong" (or vice versa), do not waste your time negotiating. Values, ideologies and religious issues make the parties stubborn and inflexible. With these types of issues "on the table" the chances are that you will end up with an impasse. It is better to look for your *BATNA* before, instead of getting involved in such a negotiation process.

- In the event that you choose (?) to cooperate, make sure the other party is not unwilling or unable to reciprocate. Adversary reciprocation may lead to an impasse or even worst results, such as present rivalry or a future lack of desire to negotiate.

- Interdependence between you and the other side is embedded in the very nature of negotiation. You always have to calculate not only your own moves, but also (and even more importantly) the other side's intentions and moves. Taking into account the other side's intentions may lead to better relationships and a pleasant atmosphere. However, it may also lead to a surprise "sting". Be cautious! Participate with positive motivation, but be careful when a vicious sense of interdependence develops.

- When the conflict intensity level is low, you can afford to be generous and more cooperative in your negotiation behavior than when the conflict intensity level is high.

Chapter 3

A Matter of Perception: Subjective Rationality and Its Effects

"In every man there are two minds that work side by side, the one checking the other: Thus emotion stands against reason, intellect corrects passion..."

Ford Madox Ford

Negotiators do not always make their decisions based on objective facts or an objective rationality. They rather behave according to their own individual perceptions of the situation. Over the past decades, such decision-making has often been perceived as negotiators' *irrational behavior* or, in other words, a result of negotiators' *biases.* The list of such biases has only grown longer over the years, to include even completely natural and objectively rational behaviors, such as self-serving behavior or toughness.[1] It is, however, possible that all biases are not really irrational, but can be perceived as a certain type of rationality — *subjective rationality.*

Negotiators' biases are perceived as a deviation from rational behavior, which may lead negotiators to lower-quality decisions, possibly ending in a negative outcome. However, it is not accurate to always judge negotiators' behaviors as irrational when they are trying to reach the best outcome for themselves — of course, from their subjective point of view. Take, for example, *self-serving* behavior. Is it truly a *"bias"* or merely a subjective natural behavior often seen during a negotiation process? Take another example — *escalation of commitment.* Escalating commitment in the face of negotiators' continuing losses, which outweigh the current benefits, is usually considered a classic bias. An apt metaphor is that of a Casino player who keeps on

---

[1] See Caputo, A. (2013), A Literature Review of Cognitive Biases in Negotiation Processes, *International Journal of Conflict Management*, Vol. 24(4), pp. 374–398. In this paper, all mentioned biases are conceived as irrational.

gambling, despite ongoing losses. The more he loses, the more he decides to keep on playing. Objectively, of course, these are low-quality decisions which, in the end may leave the player with an empty purse. However, what about the subjective hope — to win a lot of money in the next round — which will allow the player to recover his previous losses? It can happen, despite the low statistical probability. Is this not the subjective rationality of the Casino player? In the same way, negotiators' rationality to continue negotiating — after investing money, time, preparations and even emotions — is often decided with the hope that by continuing the negotiation process, they will recover their losses or at least minimize them. Is such a subjective hope — to minimize one's losses by continuing to negotiate — a "bias" — a deviation from rationality — or is it rather simply a subjective, rational consideration?

It seems that many negotiators' behavior, often considered as biases, are actually subjective rational behaviors, which do not necessarily lead to low-quality negotiation decisions and outcomes. In fact, sometimes, quite the opposite is true. Subjective rationality behavior may, at times, lead to better outcomes than making decisions based on objective rationality. For example, *anchoring*, which is the tendency to make decisions based on the first offer or preliminary information, is traditionally considered a "bias". However, presenting an initial price that is extremely high during negotiation, as an "anchor", may change the opponents' subjective attitudes about the proper agreement and, in the end, negotiators may achieve a higher outcome than a reasonable so-called "rational" price. Of course, offering an extremely high price can also cause a negotiation impasse; however, there is always the chance to reach an impasse when negotiating, whatever the offered price is. In other words, the so-called biases are not necessarily a deviation from rationality. Generally, subjective efforts to minimize losses or to maximize outcomes cannot always be considered a "bias". In most cases, these are logically right decisions, which are based on negotiators' subjective emotions, interests and objectives, which can be perceived as subjective rational behavior.

1. Subjective Rationality: A Metaphor and Its Implications

The best deal, according to the rational conception, is when negotiators give up the objects that are of the least importance to them, but of the highest importance to their opponents, in exchange for objects of the highest importance to them, but the least importance to their opponents. Therefore, it is considered quite irrational if, as a result of the negotiation, each of the sides gives up highly important objects and, in exchange, receives objects that are of minor importance or even useless — a Lose–Lose negotiation outcome. Yet, in the real world of negotiation one can observe many negotiators behaving in exactly this manner. Such behaviors are characterized by what can be referred to as "*subjective rationality*". "Subjective rationality" may yield a negotiation outcome that is a loss for one or both negotiating parties, in terms of "on-the-table" tangible achievements, but is still considered a gain in terms of their immediate or long-term interests or benefits. In such a case, even giving up an important item, which is reciprocated with a useless item, can be subjectively perceived by the involved parties as **rational.** It is, of course, a subjective rationality, but it is still a kind of rational behavior, rather than a bias.

An interesting classical metaphor, which illustrates just such a subjective rationality behavior, is portrayed in the negotiation literature as the O. Henry Effect,[2] along the lines of O. Henry's, famous story, "The Gift of the Magi".

In short, the story describes Jim and Della, who loved each other very much, but were very poor. They only had two great treasures, in which they both took pride. One was Jim's gold watch, which had been in his family for generations, and the other was Della's beautiful long hair. On Christmas day, Della cut her hair and sold it, in order to buy a chain worthy of Jim's watch, while Jim sold his watch in order to buy Della the shell hair combs she had wanted for ages, for her beautiful hair, which was now gone. Unfortunately, in the end, both presents were useless. Still, both Jim and Della gained something much more important, at least from their subjective point of view.

This, of course, is not a true negotiation scenario, but just a metaphor. Yet, if it were a real negotiation situation, according to the objective rational negotiation theories, it would be perceived as the worst possible scenario. Both Della and Jim "trade" something that is highly valued by them, in exchange for something that is worthless — has no value at all for either of them. In a negotiation context, this can be described as a Lose–Lose outcome. If we continue to analyze the O. Henry-type negotiation scenario,

---

[2]Curhan, J.R. Elfenbein, H.A. and Xu, H. (2006), What Do People Value When They Negotiate? Mapping the Domain of Subjective Value in Negotiation, *Journal of Personality and Social Psychology*, Vol. 91(3), pp. 493–512.

it is possible to conclude that it was Jim and Della's apparent irrational behavior which led them to such a miserable result. However, was it indeed irrational behavior on their part? Such a conclusion may be incorrect, since Della and Jim proved — from their subjective standpoints — that there is something even more important than an objective rational gift exchange — their love. In real negotiation scenarios, there are often also more influential aspects than the tangible "on-the-table" exchange, such as maintaining a long-term relationship.

1.1. *"Positive" Subjective Rationality*

Imagine the following three scenarios, all dealing with the sale of an apartment. In the first scenario, a father negotiates with his daughter about selling her his apartment. During the negotiations, he requests a substantially lower price than the estimated value of the apartment. In addition, he does not demand any advanced payments or guarantees from his daughter. Assuming that the daughter is not interested in the apartment, the father then offers it to a real estate agent. In this second scenario, the father's initial offer is 20% higher than the apartment's current estimated value, plus a big advance payment, and various guarantees for the following payments. In a third possible scenario — through an internet advertisement — a buyer, who is a complete stranger, wants to purchase the apartment. During their first "preliminary talk" before negotiating, the father detects several similarities between himself and the new buyer. For example, he discovers that they both studied in the same high school, (but in different years), their children have similar professions, and they share similar political orientations. As a result, during the negotiation the initial price of the apartment is reduced to its estimated value, and the father is ready to make further compromises regarding the advance payment and the required guarantees. In which one of the three scenarios, in your opinion, is the father's behavior "irrational"?

In the first scenario, the father's relation and emotions regarding his daughter influenced his behavior. In the second scenario, it may be that the stereotype of the greedy real estate agents shaped his behavior. In the third scenario, the closeness that he felt to the stranger/ buyer, due to their similarities, caused his flexible behavior. In all three scenarios, the father's actions reflect acceptable, rational human behavior, although in the first and third scenarios, the father's behavior is typical to that of subjective rationality.

Objective rationality can be measured by achieving the maximum available value of the negotiation outcomes. For example, a behavior whose aim is to get the maximum price for selling an apartment, can be measured objectively by how much money the negotiators received and the amount of the advance payment. However, "subjective rationality" can be measured by the parties' success in establishing a positive rapport and the satisfaction received from attaining a sense of friendship. For example, similarity found between strangers may result in an urge to establish a mutual long-term relationship. This, in turn, can lead to a substantial reduction in the price of the negotiated object, in exchange for a good relationship in the future. In this case, subjective rationality cannot be measured by the high "on the table" outcome, but rather by the parties' satisfaction with their "off the table" intangible gains. In addition, subjective rationality enables negotiators to make excuses, and even justify a loss in terms of economic gains, in exchange for other desired outcomes.[3]

1.2. *"Negative" Subjective Rationality*

Subjective rationality does not have only positive connotations, such as achieving rapport. It also has another side, with somewhat "negative" connotations. For example, negotiators who enjoy a high level of rapport with their opponents do not always make efforts to preserve it. On the contrary, they are more likely to behave unethically and exploit their opponents, compared to negotiators who enjoy low levels of rapport. Furthermore, when their own reputation is at stake due to the negotiation, these negotiators show no satisfaction with the current negotiation or any desire to work in the future with their opponents.[4] In such cases, maintaining their own good reputation, which is a kind of intangible asset, is more important to negotiators than preserving or establishing good, long-term relationships with their opponents.

Moreover, negotiators do not always engage in a negotiating process in order to reach an agreement — sometimes, they have other subjective

---

[3] See also, Curhan, J.R. Neale, M.A. Ross, L. and Rosencranz-Engelmann, J. (2008), Relational Accommodation in Negotiation: Effects of Egalitarian and Gender on Economic Efficiency and Relational Capital, *Organizational Behavior and Human Decision Processes*, Vol. 107(2), pp.192–205.

[4] Jap, S. Robertson, D.C. Hamilton, R. (2011), The Dark Side of Rapport: Agent Misbehavior Face to Face and Online, *Management Science*, Vol. 57(9), pp. 1610–1622.

considerations, for example, negotiators may engage in negotiation in order to obtain confidential information from their opponents during the negotiation process. After this information has been attained, there is no subjective rationale to continue the negotiation process. This example as well as others,[5] cannot be explained by objective rationality, but may be clearly understood by "negative" subjective rationality.

A "dark side" of "subjective rationality" can be demonstrated by the motivations of revenge and even terror. Subjective motivation of this kind can cause negotiators to bring about a negotiation failure, a Lose–Lose outcome. In real-world negotiations, it is possible to observe negotiators who are ready to accept a small loss in order to cause their opponents a bigger and far bitter loss — in extreme terms — a sort of "accepting the loss of one eye in order to cause the opponents the loss of both". Of course, from a subjective point of view, there are several benefits of revenge, such as the signaling of power, as in: "no one messes with me and gets away with it" or in relation to the restoration of self-esteem. Sometimes, the emotions associated with revenge in negotiation are created by the opponents' actions, which are interpreted as signs of disrespect and rejection.[6] Moreover, subjective satisfaction and even a feeling of triumph may be associated with vengeful actions.[7] The satisfaction such negotiators take from their revenge may be even stronger if the opponents understand that the act of revenge has actually been an act of punishment.[8]

To conclude, although "objective rationality" is probably more salient among negotiating parties, and tangible gains are more frequently used as a measure of a "successful" negotiation, "subjective rationality" can also be observed in day-to-day negotiations. Such subjective rationality sometimes has a "bright side" (as in the O. Henry Effect), which helps the parties to make concessions and cooperate. However, at times, it also has a "dark side". The "dark side" of subjective rationality is demonstrated in its most extreme

---

[5]See the section on "pretence strategy", in Chapter 7 of this book.

[6]Mcdonald, K.L. and Asher, S.R. (2013), College Students' Revenge Goals Across Friends, Romantic Partners, and Roommate Contexts: The Role of Interpretation and Emotions, *Social Development*, Vol. 22(3), pp. 499–521.

[7]Schumann, K. and Ross, M. (2010), The Benefits, Costs and Paradox of Revenge, *Social and Personality Psychology Compass*, Vol. 4(12), pp. 1193–1205.

[8]Gollwitzer, M. Meder, M. and Schmitt, M. (2011), What Gives Victims Satisfaction When They Seek Revenge? *European Journal of Social Psychology*, Vol. 41(3), pp. 364–374.

form by the subjective satisfaction (and sometimes even a sense of triumph) negotiators may derive from revenge and acts of terror.

Thus, each individual negotiator has various rationalities that exist at and beyond the negotiation "table". Objective and subjective rationalities sometimes operate in opposite directions; yet, often exist side by side during the negotiation process. Both objective and subjective rationality stand side-by-side during negotiation processes and influence their outcomes. The following chapter discusses, at length, just a few examples of negotiators' subjective rational behaviors.

2. Feelings as a Cause for "Subjective Rationality"

Emotions and moods are good examples of causes of subjective rationality. Moods are a temporary state of mind that generates some sensation towards situations or the parties involved in this situation. Moods are reactions to everyday experiences in various situations, such as work aggravation, satisfaction over winning the lottery or empathy with others. *Emotions* are similar to moods; however, moods tend to change when the situation transforms, whereas emotions are stronger and not very temporal. Emotions can influence moods, just as moods can influence emotions. It is possible, therefore, to refer to both moods and emotions as "feelings". Negotiators who act in accordance with their feelings are not irrational negotiators. Subjective feelings are triggers that affect negotiators' subjective perceptions and behavior during and after the negotiation process.

2.1. *Positive and Negative Feelings*

Some examples of feelings that may influence relationships, in general, and negotiators' behavior, in particular, are: Joy, compassion, surprise, fear, sadness, anger, disgust and contempt. Some of these feelings, such as happiness, compassion and empathy, are often classified as "positive" feelings, whereas anger and disgust are often classified as "negative" feelings. All kinds of feelings are not necessarily typical to negotiation situations and are not necessarily generated at the negotiation "table". It is also worth noting that feelings are usually spontaneous, involuntary and sometimes even uncontrollable.[9]

---

[9]Dubin, R. (1992), *Central Life Interest*, New Brunswick Transaction Publishers, pp. 23–29.

There is no need to delve deeply into the negotiation process in order to realize that feelings, including those which are not generated during negotiation processes, might have an impact on negotiators' behavior. Yet, in what way do feelings influence negotiation processes and outcomes? Does emotional involvement in negotiation — from angry outbursts to expressions of sympathy and happiness — create uncertainty among negotiators? Alternatively, does the actual expression of feelings during the negotiation process create a "road map" for negotiators, enabling them to understand hidden cues and adapt themselves to problematic situations? Do "positive" feelings — such as joy and sympathy — affect the negotiation process in a different way than "negative" feelings? And when do feelings help negotiators solve problems, and when do they escalate negotiation difficulties?

2.2. *"Negative", "Positive" and Mixed Feelings — Their Influences on Negotiations*

Feelings can either assist or damage the negotiation process. Even feelings not linked to the negotiation itself or incidental feelings may serve to influence the negotiation process and therefore its outcome. On the positive side, feelings play an important role as information conveyers. They may convey significant signals regarding the opponent's intentions, positions and preferences. They also provide impressions such as the impatience and aversions of the other side, which may increase negotiators' motivation to adapt their behavior to their opponents' moods. This type of adaptation to the opponent's feelings may improve the negotiators' capability to avoid unwanted developments. Dana's story is an example of this point. Dana had been negotiating with her boss for a promotion, as well as for a raise in salary, for some time. Dana claims that throughout the negotiations she tried to be as pleasant and empathetic as possible. However, her boss never stopped insulting her and behaved in a very tough manner. During their last negotiation meeting, Dana could no longer bear it. She burst into tears and left the negotiation room, slamming the door behind her. Dana said she was sure she would be fired, but this did not happen. To her surprise, her boss stopped insulting her and gave her everything she asked for. Dana was not aware that it was her anger at her boss — her subjective rational behavior — which would finally cause him to accept her demands. She did not realize that her anger provided her boss with information regarding the possibility of her leaving the job. This probably caused her boss to react in a subjective rational way and accept her demands. Of course, an "objective rational" boss would probably have rejected Dana's demands, leading to a negotiation impasse, taking the risk of her resignation. However, ignoring opponents' feelings may lead to an impasse which, in turn, may lead to negotiators being caught in a competitive-behavior spiral: i.e. they become less cooperative, share less information, have less faith in negotiation as a way to solve their conflict, and end up with no agreement.[10] Negotiators' feelings, such as anger and disgust, may threaten the relationship between the parties and call for a change in their behavior.[11]

2.3. On the "Mixed" Influences of Positive and Negative Feelings

It has been traditionally accepted to differentiate between the subjective influence of "positive" and "negative" feelings on negotiations processes. It has been argued that "positive" feelings, such as joy and sympathy, contribute to increased cooperation between parties, greater concession-making, reduce the use of hard tactics, and generally contribute to cooperation and integrative negotiation outcomes i.e. *expanding the "Pie"*, and finally creating joint gains. In contrast, "negative" feelings, such as anger and disgust, supposedly enhance competitiveness among parties, cause negotiators to be self-centered, and decrease the possibility of reaching an integrative agreement and joint gains.[12] Notwithstanding Dana's example, angry negotiators may reject reasonable offers, make few concessions, and refuse to further negotiate with their opponents. Anger may also influence a negotiator's judgment, causing it to become inconsistent and harsh, especially where the opponent's interests are concerned.[13] Anger causes negotiators to be inflexible and propose fewer integrative offers.[14]

---

[10]O'Connor, K.M. and Arnold, J.A. (2001), Distributive Spirals: Negotiation Impasses and the Moderating Role of Disputant Self-Efficacy, *Organizational Behavior and Human Decision Processes*, Vol. 84(1), pp. 148–176.

[11]Druckman, D. and Olekalns, M. (2007), Emotions in Negotiations, *Group Decision and Negotiation*, Vol. 17(1), pp. 1–11.

[12]Van Kleef, G.A., De Dreu, C.K.W. and Manstead, A.S.R. (2004), The Interpersonal Effects of Anger and Happiness in Negotiations, *Journal of Personality and Social Psychology*, Vol. 86(1), pp. 57–76.

[13]Allred, K.G. Mallozzi, J.S. Matui, F. and Raia, C.P. (1997), The Influence of Anger and Compassion on Negotiation Performance, *Organization Behavior and Human Decision Processes*, Vol. 70(3), pp. 175–179.

[14]Liu, M. (2009), The Intrapersonal and Interpersonal Effects of Anger on Negotiations Strategies: A Cross Cultural Investigation, *Human Communication Research*, Vol. 35(1), pp. 148–169.

However, the clear differentiation between the influence of the two categories — "positive" feelings and negative feelings — is somewhat overly rigid, since various differences exist within each category. It is possible that, at times, negative feelings might have some "positive" influence on negotiators' decision-making, whereas "positive" feelings might sometimes have a negative influence. In other words, depending on the situation, the distinction between the impact of "negative" and "positive" influences is not completely clear-cut. Several examples can demonstrate this kind of mixed influence.

2.4. *On the Negative Effect of Positive Feelings*

Positive feelings do not always contribute to cooperation. Positive feelings can, for example, contribute to negotiators' *overconfidence* and high *self-estimation*. Negotiators with too much confidence in their own judgment and abilities may underestimate their opponents. They are also more likely to experience the "illusion of control", distort information and feedback, and are often reluctant to reach an agreement.[15] Overconfidence as a result of good feelings also reduces negotiators' concessionary behavior, enhancing rivalry and often causing negotiation crises. In addition, positive feelings may lead to greater risk taking.

However, it is possible to notice precisely the opposite effect of positive feeling. Due to positive feelings, negotiators tend to make many concessions; they also become risk-averse and, as a result, might become the losers in the negotiation process.[16] Empathy, the capacity to take the role of the other, is also included in the positive feeling category, and is supposed to smooth the path in regard to negotiation problems solving. Indeed, empathy can make negotiations easier by smoothing the way to agreement. Yet, empathy might be rejected by the opponent due to various reasons, such as lack of trust or the desire to gain control over the negotiation process. When empathy is rejected, it may incur increased risk and high demands.[17] Thus, the "positive feelings" negotiators experience can, on the one hand, lead to enhanced cooperation.

---

[15] Kramer, M.R., Newton, E. and Pommerenke, P.L. (1993), Self-Enhancement and Negotiator Judgment: Effects of Self-Esteem and Mood, *Organizational Behavior and Human Decision Processes*, Vol. 56(1), pp. 110–133.

[16] Morris, W.N. (1989), *Mood, the Frame of Mind*, Springer-Verlag, p. 102.

[17] Maritinovski, B. Traum, D. and Marsella, S., (2007), Rejection of Empathy in Negotiation, *Group Decision and Negotiation*, Vol. 16(1), pp. 61–76.

On the other hand, it can lead to high demands and low concessions on the part of the opponents.

2.5. *On the Positive Effects of Negative Feelings*

Negative feelings may also have positive effects on negotiators and the negotiation process. The impact of specific feelings on negotiations may vary according to different dimensions, such as whether they are endogenous or were caused incidentally.[18] Negative feelings influence the negotiation process; for example, displays of anger lower the opponents' demands and enhance opponents' concessions.[19] This may, however, promote a rapid agreement, either integrative or non-integrative.[20] In a more positive light, negative feelings may help adjust the manner of interaction between the negotiating parties. For example, sending signals of dissatisfaction, such as displays of anger or sadness, serves as a warning. It is a strong signal to the other parties involved in the negotiation process to somehow change their behavior — give more respect or make some concessions — otherwise; they risk a negotiation crisis or complete impasse. Negative feelings may also help negotiators to understand their opponents' abilities and power. For example, showing anger or hostility is a luxury, usually available only to the powerful negotiator. Less powerful negotiators hesitate and even fear to show negative feelings during the negotiation process. Thus, showing anger may give some indication of the opponents' power or intentions, such as walking away from the negotiation "table".

2.6. *The Manipulation of Feelings During the Negotiation Process*

It is noteworthy that the display of feelings expressed during the negotiation process is not always genuine. Anger, sadness and disgust, for example, can be triggered incidentally or used intentionally as a systematic tactic to

---

[18]Polman, E. and Kim, S.H. (2014), Effects of Anger, Disgust and Sadness on Sharing with Others, *Personality and Social Psychology Bulletin*, Vol. 39(2), pp. 683–692.

[19]Barry, B. (2008), Negotiator Affect: The State of the Arts (and Sciences), *Group Decision Negotiation*, Vol. 17(1), pp. 97–105, see also Van Kleef, G.A. De Dreu, C.K.W. and Manstead, A.S.R. (2004), The Interpersonal Effects of Anger and Happiness in Negotiation, *Journal of Personality and Social Psychology*, Vol. 86(1), pp. 57–76.

[20]Tsay, C.J. and Bazerman, M. (2009), A Decision-Making Perspective to Negotiation: A Review of the Past and a Look to the Future, *Negotiation Journal*, Vol. 25(4), pp. 467–480.

force the opponents' hand. Feelings are, in many cases, manipulated and used as tactics in negotiation, in order to change participants' perceptions and influence their actions. Pretending to have negative or positive feelings or, alternatively, the inhibition of such genuine feelings are strategies used to change the negotiation process. The following are some examples of possible results of an unauthentic exhibition of feelings. The display of negative or positive feelings, as a reaction to opponents' demands, serves to stress the level of importance that negotiators ascribe to these demands. Displays of anger or enthusiasm indicate high importance, whereas boredom or indifference indicates low importance. Faking certain negative emotions, such as anger, may be used to convey dissatisfaction. In contrast, suppressing positive emotions, such as pleasure at the opponent's concessionary behavior, may be used to prevent the opponents' reconsidering their concessions. A false emotional outburst is a signal that, from now on, the negotiators' behavior may be unpredictable and they would not have much control over future developments. A quick shift in feeling from negative to positive, i.e. from hostility to warmth, is intended to deceive the opponent by disguising the negotiator's real intentions. It is interesting that research findings indicate that negotiators perceive the use of positive feelings as a better tactic than the use of negative feelings.[21] Moreover, negotiators look upon intentional emotional deception as more suitable than other planned deceptions in negotiation, such as conveying disinformation or making false threats.

To conclude, negotiators do not express bias or irrationality when they behave emotionally. The use of feelings during the negotiation process is an expression of their subjective rationality. This is especially noticeable when feelings are used to manipulate the process. It is noteworthy, however, that both genuine and unauthentic feelings serve as tactics, intentionally or unintentionally, thus influencing the relationship among the negotiating parties, as well as the negotiation process itself.

3. The Endowment Effect — An Example of Subjective Rationality

The Endowment Effect has attracted much attention in the literature, due to its influence on a wide variety of fields and, in our case especially, its influences on the negotiation process and outcomes.

---

[21]Barry, B. (1999), The Tactical Use of Emotion in Negotiation, *Research in Negotiation in Organization*, Vol. 7, pp. 93–124.

Imagine you are going to sell your apartment to a stranger. You have lived in it for 15 years and are now moving to a house. How much would you ask for your apartment? Would you ask for its "market" value? Would you ask for more than its "market" value? For less?

According to the objective rational theories (such as economics, game theory, decision-making), ownership of an object, should not affect its valuation. The Endowment Effect,[22] however, implies that people value their own assets higher than their market value — and higher than what they would be ready to pay if they were to buy the same assets from someone else.[23] As a result, the Endowment Effect is considered a bias, a deviation from rational behavior. However, is high valuation of an object we possess really irrational? First, the market valuation is not static; it varies according to the specific sellers and buyers, depending, among other things, on the specific sellers' willingness to sell and the buyers' willingness to buy. From this point of view, the high price asked for the sellers' own assets is not irrational from a subjective point of view; second, it is more than reasonable to assume that the mere ownership of an object creates some psychological association between the owner and its object,[24] which may be the cause for the higher valuation. This is exactly what was previously referred to as *subjective rationality*.

Thus, as a result of ownership, object possessors when negotiating, often tend to exaggerate their demands at the negotiation "table", relative to the market price. It is noteworthy, however, that the mere 'sense' of ownership — as opposed to actual ownership — is enough to cause negotiators' high demands.[25] As a result, due to the subjectively high valuation of their owned assets and ensuing demands, negotiators can either achieve a high outcome or end their negotiation in a deadlock.

---

[22]Kahneman, D. Knetsch J.L. and Thaler, R.H. (1990), Experimental Tests of the Endowment Effect and the Coase Theorem, *Journal of Political Economy*, Vol. 98(6), pp. 1325–1348.

[23]Belk, R.W. (1988), Possessions and the Extended Self. *Journal of Consumer Research*, Vol. 15(2), pp. 139–168.

[24]Beggan, J.K. (1992), On the Social Nature of Nonsocial Perception: The Mere Ownership Effect, *Journal of Personality and Social Psychology*, Vol. 62(2), pp. 229–237. See also Feys, J. (1991), Briefly Induced Belongingness to Self and Preference, *European Journal of Social Psychology*, Vol. 21(2), pp. 547–552.

[25]Gimpel, H. (2007), Loss Aversion and Reference-Dependent Preferences in Multi-Attribute Negotiations, *Group Decision and Negotiation*, Vol. 16(4), pp. 303–319.

3.1. *Explaining the Endowment Effect from Several Perspectives*

There are several proposed explanations of the Endowment Effect. The most conventional explanation is based on *Prospect Theory*.[26] According to this theory, identical gains and losses have different meanings for negotiators, since losses typically loom larger than gains. For example, if you your salary is increased by 10%, you will probably be satisfied. However, if your salary is cut by an **identical** 10%, your distress from the salary reduction would probably be bigger and far more bitter than the satisfaction experienced from your salary increase. This characteristic leads to interesting negotiation behavior. On the one hand, when gains are expected, negotiators will avoid risk and become "loss aversion" negotiators. On the other hand, when losses are expected, negotiators will become "risk-seeking" negotiators. To be a risk-seeking negotiator means to be rigid and non-concessionary, behavior which may result in a negotiation impasse. Generally, negotiators' subjective perception of their outcome, as either gain or loss, may determine their behavior and demands when selling.[27]

Imagine you are selling an expensive painting that you bought for 150,000. You know that its current market value is about 170,000. Yet, the best offer you have received until now is 160,000. Would you perceive this as a gain or a loss? According to Prospect Theory, object possessors — or those who have a sense of possession — are most often "affected" by the Endowment Effect. They usually sustain the view that "selling" their own object is a "loss", and thus become "risk-seeking". To compensate for their feelings of loss, they risk the negotiation by demanding a high, and sometimes even unreasonable, price — a price which they themselves would not be willing to pay if they were the "buyers".[28]

---

[26]Kahneman, D. and Tversky, A. (1979), Prospect Theory: An Analysis of Decisions under Risk, *Econometrica*, Vol. 47(2), pp. 263–291.

[27]Kahneman, D. and Knetsch, J.L. (1992), The Endowment Effect, Loss aversion, and the *Status Quo* Bias, in Thaler, R.H. (Ed.), *The Winner's Curse*, Princeton University Press, Princeton, New Jersey, pp. 63–79. See also Van Boven, L. Loewenstein, G. and Dunning, D. (2003), Mispredicting the Endowment Effect: Underestimation of Owners' Selling Prices by Buyer's Agents, *Journal of Economics Behavior and Organization*, Vol. 51(3), pp. 351–365.

[28]Neale, M.A. and Bazerman, M.H. (1998), Negotiating Rationally: The Power and Impact of the Negotiators' Frame. In Lewicki, R.J. Saunders, D.M. and Minton J.W. (eds.), *Negotiations — Readings, Exercises and Cases*, McGraw-Hill Education, Irwin, pp. 149–159.

Therefore, if you perceive selling your painting for 160,000 (150,000 is your anchor) as a *gain*, then you will be relatively flexible, tend to make concessions during the negotiation process, and probably end up with an agreement. However, if you perceive the 160,000 offer (170,000 is your anchor) as a *loss*, then you will probably end up being a rigid negotiator and will risk looking for a better offer. The Endowment Effect indicates that when selling your own painting, there is a high probability that you will feel a subjective loss rather than a gain, and therefore take the risk of being a rigid negotiator, which may lead to an impasse.

There are other explanations for the Endowment Effect phenomenon. One such explanation emphasizes the difference in valuation, simply due to the different attitudes of buyers and sellers regarding the features of a negotiated object.[29] Of course, sellers want to sell at a bit higher than "market price", while buyers want to buy at a bit lower than market price. The gap between the sellers' high demands and the buyers' low offers is typical "market" behavior. These are the subjective rationalities of buyers and sellers. Other explanations of the Endowment Effect refer to asymmetric market information,[30] uncertainty and ambiguity,[31] the desire to discover the asset value of an object in the marketplace[32] or curiosity regarding discovering an uncertain value.[33]

3.2. Is it Possible to Moderate the Endowment Effect? Some Research Findings

Whatever the explanation of the Endowment Effect is, it seems to play a key role in many negotiation decisions, as sellers' demands made by owners tend

---

[29]Nayakankuppam, D. and Mishra, H. (2005), The Endowment Effect: Rose-Tinted and dark-Tinted Glasses, *Journal of Consumer Research*, Vol. 32(3), pp. 390–395.

[30]Dupont, D.Y. and Lee, G.S. (2002), The Endowment Effect, *Status Quo* Bias and Loss Aversion: Rational Alternative Explanation, *Journal of Risk and Uncertainty*, Vol. 25(1), pp. 87–101.

[31]Inder, B. and O'Brien, T. (2003), The Endowment Effect and the Role of Uncertainty, *Bulletin of Economic Research*, Vol. 55(3) pp. 289–301.

[32]Brown, T.C. (2005), Loss Aversion Without the Endowment Effect, and Other Explanations for the WTA–WTP Disparity, *Journal of Economic Behavior & Organization*, Vol. 57(3), pp. 367–379.

[33]van de Ven, N. Zeelenberg, M. and van Dijk, E. (2005), Buying and Selling Exchange Goods: Outcome Information, Curiosity and the Endowment Effect, *Journal of Economic Psychology*, Vol. 26(3), pp. 459–468.

to be significantly higher than those expected by buyers. Since this may result in a negotiation impasse, it is important to better understand the Endowment Effect moderators. Any successful attempt to reduce this effect could prevent a negotiation deadlock.

Market experience as an Endowment Effect moderator: It would have been logical to assume that "market" experience could mitigate the Endowment Effect, as negotiators gain more experience in the "market". Accordingly, negotiators experiencing many deadlocks resulting from their high demands would be more concessionary and less affected by the Endowment Effect. However, a reduced Endowment Effect has not been found with greater market experience.[34] On the contrary, it has been found that negotiators who reached an impasse in previous negotiations are more likely to reach an impasse in their next negotiations, even with different opponents.[35] Thus, "market" experience does not serve as a moderator for the Endowment Effect. Subjective rationality does not change much with experience.

On-going negotiation as an Endowment Effect moderator: Another possible moderator of the Endowment Effect is an on-going repetitive negotiation. The "default" belief is that in a one-shot negotiation, the parties are guided by their intentions to immediately achieve as much as possible, whereas in on-going, repetitive negotiations the negotiators are more restrained, expecting to get future rewards. In regard to the Endowment Effect theory in a one-shot negotiation, negotiators should present much higher demands than the on-going repetitive negotiators. Accordingly, the long-repetitive negotiators who apparently make much lower present demands moderate the Endowment Effect. However, such a difference between one-shot and long-term negotiations has only been partially proven.[36] It seems that long-term negotiators, in accordance with their subjective rationality, are

---

[34]Harbaugh, W.T. Krause, K. and Vesterlund, L. (2001), Are Adults Better Behaved than Children? Age, Experience, and the Endowment Effect, *Economics Letters,* Vol. 70(2), pp. 175–181.

[35]O'Connor, K.M. Arnold, J.A. and Burris, E.R. (2005), Negotiators Bargaining Histories and their Effects on Future Negotiation Performance, *Journal Applied Psychology,* Vol. 90(2), pp. 350–362.

[36]Galin, A. Gross, M. Sapir, S. and Kela-Egozi, I. (2006), The Endowment Effect on Academic Chores Trade-OFF (ACTO), *Theory and Decision,* Vol. 60, pp. 335–357.

not always prepared to make "sacrifices" for the sake of future achievements. Thus, on-going, repetitive negotiations are only a limited moderator of the high demands of "endowed" negotiators.

The negotiation proposal sequence as an Endowment Effect moderator: Can the proposal sequence — or the sequence in which the demands are presented at the negotiation "table" — serve as an Endowment Effect moderator? And if so, which sequence is a better Endowment Effect moderator? It was found that negotiators are willing to lower their demands and make concessions when the gain proposal follows the loss proposal, i.e. a loss–gain sequence.

The subjective impact of a "loss-gain" demand sequence is in line with the "contrast effect". Imagine you have to carry a heavy parcel and afterwards a light parcel. Would you not feel that the light parcel is lighter than it actually is, objectively? The contrast of the heavy parcel followed by the light parcel amplifies the subjective sense of a lighter parcel. Obviously, if you carry a light parcel first and then a heavy one, your subjective sense of a greater weight is amplified. In the same way, if negotiators experience a loss after a gain, the negotiators' subjective sense of the loss is amplified, leading to risk-seeking behavior and higher demands. If, however, the situation is reversed and the subjective sense of gain follows the sense of loss (a loss–gain sequence); then, the negotiators' sense of gain is amplified, leading to the negotiators' loss-aversion and decreased demands.[37] In other words, the negotiation sequence of subjective feelings — either a gain–loss or loss–gain sequence — may change people's subjective decisions to increase or decrease their demands, and consequently serve as an Endowment Effect moderator.

Individuals versus groups as an Endowment Effect moderator: Many studies on the Endowment Effect have mainly focused on its relation to individual owners rather than groups. Yet, many negotiations involve negotiating groups rather than negotiating individuals. Imagine a scenario in which a group representing graduate students is negotiating with the university authorities about the students' leisure time. Would the group be a more or less demanding negotiator than each individual student? It was found that groups

---

[37]Galin, A. (2009), Proposal Sequence and the Endowment Effect in Negotiation, *International Journal of Conflict Management*, Vol. 20(3), pp. 212–227.

significantly amplified the Endowment Effect in comparison to individuals, at least in the case of "selling" their leisure time. Since groups are inclined to be much more demanding in comparison to individuals, negotiation with individuals may moderate the Endowment Effect and thus ease the difficulty of reaching an agreement.[38]

To conclude the Endowment Effect, its effects on negotiation, as well as its moderators are dependent on the subjective perceptions of the negotiators, rather than on the objective situation.

4. Perceived Similarities and Attraction as a Subjective Rationality

Has it ever occurred to you that similarity, even coincidental similarity such as a similar dress or identical name, can affect the negotiation process and its outcomes, increase the likelihood of your compliance with opponent's demands or increase the likelihood of reaching an agreement? While it sounds a bit bizarre, there is evidence that such a phenomenon does exist in the real world of negotiations.

4.1. *Similarity Perception in Negotiation*

The similarity perception is another example of subjective rationality. People, in general, and negotiators, in particular, are attracted to others whom they perceive to be similar to them. The similarity that attracts negotiators to opponents could relate to various life aspects, such as a similarity in personality traits, attitudes, life experience, values and even similar pronunciation. Due to the similarity perception, negotiators tend to prefer, comply, agree and even help opponents who are similar to them. Similarity also induces increased empathy, leading negotiators to think about their opponents' problems as their own, and identify with them. Moreover, conceived similarity may reinforce negotiators' attitudes shared by all sides and thus contribute to a joint gains agreement.

The nature of similarity is of the highest importance when it comes to negotiators' inclination to identify with others. The more incidental and common the similarity — for example, a similar first name, a similar or

---

[38] Galin, A. (2013). Endowment Effect in Negotiating Group versus Individual Decision-Making, *Theory and Decision*, Vol. 75(3), pp. 389–401.

even identical date of birth — the less influence it has on negotiators.[39] On the other hand, the more distinctive the similarity — such as similar communal values shared by a specific group — the stronger the impact of similarity on negotiators. When negotiating with unfamiliar opponents, distinct similarities may induce cooperation. However, since cooperation may involve unwanted and undesirable costs and obligations, cooperation due to similarity also has some limitations.[40] Naturally, perceived dissimilarity may induce an opposite reaction,[41] such as rejecting cooperation.

4.2. Motives Underlying the Perceived Similarity Effect

There are various motives underlying the perceived similarity effect. First, in the absence of information regarding the opponent's traits, attitudes, values and background some manifest traits, such as gender, race and culture may create perceived similarity or dissimilarity. When information regarding opponents' attitudes and other personal attributes is available and favorable in terms of similarity, attraction often results. Second, is a sense of liking one's opponent, due to the perceived "reciprocity effect". Negotiators may "like" opponents with similar attitudes because they expect them to "like" them back.[42] A third motive is the creation of a generic prototype opponent, which serves as a model. When the model is conceived as being similar to the opponent, a favorable attitude towards the opponent may arise. Finally, the negotiators' self-judgment may provide a basis for conceived similarity or dissimilarity.[43] Generally, negotiators perceive greater

---

[39] See also an article by Simonsohn in which he criticizes the assumed influences of incidental similarities, such as first name, birth date, etc. Simonsohn, U. (2011), Spurious? Name Similarity (Implicit Egotism) in Marriage, Job and Moving Decisions, *Journal of Personality and Social Psychology*, Vol. 101(1), pp. 1–24.

[40] Locke, K.D. Craig, T. Baik, K.D. and Gohil, K. (2012), Binds and Bounds of Communication: The Effect of Interpersonal Values on Assumed Similarity of Self and Others, *Journal of Personality and Social Psychology*, Vol. 103(5), pp. 879–897.

[41] Hung, I.W. and Wyer Jr., R.S. (2014), Effects of Self-Relevant Prospecting-Taking on the Impact of Persuasive Appeals, *Personality and Social Psychology Bulletin*, Vol. 40(3), pp. 402–414.

[42] Montoya, R.M. and Horton, R.S. (2012), A Meta-Analytic Investigation of the Processes Underlying the Similarity–Attraction Effect, *Journal of Social and Personal Relationships*, Vol. 30(1), pp. 64–94.

[43] Cho, J.C. and Knowles, E.D. (2013), I'm Like You and You're Like Me: Social Projection and Self Stereotyping both Help Explain Self-Other Correspondence, *Journal of Personality and Social Psychology*, Vol. 104(3), pp. 444–456.

similarity with opponents they are already familiar with, and with whom they have shared past cooperative experience.

4.3. *Symbolic Interaction, Similarity and Negotiation*

The theory of *symbolic interaction* is a framework for understanding how individuals, and in our case negotiators, interact with each other through the meanings of symbols — both verbal and nonverbal.[44] Thus, negotiators mediate their communication with opponents by interpreting symbols, such as voice,[45] facial expressions, physical gestures and even similar attire. All these symbols, which are interpreted by the negotiators during a process of similarity formation, influence not only perceptions about the opponents' behavior, but also about their intentions.

As a result of the symbolic interaction, imitation affects negotiators and the negotiation process. Negotiators may imitate their opponents' verbal or nonverbal behavior in order to create similarity. Imitating is performed by using identical words or the opponents' tone of voice, accent or clothing. Thus for example, sellers imitating customers' verbal and nonverbal behavior results in a higher sales rate and greater compliance with the sellers' proposals during the negotiation process. Moreover, imitation (or faked similarity) results in the greater valuation of the sellers.

4.4. *Physical Attractiveness and Negotiation*

People, in general, and in our case negotiators, often prefer attractive individuals over those who are less attractive. The "attractiveness effect" has been reported to influence the process of negotiation during selection interviews. It is fairly common that such interviews end in favor of attractive applicants of both sexes. Perceived attractiveness of applicants in negotiation interviews was found to have a higher predictive value than other selection criteria. Furthermore, the considerable experience of interviewing specialists does not neutralize the favoring of attractive applicants.[46] Professionals are just as

---

[44]Herman-Kinney, N.J. and Reynolds, L.T. (2003), *Handbook of Symbolic Interaction*, Alta Mira, New York.

[45]Korsgaard, M.A. and Robertson, L. (1995), Procedural Justice in Performance Appraisal: The Role of Instrumental and Non-Instrumental Voice in Performance Appraisal Discussions. *Journal of Management*, 21(4), pp. 657–669.

[46]Chiu, R.K. and Babcock, R.D. (2002), The Relative Importance of Facial Attractiveness and Gender in Hong Kong's Selection Decision, *International Journal of Human Resource Management*, Vol. 13(1), pp. 141–155.

susceptible to attractive people as college students, and attractiveness is as important for men as it is for women. In a meta-analysis review of physical attractiveness in a variety of job-related scenarios, attractive individuals were found to perform better than unattractive individuals.[47] Apparently, there is a universal attractiveness effect, even though the attractiveness perception varies from culture to culture. However, it seems that physical attractiveness also has some negotiation limitations. Physical attractiveness may be an obstacle for women or men negotiators attempting to cross traditional gender barriers. For example, attractive women can be perceived as too feminine to be truly clever negotiators.

To conclude, similarity and attractiveness may be a cause for subjective rational decisions during the negotiation process. Similarities can create a kind of familiarity and, at times, even intimacy between negotiators and their opponents. Similarities and attractiveness may therefore trigger negotiators' favorable decisions and encourage cooperation. Dissimilarity and unattractiveness, of course, act in the opposite direction.

Practical Applications

- "Winning" or achieving the maximum available gains in negotiation does not always guarantee your desired benefits or satisfaction. It is sometimes better to achieve less — even much less — than the available maximum or any other achievement, in exchange for a good long-term relationship with your opponent.
- Beware of your opponents' intentions. Sometimes your opponents negotiate not in order to achieve a mutual agreement, but rather to obtain some confidential information you might possess or gain time to establish facts. In addition, your opponents may have other inappropriate intentions on their agenda, which will help them, but may harm you.
- Expressing your feelings during the negotiation process serves as signals to your opponents, enabling them to understand how they can adapt themselves to your positions. Do not put on a "poker face" while negotiating; without emotional signals, such as anger, which

---

[47]Hosoda, M. Stone-Romero, E.F. and Coats, G. (2003), The Effects of Physical Attractiveness on Job-Related Outcomes: A Meta–Analysis of Experimental Studies, *Personnel Psychology*, Vol. 56, pp. 431–462.

signals to your opponents to change their behavior, they might continue pressuring you.

- Remember, feelings can be faked and used as a negotiation tactic. Be sensitive and carefully examine your opponents' emotional signals. For example, a rapid transformation of feelings from negative to positive — i.e. from hostility to warmth — may be displayed in an attempt to "anesthetize" you by disguising your opponents' real intentions.
- During the negotiation process, if you are in a good mood (such as happy), there is a high probability that you'll make more concessions to your opponents than you are expected to do. However, if you are in a bad mood (such as angry), there is a high probability that your opponents will make more concessions than they are expected to do. Carefully examine your decisions, especially on a day when you feel happy.
- If the "price" you require substantially exceeds the market price, it is most likely that you are "affected" by the Endowment Effect (what belongs to me is worth more). Take this into consideration, as it may lead you directly to a negotiation impasse.
- Do not try to "sacrifice' your current requirements for future potential profits. You do not know what the future will bring. At least as far the Endowment Effect is concerned, no fundamental difference exists in negotiators' demands between one-shot negotiations and on-going negotiations. In on-going negotiations, your opponents' demands can be just as high as in one-shot negotiations.
- It is better for you to avoid negotiating with groups affected with the Endowment Effect. It is better to negotiate with individuals, even when they are also "endowed". Groups are more extreme in their Endowment Effect and have significantly higher demands than individuals. Therefore, negotiating with "endowed" groups may be tougher than negotiating with individuals.
- In the absence of information regarding the opponent's traits, attitudes, values and background, assuming your opponent is similar to you (on the basis of gender, ethnic group, etc.) is a mistake, which may lead you to make wrong decisions. However, on the basis of solid information regarding mutual interests or experience (such as the same hobbies or education), a sense of similarity between you and your opponents may produce good feelings and cooperation.

Perceived similarity with your opponents can make negotiations easier on both of you.

- As a female negotiator, do not make an effort to emphasize your attractiveness. There are limitations to the attractiveness in negotiation for men as well, but this is especially true for women.

PART TWO

Becoming Acquainted
with the Negotiation Process

Chapter 4
Preparing for Negotiation

"By failing to prepare, you are preparing to fail".

Benjamin Franklin

Tania was one of the founders and had been the manager of a flourishing hi-tech firm for 20 years. After 20 successful years, she felt she had made the most of it. Therefore, when she was offered a prestigious job in public administration, she readily accepted, despite the fact that her income would be substantially reduced. She believed that she could afford to take on the public administration job with the money she had saved over the years and the money she would receive by selling her share in the firm to her partners. As a result of her decision, she immediately offered the shares to her partners, convinced that they would buy them without delay. She did not prepare for the negotiation with her partners, as she had many years of experience in negotiations and, therefore, evaluated herself as a good negotiator. Furthermore, she believed that due to her experience with her partners, she should not expect any problems. To her surprise, however, her partners were reluctant to buy her share, especially at the price she offered.

The negotiation process got tough, and she found herself giving in at each stage of the negotiation. She ended up with a poor deal, far below her original expectations. Had Tania been overconfident? Had she relied too much on her experience to achieve a lucrative agreement with her partners? Had she believed that preparation for negotiation is time consuming and that "time is money", which she should save? Or as a negotiator had she simply chosen to save her time for more important issues than pre-negotiation preparation with her own partners? No one will ever know the answers to these questions, except perhaps Tania herself. However, the facts are obvious: the first fact is that Tania did not prepare for the negotiation, and the second is that she ended up with a very poor deal. Could there be some correlation between these two facts?

Surprisingly enough, many negotiators engage in negotiations without first making sufficient preparation. They make important decisions under conditions of uncertainty because they rely on their experience. Indeed, experience plays an important role in pre-negotiation processes. Relying on previous experience is seemingly helpful, as it can save negotiators time and effort, but as Otto von Bismarck said long ago: "*Fools learn from experience. I prefer to learn from the experience of others*".

As each negotiation has its own "characteristics", negotiators should decide whether they would like to explore the forthcoming negotiation, or make use of what is already known from previous negotiation. Negotiators may have a hard time linking different situations.[1] Moreover, relying on previous experience provides a somewhat myopic view of the forthcoming negotiation. Preparation can provide negotiators with information and knowledge about both their immediate and long term costs and benefits. Preparation can also provide negotiators with better insight into their possible best and worst alternatives (their *BATNA* and *WATNA*).

Unfortunately, just like Tania in the previous scenario, in many cases negotiators who have prior negotiation experience are not motivated to invest time and effort in preparation, which may result in poor performance during their current negotiations.[2] Thus, preparing for both one-shot and long-term negotiations plays a crucial role in negotiators' performance and successful outcomes.

The preparation process includes several stages: Collecting information (or intelligence gathering)[3], choosing the negotiation location, organizing external human support and choosing a E-negotiation support system.

---

[1] Barnett, S.M. and Ceci, S.J. (2002), When and Where Do We Apply What We Learn? A Taxonomy for Far Transfer, *Psychological Bulletin*, Vol. 128(4), pp. 612–637.

[2] Huang, Y. and Hutchinson, J.Y. (2013), The Role of Planning, Learning, and Mental Models in Repeated-Dynamic Decision Making, *Organization Behavior and Human Decision Processes*, Vol. 122(2), pp. 163–176.

[3] See also Peterson, R.M. and Lucas, G.H. (2001), Expanding the Antecedent Components of the Traditional Business Negotiation Model: Pre-Negotiation Literature Review and Planning-Preparation Propositions, *Journal of Marketing Theory and Practice*, Vol. 9(4), pp. 37–49.

The more complex the negotiation, the more important the preparation process is.[4]

1. On Intelligence Gathering

Is it worthwhile to collect information in the pre-negotiation stage? What kind of information should negotiators look for? What are the advantages of such information? What are the effects of asymmetrical information? Does pre-negotiation information offer only advantages or are there some disadvantages as well?

1.1. *On the Importance of Information-Gathering*

Negotiation may be described as an uncertain, unpredictable process. Uncertainty exists regarding economic, social and other relevant developments. There may also be a certain extent of uncertainty regarding the negotiators' interests, even in relation to their own interests. Negotiators' preferences are often unknown, and there is uncertainty regarding the negotiation development, especially its outcomes. Information enables negotiators to predict, as far as possible, the negotiation developments; it enables them to trace opportunities, evaluate potential risks, find out more about competitors and discover the strengths and weaknesses of the involved parties. In short, information can, to a great extent, reduce the uncertainty embedded in the pre-negotiation stage. There is evidence suggesting that the average price achieved by buyers/negotiators with pre-information about the sellers is lower in comparison to buyers without pre-information.[5] Of course, negotiators who do not have information or those who have only partial information can obtain the necessary information later on, through the opponents' offers and especially through the signals that are sent and received during the negotiation process. However, late learning can cause crucial difficulties, such as costly delays and failures to reach an agreement when an agreement is profitable and desired.

---

[4]Schoop, M. Jertila, A. and List, T. (2003), Negoist: A Negotiation Support System for Electronic Business-to-Business Negotiation in E-Commerce, *Data & Knowledge Engineering*, Vol. 47(3), pp. 371–401.

[5]Brodt, S.E. (1994), Inside Information and Negotiator Decision Behavior, *Organization Behavior and Human Decision Processes*, Vol. 58(2), pp. 172–202.

1.2. What Kind of Information Should the Negotiator Look For?

There are three significant categories of information that negotiators should be aware of: information about the opponents, information on the negotiators themselves and objective information.

Information about the opponents: The negotiator should collect and interpret all relevant information regarding their negotiation opponents; for example, information regarding the opponents' interests in the current negotiation. Are they really interested in reaching an agreement at the end of the negotiation or do they simply wish to gain time in order to establish certain facts meanwhile? The opponents' financial condition and cash flow is also an important issue (is their financial situation stable or are they threatened by bankruptcy?). Time constraints and deadlines should be looked into (is an agreement in this case urgent or do they have all the time in the world to negotiate?). What are the opponents' power sources and who supports them (do they have the support of other groups, such as government agencies, private investors or solid banks behind them?). And finally, what is the opponents' negotiation style; are they known for their cooperative or competitive negotiation style?

Information on the negotiators themselves: Sometimes negotiators are not aware of the importance of systematically and consciously "collecting" information about themselves. For example, are negotiators really aware of their alternatives to a negotiated agreement — what are their *BATNA* and *WATNA*? Do they have a better, equal or worse alternative to the current negotiation? What are the negotiators' priorities in the current negotiation? Is it, first and foremost, a matter of immediate gains, future gains or a long-term relationship? Who are the negotiators' competitors and what is known about them? Are they competitors who can present serious alternatives?

Objective information: For example, the state of the market — are we in a recession, a boom or any other financial state during the negotiation period? Legal regulations — do they limit the negotiation (such as a legal demand not to negotiate at the same time with two or more negotiators)? The cultural framework within which the negotiations take place — is it an individualistic or collectivistic culture?[6] Even the weather at the time of the negotiations

---

[6]See Chapter 9 of this book.

may play a part — is it very hot with no air conditioning to be found or is it perhaps an extremely cold and foggy day with no heating?

All of the factors in the earlier three categories may have an influence on the negotiation process; and these are only a few examples.

Going back to Tania's miserable negotiation, Tania counted on her past experience and long-standing friendship with her partners to ensure a successful negotiation process. This shaped her conception that there was no real need to invest any time or effort in preparing for the forthcoming (easy, in her opinion) negotiation. As a result, she did not collect any information regarding her partners' actual interest in buying her shares in the firm. If she had known about their objections in regard to buying her shares, she probably would have acted differently. She also failed to gather information about her own *BATNA* in the event that she would not be able to sell her shares in the firm. Thus, she was left with no immediate alternative, except for the bad deal she made in her negotiation with her partners. The lethal combination of overconfidence and lack of information, in many cases, guarantees a poor negotiation outcome.

2. Some Problems Related to Information Gathering

The importance of pre-negotiation information gathering is unquestionable. However, there are several obstacles that may present themselves during such a process, which every negotiator should be aware of. We live in a world of rapid changes, uncertainty and almost unlimited information. It is possible and probable to receive information from a variety of sources: The Internet, e-mail, Facebook, Google, Microsoft, e-libraries, protocol reports, accounts, interviews and observations, among many others. The numerous amounts of available data make it impossible for negotiators to process all of the available information. Sometimes, it is a simple case of "not being able to see the forest for the trees" or, in other words, it is very difficult to filter all of the important pre-negotiation information. Time constraints often make it even harder to efficiently collect and analyze information. Thus, knowing how to select from among the available kinds of information becomes essential and can be achieved with the help of E-negotiation support systems, which will be discussed later on in this chapter. However, as a result of pre-negotiation time constraints and the need to select the "right" relevant information, several disturbing obstacles must be dealt with, as they may have undesirable implications on the negotiation process. Such obstacles include: asymmetrical information, conception and framing, negotiators' "short" memory, and the possible intimidation factor linked to pre-negotiation information.

2.1. *Asymmetrical Information*

Asymmetrical information exists when one party has gathered information before negotiation, while the other party has not or when one party has access to important information, while the other party does not.

In the case of such asymmetrical information, the informed party may be motivated to deceive the other party, and even exhibit unethical behavior. This deceit may occur by convincing the uninformed party into believing that the available negotiated "pie" is smaller than it actually is.[7] For example, to examine the results of asymmetrical information, a sort of "Dictator Game" was used.[8] In this game, two sides negotiate over a certain amount of money; yet, the available amount of money is known only to one party, which also "owns" the money. At the end of each negotiation, both parties have to agree on how to divide the money between them. If they reach an agreement, the money is divided between them, as agreed. If they cannot reach an agreement, the money is confiscated and they both lose. During the asymmetrical negotiation, the uninformed party usually demands a "fair" share of 50% of the available money. Indeed, the informed party usually pretends to give the uninformed party 50%. However, in most cases the party's description of the "fifty percent" is substantially reduced. The "fifty percent" offered by the informed party is not really 50% at all. The sum of money usually obtained by the uninformed party is much less than half of the actual amount of money which the other party owns. To be more precise, the uninformed party is deceived by the informed party. The higher the amount of available money, the higher the motivation of the informed party to deceive the uninformed party is. Yet, when both sides are fully informed regarding the available amount of money, in most cases no deception takes place and both sides often agree to share the money equally. A real life example is a salary negotiation between employer and employee.

---

[7]Srivastava, J. (2001), The Role of Inference in Sequential Bargaining with One-Sided Incomplete Information: Some Experimental Evidence, *Organization Behavior and Human Decision Processes*, Vol. 85(1), pp. 166–187.

[8]Galin, A. Unpublished experiments, Faculty of Management, Tel Aviv University, Israel.

Of course, the employer has more information than the employee regarding the firm's resources, but presents a situation that is much worse than the reality. Under such conditions of asymmetrical information, the final agreed salary level of the employee is lower than if it were agreed under symmetrical information.

However, it may occur that the relatively uninformed negotiators will have high demands, be stubborn and slow to concede, as they hesitate about the appropriate solution.[9] It is possible that in such a case the informed negotiators may lower their demands in order to avoid a negotiation impasse; on the other hand, it also possible that the informed negotiators will reciprocate with a competitive response. As a result, there is a high probability that the negotiation will reach an impasse anyway, as the uninformed negotiators do not realize that their stubbornness and demands are unreasonable. All these problems, related to asymmetrical information, could have been avoided by proper preparation, which can eliminate or at least reduce such problems.

2.2. *Framing*

The concept of *"framing"* generally refers to the negotiators' schematic manner of dealing with new information. Negotiators subjectively narrow down new information volume on the basis of a pre-existent mental schema, formed by their subjective perceptions, dispositions, previous experience and interests. They perceive any new information by fitting it into their schema, in a way that does not distort or reject their preconceived ideas in any way, shape or form. Any truthful information that contrasts with negotiators' schema may be rejected or ignored, whereas any false information or disinformation that is compatible with the schema may be accepted. For example, a wife who is pre-disposed to believe in her husband's loyalty would not accept true information, even hard evidence, disclosing his betrayal, and therefore would not negotiate divorce. A wife, on the other hand, who suspects her husband's infidelity may readily accept disinformation regarding his betrayal and may negotiate divorce, despite the (rejected) fact that he has truly been loyal to her. Thus, framing not only shapes negotiators' perceptions, it may also guide them to a wrong way of dealing with their co-partner or opponent.

---

[9] See Beisecker. T. Walker, G. and Bart, J. (1989), Knowledge versus Ignorance as Bargaining Strategies: The Impact of Knowledge "About Others" Information Level, *The Social Science Journal*, Vol. 26(2), pp. 161–172.

"Conception" or "framing" also refer to a mental structure that helps negotiators interpret new, incoming information about the current situation and negotiation issues. They can distort new information, due to its wrong interpretation and can also shape or limit negotiators' comprehension and expectations of the negotiation process. For example, due to framing, a 10% share in a firm can be interpreted as a good investment, if it fits into the negotiators' conception. The same 10% share in the same firm can be interpreted as a bad investment, if it does not fit into the negotiators' accepted conceptions. It is noteworthy that framing can change over time, due to new information which, although it does not fit into the existing frame, still makes sense. Therefore, frames do not always remain stable over a long period of time; they may change and incorporate new information, leading to new interpretations and changing negotiators' behavior.[10] In order to avoid framing or conception, various techniques, such as simulations and a "devil's advocate" approach, should be employed. These techniques will be discussed in further detail later in the book.

2.3. *Negotiators' Memory*

Human memory information storage is quite limited.[11] Thus, there are great limitations when it comes to remembering items presented at the negotiating "table". Only very few items presented in a long "lecture" describing the advantages of negotiators' proposals would be perceived and remembered by the other party. In order to enhance or retrieve negotiators' information regarding the other party's proposals, it is necessary to increase the negotiators' focus of attention. Information which is not in the negotiators' area of interest will not trigger their attention and thus, their memory. On the other hand, when negotiators are exposed to information that contradicts their impression of the other party, the inconsistency between their pervious impressions and the recently acquired information, may trigger their

---

[10]For an interesting discussion of the traditional approach and the interactional approach of framing in conflict and negotiation, see: Dewulf, A. Gray, B. Putnam, L. Lewicki, R. Aarts, N. Bouwen, R. and Woerkum, C.V. (2009), Disentangling Approaches to Framing in Conflict and Negotiation Research: A Meta-Paradigmatic Perspective, *Human Relations*, Vol. 62(2), pp. 155–193.

[11]Cowan, N. (1988), Involving Conceptions of Memory Storage, Selective Attention and their Mutual Constraints Within the Human Information Processing System, *Psychological Bulletin*, Vol. 104(2), pp. 163–191.

curiosity, and thus their attention to the recent information.[12] Another example of increasing negotiation attention focus relates to the use of emotions.[13] Angry opponents, in contrast to those who do not show emotions, may attract more attention and trigger retrieval information, thus making better use of the negotiators' memory storage faculties. Rage and other dramatic outbursts are easily engraved on the negotiators' memory and thus impact their behavior. For example, the increased attention attributed to information related to previous losses or previous success may distort the negotiators' judgment in regard to forthcoming information. Thus, by and large, the limitations of memory and selective attention can influence negotiators' behavior, harming their performance. In order to overcome the problems of negotiators' short memory, pre-negotiation preparation can be of help — internally as well as externally — in storing and retrieving important information. Pre-negotiation is also a good time to reexamine information and check its accuracy, level of significance, and its possible application during the negotiation process. The storage and retrieval of information can best be done by employing an E-negotiation support system (see the following sections), but this can also be done manually.

2.4. *The Intimidating Aspect of Information*

Pre-negotiation information can, at times, be intimidating. Here are some examples of real life situations. First, if negotiators receive pre-negotiation information relating to the fact that their opponents are known for their deceptions, which may also include intentional disinformation, it is possible that they will keep away from the negotiation altogether, despite the possible great advantages they had expected from this negotiation. Second, negotiators receive information along the lines that if they do not accept their opponents' proposals, then their opponents will sue them in court (in which case they might lose everything). Third, the prosecutor informs negotiators that if they don't agree to negotiate a plea bargain and turn state's witness,

---

[12]Palma, T.A. Garrido, M.V. and Semin, G.R. (2014), Situating Person Memory: The Role of the Visual Context of Memory for Behavioral Information, *Journal of Experimental social Psychology*, Vol. 52(2), pp. 32–43.

[13]Pietroni, D. Van Kleef, G.A. De Dreu, C.K.W. and Pagliaro, S. (2008), Emotion as Strategic Information: Effects of the Other's Emotional Expressions on Fixed Pie Perception, Demands, and Integrative Behavior in Negotiation, *Journal of Experimental Social Psychology*, Vol. 44, pp. 1444–1454.

they might find themselves in jail for a long period of time. Such intimidating information, be it reliable or unreliable, may cause the negotiators to simply give in.

To conclude, it is most important to gather information during the preparation stage and even later on during the negotiation process. However, collecting information may lead to some problems that negotiators should try to resolve. Once negotiators are aware of such problems, it is possible to overcome them.

3. Choosing the Location — Is the Meeting Place Important?

Does the location really matter during the negotiation process? People often assume that negotiation is about interests, strategies and tactics and that the location — where the negotiation is held — has less importance, if any. Nonetheless, the location does have at least some influence on the negotiation process, and even on its outcomes. The negotiation location can also create an atmosphere, which increases or decreases the parties' achievements.

It seems that negotiators believe that the location issue is important; otherwise, why do they often conduct, before the main negotiation, a lengthy intensive negotiation regarding the "appropriate" location site? And what does an "appropriate" negotiation site actually mean? Sometimes, negotiators believe that, just as in sport games, their "home" territory is the most appropriate negotiating location, because it provides them with an advantage over their opponents.

In face to face negotiation, there is a need to choose a physical location. This physical location can either be the negotiators' home "territory", the other side's "territory" or a neutral site. However, nowadays many negotiations do not take place face to face. Instead, they are conducted using one or several media devices, such as e-mailing, video conferencing, telephone negotiations, etc. In such long-distance negotiations, each of the parties' remains on its own "territory", but there are no real face to face negotiations. The use of media devices does not exclude a combination that includes real face to face negotiation. For example, a negotiation can begin with an e-mail and end up with face to face negotiation, vice versa or any other combination. As the parties have to decide where and how they would like to conduct their forthcoming negotiation, they should choose the location and consider the media via which they would like to negotiate.

The following section addresses the advantages and disadvantages of a face to face negotiation location, as well as the advantaged and disadvantages of e-mail negotiation. The advantages and disadvantages of each location or an e-negotiation are described separately. However, by shifting from one negotiating site to another or by combining face to face locations with e-mail negotiation, it is possible to avoid or enhance certain advantages and disadvantages of each method.

3.1. *Choosing a Location for Face to Face Negotiation*

The decision regarding the negotiation location in face to face negotiation can be of great importance. Therefore, considering the advantages and disadvantages of each negotiation location is necessary.

Rico and Rana have been purchasers for their medical firm for many years. At a certain time, they were requested to negotiate a very big deal with a medical devices firm — a deal which was highly desired by their own firm. The supplier's firm demanded that the negotiation take place on their premises. Rana and Rico counter-suggested a neutral location. The deliberation about the negotiations' location took a long time. Finally, Rana and Rico gave up and the negotiation took place on the supplier's premises. The negotiation was tough and lengthy, and ended with no agreement. Did the fact that the negotiation took place on the other party's premises contribute to the negotiation's failure? Rico and Rena both had strong feelings that the negotiations' location significantly contributed to their failure to reach an agreement.

3.2. *Negotiating on the Negotiators' Home "Territory"* *(My Premises)*

The most widely held view is that negotiators are at an advantage when negotiating on their own "territory". Indeed, the home "territory" has many advantages, including saving the time lost as a result of work absence and the expenses of traveling outside of the work site. Moreover, having the opponents come to the negotiators' home "territory" symbolizes an imbalance of power, making the opponents seem the weaker party. Negotiating on one's home "territory" gives negotiators an opportunity to display the firm's knowledge, technological resources and human resources, to impress the opponents. However, the most important advantages are the following features: familiarity with the premises and self-confidence.

Negotiators who are familiar with their own premises are in control of all local arrangements — such as negotiation timing; planned interruptions; type of refreshments served and its timing; type of entertainment provided, if any; and easy access to the negotiators' personal experts. The ability to control both the physical environment and the events during the negotiation process lends the "home" negotiators a sense of confidence. This sense of confidence apparently enhances negotiators' aspirations level, their efforts to achieve these aspirations and, as a result, at times also leads to higher achievements. Thus, it was found[14] that negotiators who negotiate on their home "territory" reached substantially higher negotiation achievements than their visiting opponents since, in addition to all the other advantages of the home "territory", the visitors usually have low self-confidence.

Despite the notable advantages of negotiating on one's home territory, there are also some disadvantages one should be aware off. The hosting of the negotiations creates certain obligations on the part of the host, such as taking good care of the visiting party, being polite and sometimes even making some concessions. The host must also contend with both the usual work load obligations, as well as the special responsibilities of being a host negotiator, as a result of conducting negotiations on one's "home" territory. However, the worst disadvantage might be the exposure of undesirable aspects of the negotiators' premises to the eyes of their visiting opponents. For example, opponents visiting the negotiators' premises may accidentally overhear important information and collect data that may prove to be very useful during the negotiation process. Visiting opponents can also observe new products or glimpse a list of clients that the home negotiators' would prefer they not see. The physical condition of the premises — poor, reasonable or luxurious — as well as the local organizational culture, may also be revealed to the negotiating visitors and somehow influence their decision-making. Aside from the threat of potential exposure, being the guest negotiators is also an opportunity to develop relationships with the home employees (the host negotiators' employees) and even obtain their help. Thus, for example, it would be very hard for a supplier's firm to demand a substantial increase in their prices, claiming financial difficulties, when their premises are luxurious and the information received from their employees indicates substantial

---

[14]Brown, G. and Baer, M. (2011), Location in Negotiation: Is There a Home Field Advantage? *Organization Behavior and Human Decision Processes*, Vol.114(2), pp. 190–200.

profits. Other disadvantages include the host's difficulty to "walk away" from the negotiation table when on his home premises. Furthermore, if the host becomes over-confident, it may lead to a false sense of security, associated with some kind of lack of sensitivity regarding undesired developments during the negotiation process.

Therefore, Rena and Rico may partially attribute their failure to reach an agreement to the fact that the negotiations took place on the other party's premises. It might be that their lack of ability to control the events and their relatively low confidence at being away from their home "field", somehow contributed to the negotiation impasse. Yet, if they had been more aware of the importance of boosting their low self-confidence, as well as utilizing their other advantages, while negotiating on the other party's territory, the negotiation might have ended differently.

It can be concluded, then, that deciding to negotiate on one's home "territory" is important, but it also has some limitations that negotiators should be aware of and try to avoid, if the home negotiators are to fully enjoy their home "territory" benefits.

3.3. *Negotiating on the Opponents' "Territory"* (*Your Premises*)

It goes without saying that most of the advantages and disadvantages of negotiating on the negotiators' home "territory" (my premises) are reversed when the negotiation takes place on the opponents' "territory".[15] For example, the advantages are that it is relatively easy to "walk away" from negotiations held on the opponents' premises, an act which is rather complicated to carry out when the negotiations take place on the negotiators' home territory. Regarding further disadvantages, the most problematic issue is that of expenses. It is expensive to take managers or even employees (in many cases essential employees) away from work and send them to negotiate elsewhere. This problem is amplified if a team is sent to negotiate, especially if the other territory is far away. The larger the negotiating team and the farther away the opponent's "territory", the greater the expenditures. Due to the high cost of sending negotiators to the opponent's site, negotiators are highly motivated to keep the negotiation period as short as possible. Such time pressures

---

[15] Salacuse, J.W. and Rubin, J.Z. (1990), Your Place or Mine? Site Location and Negotiation, *Negotiation Journal*, Vol. 6(1), pp. 5–10.

may lead to concessions or to a negotiation impasse. It may take time to successfully bridge differences of interest.

3.4. *Negotiating on a Neutral "Territory" (Neutral Premises)*

Negotiating on neutral "territory" cancels out the advantages of the negotiators' home "territory " and maintains a conceived balance of power between the parties. No one has to negotiate on the other side's home territory, and therefore be considered the "weaker" party. Negotiating on a neutral territory means neither party has an advantage connected to location; thus, the location should be acceptable to all parties. Moreover, if the relations between the negotiating parties are hostile, a neutral location might be the only feasible place in which the parties may agree to meet.

However, a neutral location also has its shortcomings. Both parties are unfamiliar with the location and may find it hard to control both events and developments; in addition, costs are high for both parties. Necessary communication with home consultants and headquarters are sometimes problematic, and the parties may be dependent upon a third party to provide their other requirements. Even worse, the host of the "neutral" site may sometimes intervene, unexpectedly complicating the negotiation.

To conclude, each location has its advantages and disadvantages; however, there is no need to adhere to one location. Shifting locations may change the advantages and disadvantages of one site, and neutralize the effect of location on the negotiators' balance of power.

4. Choosing the Negotiation Media: E-mail versus Face to Face Negotiation

American businessmen situated in New York City would like to purchase electronic devices from a German firm. What is the best way to negotiate with the Germans? Should they go to Berlin and negotiate face to face with the electronics firm's representatives or stay home and negotiate by e-mail? What are the advantages and disadvantages of face to face negotiations, versus e-mail negotiation? And what is the best way to make the deal with the German firm successful and satisfactory?

E-mails play a growing role in our daily negotiations. However, due to globalization and geographical distances, growing expenditures and negotiators' time constraints have made e-mail negotiations even more attractive.

Yet, does this electronic medium really serve negotiators better than face to face negotiation and if so, in which ways?

4.1. *The Perceptions of Face to Face Negotiations versus E-Negotiation*

The common perception is that face to face negotiation is more effective than e-negotiation. The main argument is that face to face communication is "richer" than e-mail communication,[16] and therefore facilitates elevated rapport, and strengthens trust between opposing parties.[17] It has also been argued that verbal and especially non-verbal cues typical to face to face negotiation lead to better understanding of the opponents' messages and thus enhance credibility and accuracy of decision-making.[18]

Another point of view is that e-negotiation offers a better medium for the negotiating parties, E-mail negotiations are characterized by the ability to write, rewrite and frequently review the written messages. It is direct and to the point, and provides sufficient time to reverse the messages, and also helps the parties separate the negotiated issues from personal egos. Moreover, negotiators' sense of rapport is not affected mainly by non-verbal cues as in face to face behavior. Documented interaction, which is typical of e-negotiations, plays an important role in creating accessibility between the involved parties.[19] Furthermore, many of the negotiating "tricks" that negotiators use in face to face negotiating in order to mislead their opponents, are not possible in e-negotiation.[20] Thus, due to the absence of face to face contact, e-negotiation can prevent suspicion and, of course, bridge geographic boundaries. This is precisely why the absence of non-verbal cues in e-negotiations may reduce the level of conflict, whereas the depersonalized

---

[16]Purdy, J.M. and Nye, P. (2000), The Impact of Communication Media on Negotiation Outcomes, *International Journal of Conflict Management*, Vol. 11(2), pp. 162–187.

[17]Drolet, A.L. and Morris, M.W. (2000), Rapport in Conflict Resolution: Accounting for How Face to Face Contact Fosters Mutual Cooperation in Mixed-Motive Conflicts, *Journal of Experimental Social Psychology*, Vol. 36(1), pp. 26–50.

[18]Citera, M. Beauregard, R. and Mitsuya, T. (2005), An Experimental Study of Credibility in E-Negotiation, *Psychology & Marketing*, Vol. 22(2), pp. 163–179.

[19]Bronstein, I. Nelson, N. Livnat, Z. and Ben-Ari, R. (2012), Rapport in Negotiation: The Contribution of the Verbal Channel, *The Journal of Conflict Resolution*, Vol. 56(6), pp. 1089–1115.

[20]Croson, R. (1999), Look At Me When You Say It: An Electronic Negotiation Simulation, *Simulation and Gaming*, Vol. 30(1), pp. 23–37.

nature of e-negotiation may eliminate status differences between negotiating people and groups.

4.2. *The Main Difference Between Face to Face Negotiation and E-Mailing*

The main difference between face to face negotiation and e-mailing is not in the outcome, but in the process — in the time duration of the process and the tactics used during the process. Time duration in e-negotiation can be substantially longer — more than double the time — of face to face negotiation. *Prima facie*, this could be explained by the fact that e-negotiations require the parties to be precise, to check and double-check every written word. Moreover, negotiators via e-mail may use more "hard" tactics (such as threats) than face to face negotiators. This can be explained by the elimination of status-related "fear" in e-negotiations. However, in spite of the differences between face-to-face and e-negotiations, their outcomes seem to be very similar, barring the case of cultural influences. Face to face negotiation and e-negotiation yield similar outcomes regarding the final negotiated price, number of installments and the down payment amount.[21] However, it is noteworthy that the comfort which negotiators feel when using e-mail may influence the negotiation outcome and the negotiators' satisfaction with this outcome. Negotiators who are more comfortable using e-mails are usually pleased with their outcomes.[22]

Thus, if our American negotiators (in the above scenario) are comfortable using e-mail, they can stay at home and conduct negotiations via e-mail. The outcome will be similar to what they would have achieved in face to face negotiations. Of course, they could also combine e-mailing together with some face to face negotiation, perhaps at the beginning stage of the negotiation or at any other time during the process. This may help them to obtain more information regarding their opponents, and provide an opportunity to achieve increased familiarity. By using e-mails during all or most of the process, they may reduce expenditures and save a lot of traveling time.

---

[21] Galin, A. Gross, M. and Gosalker, G. (2007), E-Negotiation versus Face to Face Negotiation: What has Changed — if Anything?, *Computers in Human Behavior*, Vol. 23(1), pp. 787–797.

[22] Geiger, I. and Parlamis, J. (2014), Is There More to E-Mail Negotiation Than E-Mail? The Role of E-Mail Affinity, *Computers in Human Behavior*, Vol. 32, pp. 67–78.

However, suppose our American negotiators would like to buy their electronic parts not in Germany, but in Hong Kong — would the process and the outcome be the same? Apparently, Hong Kong's Chinese when negotiating via e-mail — may react differently than the American or the German negotiators.[23] Culture influences e-mail negotiations, just as it influences face to face negotiation. Negotiators should be aware of this, and negotiation methods should be chosen in the preparation stage with knowledge and care.[24]

5. Arranging External Support

Negotiators often need external support to assist them when preparing for the negotiation and during the process itself. Such external support could be either in the form of human support, e-negotiation support systems, or both.

5.1. *Human Support*

Senior faculty members negotiated a salary increase with the university authorities. Since the deliberations did not work out well, they decided to exacerbate the negotiation by going on an unlimited strike. The public media accused the faculty members of "taking the students' hostage". Extreme local newspaper articles were written, as well as TV programs, which argued that the faculty work little and demand a lot. The students threatened to sue the University for not fulfilling its obligations and the faculty members did not have a strike fund that would have enabled them to continue the strike. Obviously, the negotiation ended in a Lose–Win situation. The faculty members lost. What should the faculty members have done, in order to avoid such a miserable ending?

During the preparation stage, certain necessary actions should be conducted by the negotiators. For example: Negotiators can collect information from various sources, choose their preferred negotiation location and negotiation medium, and carry out some simulations. Moreover, organizing

---

[23] Rosette, A.S. Brett, J.M. and Zoe, L.A. (2012), When Cultures Clash Electronically: The Impact of E-Mail and Social Norms on Negotiation Behavior and Outcomes, *Journal of Cross-Cultural Psychology*, Vol. 43(4), pp. 628–643.

[24] The impact of culture on negotiations will be discussed at length in Chapter 9 of this book.

additional external human support is often necessary during the preparation stage. This means, for example, the organization of favorable public relations or public media coverage, by convincing journalists to support the negotiators' demands in their publications. The creation of various groups that can identify with the negotiators, such as friends, unions or employers' organizations, is another example of external support. Furthermore, Organizing people or organizations that may benefit from the negotiation's positive outcome, in addition to employing a favorable lobby that can put pressure on the opponents to meet the negotiators' demands can also be helpful. Last, but not least, acquiring the aid of financial institutions, such as banks, in case there is a financial need to support the negotiators during the process.

Let us look back at the faculty members' negotiation and strike as part of their negotiation. During their preparation, they could have done some simulations on how to change the public media's hostility into support; how to continue the strike when the university stopped paying the faculty a regular salary; or how to recruit the students as a support group over to their side. During the "devil's advocate" discussions, they could have found some creative ways to deal with such problematic situations; for example, to convince a journalist to write favorably about their negotiation. Alternatively, another way would be to appoint a public relations officer and internet bloggers to introduce favorable articles into the public media, generate internet posters, as well as Facebook, Twitter activity, etc. and, if possible, to attract the interest of TV channels programs. In addition, locating a lobby or VIPs to exert some pressure on the university authorities could also have been beneficial. In order to raise financial support for the faculty, faculty members should have convinced some banks to provide them with a loan (in advance) at the rate of their net salary during the strike. In this way, the faculty members would have had enough financial support to wait out the strike, until a settlement could have been reached in their favor. Furthermore, in order to avoid an expected student opposition, they should have convinced the students that for their own good, or for the future support of the faculty members on issues involving students' interests — it is worthwhile for the students to support the strike, rather than oppose it. The students, as a support group, could have done "wonders" for the faculty's negotiation. Thus, during the preparation, negotiators should have made a point of adding the external human support of people, groups and organizations that may have helped faculty members achieve a favorable final agreement.

5.2. E-Negotiation Support System

An e-negotiation support system can significantly assist negotiators at every stage of the negotiation process. However, it has particularly special importance during the preparation stage, where uncertainty is significant and the need to acquire and analyze fundamental information quickly is essential.[25] Thus, it is precisely during the preparation stage that e-negotiation support can minimize uncertainty; therefore, its acquisition, including relevant data, is highly recommended. Of course, negotiation support systems (NSS) require an investment, especially as regards its customization and application. A quality support system, be it simple or complex should include the following features: the ability to meet negotiators' requirements, friendly comfortable human-computer interface, flexibility, effectiveness of the search mechanism and the possibility to protect information. The popularity of any support system gives some indication of the system's usefulness.[26] Information Technology (IT) and telecommunications are the basis of all e-negotiation support systems.[27] They provide the necessary tools needed to manage negotiators' information via all communication media, such as face-to face, e-mail, video conferences and telephone conferences

In general, e-negotiation support systems can be helpful in the following tasks[28]:

Supporting information processes: In light of the overload of information available to negotiators, e-negotiation support systems can serve as an internal and external memory, substantially enlarging the limited memory of humans. This can help in limiting the amount of information overload

---

[25]Lim, J. and Yang, Y.P. (2007), Enhancing Negotiators' Performance with Computer Support for Pre-Negotiation Preparation: An Experimental Investigation in an East Asian Context, *Journal of Global Information Management*, Vol. 15(1), pp. 1–25.

[26]Alavi, M. and Leidner, D, (2001), Review: Knowledge Management and Knowledge Management Systems: Conceptual Foundations and Research Issues, *MIS Quarterly*, Vol. 25(1), pp. 107–136.

[27]An interesting review of various negotiation support systems can be found in the paper of Schoop, M. Jertila, A. and List, T. (2003), *N*egoisst: A Negotiation Support System for Electronic Business-to Business Negotiation in E-Commerce, *Data & Knowledge Engineering*, Vol. 47(3), pp. 371–401. In this paper, negotiators can find the names and locations of important negotiation support systems, as well as *N*egoisst as an integrative support system.

[28]Lim, L.H. and Benbasat, I. (1993), A Theoretical Perspective of Negotiation Support System, *Journal of Management Information Systems*, Vol. 9(3), pp. 27–44.

by sorting through a dense collection of records to find specific information relevant to negotiators' queries, as well as in identifying information patterns amongst a large collection of records. Generally, relevant information can be accessed and retrieved by use of a search engine using key words and semantic investigations. The e-negotiation support system can thus assist in storing and analyzing verbal information communicated in meetings, analyzing protocols and in locating information regarding legal regulations and economic reports. It can also be very helpful in utilizing all kinds of statistics and their applications; retrieving past agreements, past sales, and past proposals and costs. By and large, e-negotiation support systems can integrate all sorts of information, increase the speed of accessing important information and help negotiating parties focus on relevant information.

Supporting information applications: Negotiators' performance often depends on their ability to apply information and use it in decision-making. Time constraints as well as individual cognitive limitations may prevent turning information into decision-making, and afterwards into actual moves during the negotiation process. E-negotiation support systems can assist in decision-making by helping to define the negotiators' targets and their preferences. Thus, the e-negotiation support system may reduce negotiators' preparation load and help implement information into negotiators' decision-making processes. It can also assist in simulating an exchange of messages or proposals. It can examine financial systems, organize scheduling systems and at later stages of the process, help monitor the negotiation process and outcome by playing a part in building the contract and following up on the fulfillment of the contract's obligations.

Supporting choice: The need to choose from among alternatives, especially when there are many alternatives, may be problematic. Support systems can quickly calculate the various alternatives' expected utility, thus helping negotiators find better options and make better choices. In addition, by calculating the expected utility of the various alternatives, an e-negotiation support system can help negotiators determine their *BATNA* and *WATNA*.

Supporting predictions: A major contribution of e-negotiation support systems is the simulation process. Having detailed information regarding costs, products, previous contracts, legal procedures and other issues helps negotiators simulate various alternatives which, in turn, allows them to predict the possible results of each alternative. The support system can also analyze and predict opponents' proposals and thus assist negotiators to simulate the result of accepting or rejecting the opponents' proposals. During simulations, it can also assist in analyzing the results of the "what if?" questions and answers.

Finally, research evidence shows that e-negotiation support systems can improve the information-processing aspects of negotiation, increase the number of negotiators' proposals and enhance negotiators' perceived satisfaction.[29]

To conclude, by supporting quicker, broader and deeper access to essential information, including clarifying situations by providing essential replies and integrating various forms of information, e-negotiation support systems can produce better negotiators' perspectives and sharpen decision-making. However, at the end of the day, decision-making and control over preparation for the negotiation and the process itself remains in the hands of the negotiating individuals themselves.

Practical Applications

- Relying on previous experience can save you time and effort. However, information regarding past negotiation can be misleading when preparing for forthcoming negotiations, as each negotiation has its own "characteristics". Thus, relying on previous experience may provide you with a somewhat myopic view of the forthcoming negotiation. When preparing for the forthcoming negotiation, carefully examine information that relates to previous negotiations with the same opponents or others.
- When you have partial or asymmetrical information, beware of deceit. Opponents may deceive you by convincing you — the uninformed party — into believing that the available negotiated "pie" is smaller than it actually is, or by intimidating you. If you know you are less informed, try to probe, ask questions, observe signals carefully and if possible, get external support. All this may help in identifying deceit and decrease your opponents' desire to mislead you.
- When you choose to negotiate face to face with your opponents on your "home territory", you have some recognizable advantages. However, you should beware of the exposure of commercial secrets

---

[29]Delaney, M.M. Forough, A. and Parkins, W.C. (1997), An Empirical Study of Efficacy of a Computerized Negotiation Support System (NNS), *Decision Support Systems*, Vol. 20(3), pp. 186–197.

or other undesired information. You should also take into consideration the unique obligations of hosting the negotiations — which may be intense and, at times, also expensive.

- Frequently, agreeing to negotiate on your opponents' "territory" may provide you with important information, but it also signals weakness on your part. In order to balance your power image, shifting from one territory to the other is preferable to a neutral territory. In a neutral territory, you will both be unfamiliar with the location and you may find it hard to control both events and developments (like when on the opponent's territory).

- Using e-mail during all or most of the negotiation process may save you money and time, especially if the opponent's "territory" is geographically far away. Another advantage of e-mail negotiation is the ability to be more precise in your communication. On the negative side, you miss out on the sense of possible familiarity with your opponent. However, some combination between e-mail negotiation and face to face negotiation may balance the advantages and disadvantages of both negotiation methods.

- Remember that both face to face and e-mail negotiation are influenced by cultural values and behavioral norms. Prepare yourself to negotiate with other cultures, (negotiation with other cultures will be discussed in detail in Chapter 8).

- During the preparation process, you would do well to look for external human support. For example, you may need the help of people who can influence your opponent or the help of a supporting group. Moreover, during your simulations of the forthcoming negotiation, you need a "devil's advocate", who will help you to reach the "right" pre-negotiation decisions.

- There is evidence that you, as a negotiator, can perform better with pre-negotiation e-negotiation support system. If you acquire the needed support later on during the negotiation process, it may be too late to postpone difficulties, such as costly delays and to identify all possible alternatives. Finally, it may be too late to reach an agreement that is profitable for you and also desirable to your opponents. Thus, you are better off acquiring a quality e-negotiation support system as early as possible.

- When deciding upon the e-negotiation support system of your choice, you should take into consideration the extent to which it is user-friendly, and ensure that the interface between you and your computer is comfortable. Other considerations are: The flexibility and effectiveness of the search mechanism; the system's support and security measures, i.e. the support system's capabilities in regard to protecting your information. The popularity of a specific e-negotiation support system can give you some indication of its usefulness.

- If possible, adding an IT professional to your negotiation team is most advisable. An IT professional can effectively search for data from various sources, and utilize his or her skills in retrieving and applying the data to suit your negotiation needs.

Chapter 5

Negotiators' Interests and Objectives

"A man will fight harder for his interests than for his rights."

Napoleon Bonaparte

Imagine a good singer at the beginning of her career: How much should she ask for a performance, in terms of payment and other conditions related to her performance? The answer is embedded in her *interests*, or what she desires — income, publicity, admiration or being invited to other performances. For example, if she is invited to sing at a wedding in a remote place, she might negotiate a high price, to cover the driving time and the cost of her guitarist. However, if she is invited to sing on a TV show, she might ask for nothing — even for a long performance, as she is mainly interested in the publicity. If, however, she is invited to sing in a theater, she might ask for a low salary and a lengthy contract because she is interested in the honor of being invited to sing in such a respectable theater, the publicity and perhaps the admiration she will receive during her performances.

Obviously, the singer's *objectives* (sometimes called *positions*), such as monetary rates as well as other conditions she may request in exchange for her performances, are shaped by her interests — income, publicity and admiration. In addition, usually only her objectives (positions) would be placed on the negotiation "table", but not her interests. The singer would not ask for admiration (interest), but she would ask for a certain amount of money and various other conditions — her objectives. Notice that her objectives (*positions*) are negotiable, whereas most of her interests are not.

1. Some Insights into Negotiators' Interests

Interests portray the needs, desires and motivations that negotiators attempt to satisfy through the negotiation process. Even though negotiators do not negotiate over interests — just their objectives (*positions*) — their interests have the potential to significantly affect negotiation processes and outcomes.

However, understanding interests — even the negotiators' own interests — is somewhat problematic, for several reasons. First, negotiators do not always consciously identify their own interests. During the negotiation process, negotiators present their objectives but, in many cases, they are not fully aware of what they really want — their interests. Alternatively, negotiators may doubt their own interests due to the reactions of others. What previously seemed to be reasonable interests to negotiators may not seem so reasonable, in face of the reactions of their opponents and other influential parties. Second, in many situations the negotiating party is a group composed of several individual negotiators, each of whom has personal and unique interests.[1] Moreover, interests can be *tangible* — such as procuring concrete resources (money, property) or intangible — such as admiration, saving face or rapport. The intangible interests are the most difficult to identify, since they are usually vague and hard to recognize. Finally, there are many types of, sometimes contradicting, interests; often making it difficult to comprehend and implement all of them. There is a long list of possible interests: short-term and long-term interests; overt and *covert interests*; practical interests and social interests. Then, too, there are the interests of other involved, yet unseen parties, which also have to be considered during the negotiation process.

1.1. *Short-Term and Long-Term Interests*

Short-term interests are typical for a one-shot negotiation, where the parties are strangers and are not interested in continuing their relationship after the deal has been concluded. Short-term interests are usually limited in number and are focused on a few specific subjects. Long-term interests, those that consider the future — are usually diversified and spread out over a variety of subjects, which also relate to the relationships between the conflicting parties in the past, present and future. Let us take, for example, a married couple that has spontaneously decided to spend the current holiday away from home. The husband's interest is to be able to respond during the holiday to any emergency that might take place at his work. As a result, he supports the idea

---

[1]Lax, P.A. and Sibenius, J.K., (2006), Chapter 5, Get All the Interests Right, in *3D Negotiation*, Harvard Business School Publishing, pp. 69–85.

of spending the holiday in a nearby village. The interest that guides the wife is having a good time (theater, concerts, shopping and good restaurants), which is only possible in the distant capital city. As a result, she would like to go the capital city, which is very far from her husband's work. Negotiations between the couple are conducted over the *objectives* resulting from their short-term interests (nearby village or capital city). However, if they consider long-term interests, their focus will shift from the current limited objectives to a variety of long-term objectives. Now, they can negotiate a more practical problem — namely, how to spend their leisure time in the future, and in general. Once long-term interests are also involved, it may be easier to set objectives which will satisfy both husband and wife. The wife can give up her immediate objective, to enjoy the advantages of the big city, in exchange for her husband's promise to join her in the future for a weekend vacation in the capital city. The cost of the various alternatives for how to spend the holiday can also be considered. However, even the long-term interests raise several fundamental problems that are important to the couple; for example, the importance of work, *vis-à-vis* leisure, or the couple's future relationship.

Short-term interests and long-terms interests are different and, at times, even contradicting. To illustrate, imagine suppliers who are interested in earning an immediate high income. Yet, their interest in developing a good relationship with the buyers for future sales may contradict their interest to earn an immediate high income. Another example is an employer who has an interest in lowering his production costs. However, his long-term interest of maintaining employees' high motivation and preventing future strikes may conflict with his interest to lower production costs. In the earlier cases, preference of long-term interests over short-term interests seems reasonable. Yet, in others cases the preference of short-term interests over long-term interests seems even more reasonable. Take, for example, a couple with no children, negotiating their divorce terms. They may prefer short-term interests, sometimes even revenge, as they don't have any interest in a future relationship.

1.2. *Overt and Covert Interests*

Some interests are openly declared by the negotiating party, while other interests are not spoken about. Yet, these covert interests are as important and influential as those which are overt. Take, for example, a negotiation regarding an organization's budget for the coming year. Each department manager expresses an interest in a greater share of the budget. However, very few managers will reveal interests such as increased influence, higher status or reputation and having a larger part of the "empire", which go hand in hand with receiving a greater share of the budget. Interests related to power, respect and appreciation are rarely announced; and if they are — they are somewhat vague and problematic in their interpretation. For example, what precisely do negotiators have to do in order to achieve or provide respect during the negotiation process? However, satisfying such covert vague interests, are at least as important as satisfying the overt interests.

1.3. *Practical and Social Interests*

Practical interests are directed at advancing and supporting the negotiation process in order to reach an agreement, such as quick profits or preventing a third-party intervention (such as a court intervention). Some interests, however, have social connotations, such as industrial security or ecological and environmental interests, which may interfere with instrumental interests; for example, entrepreneurs negotiating with the government about building hotels on a beautiful beach. The entrepreneurs' interests are instrumental — closing a deal with the government as soon as possible before "green organizations" objections may appear. The government, which is also interested in profits, may also have some social interests, such as the quality of the nearby residents' lives after the hotels have been built, preserving an open beach for public use and the survival of the natural fauna. Such social interests oppose the practical interests and may be a barrier to reaching an agreement with the entrepreneurs.

1.4. *Interests of Involved "Unseen" Parties*

There are often parties that have interests in the negotiation, but are not present at the negotiation "table". Imagine a couple with children during a divorce procedure, negotiating the division of their mutual property. Their children are not physically present at the negotiation "table", but their interests significantly influence the negotiation. A political party can negotiate with other political parties over a coalition formation, while their constituents do not participate in the negotiation. However, their interests are very much present at the negotiation "table". In the same way, the interests of the union's constituents substantially affect union–management negotiation. It is noteworthy, however, that the toughest negotiation is often not between the negotiators and their opponents — such as union *vis-à-vis* management or students *vis-à-vis* university authorities — but within each group. The various internal interests of sub-sections or even individuals within each group may prevent an agreement from being reached, even when an agreement is objectively preferable to the alternative of no agreement. In such a case, in order to reach an agreement, a consensus of interests within the group should be reached in the preparation stage, either by persuasion or through compensation of the internal opposition. However, sometimes internal conflicting interests can be quite helpful when negotiating with opponents. Experiencing problems within the group can be useful in extracting concessions from the opponents during the negotiation.[2]

Finally, since negotiators' contradicting interests are a common phenomenon, the problem can be at least partially solved by prioritizing the interest, i.e. deciding which interest is most important, which is second in importance, and so on.

2. Discovering the Opponents' Interests

Opponents' interests, just like those of the negotiators, could be manifold and diverse. If it is difficult for the negotiators to identify their own interests, identifying and understanding the opponent's interests is obviously more problematic. However, negotiators must often comprehend their opponent's interests in order to obtain the best outcome for themselves. Imagine the management of a philharmonic orchestra that would like very much to employ a talented violinist, but is uncertain about what to offer her (what salary for a certain number of performances). The philharmonic orchestra's management does not know that the violinist is predominantly interested in being famous and popular, much more than she cares about her salary. If the management had this knowledge, it could offer her extensive publicity for more performances at a lower price.

2.1. *Getting into Opponent's Head*

How can negotiators get into their opponents' heads and recognize their interests? The best way to discover an opponet's interest is simply to ask

---

[2]Mayer, F.W. (1992), Managing Domestic Differences in International Negotiations: The Strategic Use of Internal Side-Payments, *International Organization*, Vol. 46(4), pp. 793–818.

"why?" — "Why are you asking for this"? However, upon asking this question negotiators might not receive truthful answers, especially regarding their opponent's covert interests. Another indication of the opponents' interests might be their affilations, past behavior, and feedback from previous negotiators and their acquaintances.[3] *Simulations* is another way to make faster and relatively accurate predications about the opponents' interests and subsequent behavior. In simulations, negotiators take on the opponent's role in order to develop the capacity to compare the opponent's perspectives *vis-à-vis* the negotiator's own perspective. Understanding the opponent's pespectives may also enhance one's understanding of the opponent's interests and objectives. However, simulations could be substantially affected by the negotiators' values and behavioral norms. Playing the roles of dissimilar opponents (such as opponents from different cultures, ehthnic groups or races) might be difficult because of the negotiators' predispositions.[4] Such difficulties can be prevented, to a large extent, if negotiators prepare for the negotiation in a suitable manner and, as a result, are familiar with and understand these differences and how they affect their opponents' behavior. Playing the "devil's advocate", in the case of playing the role of dissimilar others, as well as in other simulations, can be useful. The role of the *"devil's advocate"* is to contradict each of the negotiator's arguments or behaviors, in order to better understand the opponent's inerests.

2.2. *Perspective Taking and Empathy*

It has also been argued that *perspective-taking* and *empathy* may also be helpful in predicting the opponent's interests and behavior. *Perspective-taking* is the ability to perceive what is in the opponents' minds, by closely observing their behavior or following their conversations. For example, if negotiators observe their opponents looking around, not paying attention to their arguments, they may understand that the opponents are indifferent, unsympathetic to the negotiators' interests or distracted for some reason. Perspective-taking is not only the ability to understand the opponents' minds, but also how it affects their action and behavior as well as how

---

[3]Lax, D.A. and Sibenius, J.K. (1986), Interests: The Measure of Negotiation, *Negotiation Journal*, Vol. 2(1), pp. 73–92.

[4]Holmes, M. (2013), The Force of Face to Face Diplomacy: Mirror Neurons and the Problem of Intentions, *International Organization*, Vol. 67(4), pp. 829–861.

it may impact on the negotiators' behavior. Empathy, which is the most popular term for "putting oneself in the other's shoes", is different from perspective-taking. While perspective-taking is the cognitive ability to understand one's opponent's interests and subsequent behavior, *empathy* points to an emotional concern with the opponent's problems. It was found[5] that perspective-taking is very helpful in uncovering an opponent's underlying interest and thus helpful in extracting concessions from opponents. Empathy, however, may reveal the opponent's emotions, which can help soften the opponent's behavior and generate an opponent's general satisfaction with the process. It is a common assumtion that empathy is always acceptable and positive, but this is not always the case. Empathy can be a source of trouble, as it might be roughly rejected by one's opponents. Therefore, empathy does not always smooth the negotiation process and its rejection may even complicate the process.[6] Thus, by and large, empathy is less helpful than perspective-taking in uncovering the opponent's interests, perspectives and emotions.

3. The Negotiated Objectives: Targets, Intentions and Resistance Points

The distinction between interests and *objectives* (positions) is significant in order to understand the negotiation process. The negotiators' objectives are often shaped by their interests; however, it is the objectives that are placed on the negotiation "table", and various objectives may be utilized to satisfy one or several interests. Moreover, interests are often abstract, ambiguous and hard to define, whereas objectives are usually concrete, precise and, in many cases, may be translated into tangible value (such as money).

3.1. *Definitions*

The term *objective*, (*position*) consists of three reference points: The negotiators' *targets*, *intentions* and *resistance* (or *reservation*) *points*.

---

[5]See the studies by Galinsky *et al.* published in Galinsky, A.D. Maddux, W.W. Gilin, D. and White, J.B. (2008), Why it Pays to Get Inside the Head of your Opponent: The Differential Effects of Perspective Taking and Empathy in Negotiation, *Psychological Science*, Vol. 19(4), pp. 378–384.

[6]Martinouski, B. Traum, D. and Marsella, S. (2007), Rejection of Empathy in Negotiation, *Group Decision and Negotiation*, Vol. 16(1), pp. 61–76.

The *targets* are the initial proposals put on the negotiation "table". The targets or initial proposals are the ideal, ambitious outcomes the negotiators would like to achieve, knowing that the probability of their opponents accepting them is low. Therefore, targets are often used as a mere tactic. Putting the targets — the initial proposals — on the "table" signifies the end of the unilateral preparation stage and the beginning of the dyad or multiple-negotiation process.

The negotiators' *intentions* (sometimes referred to as the negotiators' *aspirations*) are what the negotiators would really like to achieve through the negotiation process. The *intentions* are what the negotiators believe to be reasonable proposals or outcomes, which have a high probability of being accepted by their opponents.

The negotiators' *resistance* (*reservation*) points are the lowest or minimal proposals negotiators would be ready to accept (for example, the lowest price at which the seller is willing to sell or the highest price a buyer is willing to pay). Beyond the resistance point, negotiators would be inclined to walk away from the negotiation "table". Therefore, arriving at the resistance (reservation) point may signify an impasse or the end of the negotiation process.

For illustration purposes, imagine suppliers who prepare to sell their goods to buyers. Naturally, they would like to maximize their potential profits, so they set a relatively high ambitious target price. However, as realistic suppliers they are not confident that their buyers will accept their initial high demand; so, they set for themselves another — more reasonable — settlement price on which they can focus — their real intention price. They also decide upon a minimal acceptable settlement point — their resistance or reservation price — beyond which they would be ready to walk away from the negotiation table, as can be seen in Figure 1. It is noteworthy that that while the target — the initial proposals — are openly displayed on the "table", the negotiators' intention points and resistance (reservation) points, often remain hidden.

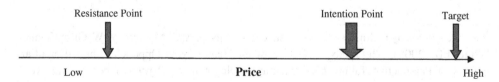

Figure 1:   Negotiation objectives (positions): Suppliers' target, intention and resistance (reservation) points

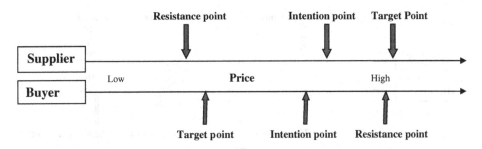

Figure 2: Negotiation objectives (positions): Targets, intention and resistance points for both suppliers and buyers

However, the suppliers are not the only ones who have prepared themselves. The buyers usually do the same. They have also set their target price, which is the lowest price they believe they can pay for the goods. Furthermore, being realistic buyers, they have also determined their intention point, and their maximum acceptable buying price, beyond which they will not buy the goods — which is, of course, their resistance point (price). It is apparent that the buyers' objectives (their target, intention and resistance points) are in the opposite direction to those of the suppliers, as can be seen in Figure 2.

3.2. *The "Acceptance Zone"*

The zone between negotiators' and their opponents' intention points — such as the zone between the supplier's and buyer's intention points — is defined as the *"acceptance zone"*. Negotiators can, with relative ease, reach an agreement that has a *"positive acceptance zone"*, i.e. where the supplier's intention point is lower than the buyer's intention point, and the buyer's intention point is higher than the supplier's intention point — as can be seen in Figure 3. Such an acceptance zone can be either very wide or very narrow.

In some cases, when the buyer's intention point is lower than the supplier's intention point — as can be seen in Figure 4 — a *"negative acceptance zone"* is evident. A "negative acceptance zone" does not mean that an agreement cannot be achieved. One party or both parties can change their intention point during the negotiation process for several reasons, such as the addition of — information, external pressure or just realizing that they have made a mistake in evaluating their own or the other party's intention point. Then, the parties can decide to generate a new "positive acceptance zone", by moving beyond their original intention point. Thus, the negative acceptance zone might make

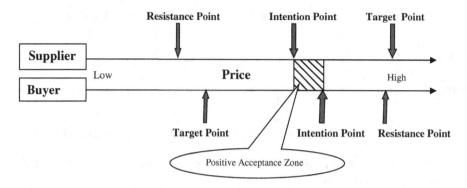

Figure 3: The "Positive Acceptance Zone": The supplier's intention point is lower than the buyer's intention point

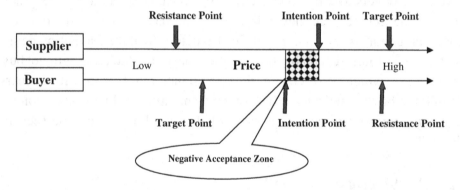

Figure 4: The "Negative Acceptance Zone": The supplier's intention point is higher than the buyer's intention point

it harder to reach an agreement, but it does not necessarily have to cause a negotiation impasse.

3.3. *The "Bargaining Zone"*

The zone between negotiators and their opponents' resistance (reservation) points — such as the zone between suppliers and buyers' resistance (reservation) points — is defined as the *"bargaining zone"*. A "positive bargaining zone" exists when the supplier's resistance point is lower than the buyer's resistance point. A positive "bargaining zone" can be either very wide or very narrow. A narrow "bargaining zone" has two possible contradictory results. On the one hand, it can cause a negotiation impasse because of the limited range in which to reach an agreement. On the other hand, if the parties are motivated to reach an agreement they can effectively reach it within a short time period, because they do not have much "room" for deliberation. When a positive "bargaining zone" is narrow, it is a case of either: Reach an agreement or fail.

It is important to mention that even if the parties' "intention zone" is negative, they may still have a "positive bargaining zone", within which they can reach an agreement, as can be seen in Figure 5.

While the *"negative acceptance zone"* can be avoided within the negotiation process, the situation of having a "negative bargaining zone" is much more problematic. Let us assume that the parties avoid their intentions when they find themselves within a negative acceptance zone. In this case, the parties may find themselves within a "negative bargaining zone" (as in Figure 6) in which, at least theoretically, reaching an agreement becomes very difficult, if at all possible. In order to reach an agreement within a *"negative bargaining"*

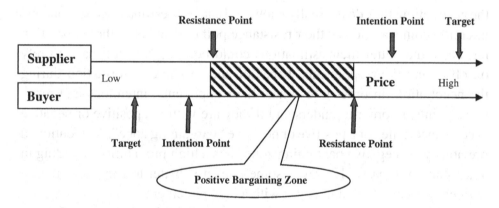

Figure 5: The "Positive Bargaining Zone": The supplier's resistance point is lower than the buyer's resistance point

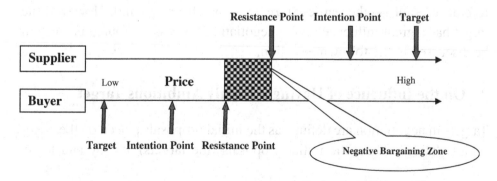

Figure 6: "Negative Bargaining Zone": The supplier's resistance is higher than the buyer's resistance point

zone" one or both parties must go beyond their resistance points to avoid a negotiation impasse. This might be almost physically painful, but it is possible under certain condition that will be discussed later on in this chapter. Thus, a "negative bargaining zone" increases the possibility of an impasse, compared with negotiation within a "positive bargaining zone.[7] However, there are some conditions, such as powerful opponents (who may impose concessions) or multiple-issue negotiations (which enable an exchange among the negotiated issues) that can cause negotiators to go beyond some of their resistance points — and still remain at the negotiation "table".

One would do well to remember that besides the negotiators' targets (the initial proposals), which are visible, clear and specific, the negotiators' intentions and resistance points are often unknown. Thus, as the negotiation process progresses, negotiators' decision-making is made mainly under conditions of uncertainty. Even if negotiators have prepared themselves well for the negotiation, they do not really know, and can only estimate, the opponents' intention points as well as their resistance points. The better the preparation has been, the better their estimations could be. Yet, they still have to rely on observing their opponents' behavior and to gather information during the negotiation, in order to estimate their opponents' intentions and resistance points, in order to understand if they are within a positive or negative "acceptance zone" or a positive or negative "bargaining zone". As mentioned previously, a "negative bargaining zone" has a high probability of ending in a negotiation impasse. However, sometimes it is better to end a negotiation with no agreement, than to end it with a bad agreement.

Up till now, the discussion has focused on the objective's two reference points — the *intention* and the *resistance* points. Both have an impact on the negotiation process and outcome. Meanwhile, the influence of the third reference point — the parties' *targets* — has been ignored. However, the target has a great influence on the negotiation process and outcome, as will be discussed in the following section.

4. On the Influence of Having a Highly Ambitious Target

Targets in negotiation are defined as the initial proposals placed on the negotiation "table". Thus, the initial proposals (the targets) are, by and large,

---

[7]Krause, D.R. Terpend, R. and Petersen, K.J. (2006), Bargaining Stances and Outcomes in Buyer–Seller Negotiation: Experimental Results, *Journal of Supply Chain Management*, Vol. 42(3), pp. 4–15.

the best outcomes negotiators can expect. Are high achievements somehow connected to the way in which the negotiation's initial proposals (targets) have been placed on the negotiation "table"? Do higher initial proposals provide better results than lower initial proposals? The literature on goal-setting in organizational behavior has emphasized the potency of high, ambitious goal-setting as a means of obtaining high results in many domains, such as education, industrial relations and organizational performance. It has been assumed and proven in organizational behavior research that high goal-setting increases effort, persistence and performance, which in the end lead to high achievements.[8] In a similar way, putting highly ambitious initial proposals (high targets) on the negotiation "table" often increases the probability of obtaining high results at the end of the negotiation process. Setting difficult targets usually demands more effort and more persistence to achieve them, especially when the goal is genuinely high. Setting a high target (initial proposal) also communicates that the negotiators are rigid and persistent in their efforts to achieve it. Such a communication may lower the opponent's aspiration level and increase their tendency towards concession-making. As a result, negotiators who set highly difficult targets are generally more profitable than negotiators who set lower and less difficult targets.[9]

4.1. The Influence of Initial Proposals

There are numerous research and observational findings indicating that the final agreements in negotiations are strongly influenced by the negotiator's initial proposals (targets) than by any other factors, such as resistance points or concession-making tendencies.[10] Setting the negotiators' targets raises another dilemma — when is the best time to put the target on the negotiation "table"? Should negotiators place their initial proposal (target) on the negotiation "table" first or wait for the opponents to move first, and then make their target proposal as a counteroffer? Letting the opponents make the first

---

[8] See Locke, E.A. and Latham, G.P. (2002), Building a Practically Useful Theory of Goal Setting and Task Motivation: A 35-year Odyssey, *American Psychologist*, Vol. 57(9), pp. 705–717. See also, Locke, E.A. and Latham, G.P. (2006), New Directions in Goal Setting Theory. *Current Directions in Psychological Science*", Vol.15, pp. 265–268.

[9] Ritov, I. (1996), Anchoring in a Simulated Competitive Market Negotiation, *Organization Behavior and Human Decision Processes*, Vol. 67(1), pp. 16–25.

[10] Kristensen, H. and Garling, T. (2000), Anchor Points, Reference Points, and Counter Offers in Negotiation, *Group Decision and Negotiation*, Vol. 9(6), pp. 493–505.

proposal may give negotiators some information regarding the opponent's aspirations and preferences; however, at the same time, the opponent's initial high proposals may become an "anchor". An anchor may serve as a benchmark to which negotiators adjust during the negotiation process. This seemingly provides an orientation point for negotiators in the uncertain negotiation process, and guides their estimations and decision-making during this process. As a result, in many cases an opponent's first proposal may cause negotiators to reevaluate their initial estimations and adjust to the opponent's anchor by decreasing their own targets and moving towards their resistance point. On the other hand, high initial first proposals made by negotiators becomes an anchor point to which the opponents might adjust their own demands. Thus, merely making the first proposal in an actual negotiation sometimes provides an advantage to the party who makes it, be it supplier or buyer. A supplier's high first proposal may increase the sale prices, while buyers profit from low first proposals.[11] The more extreme the first proposal, the larger the profits for the negotiators who make the first move will be.[12] It is noteworthy that even skilled opponents are susceptible to a negotiator's first proposal — anchoring influence — and the extremity of the proposal does not usually reduce the anchoring effect, which lowers their profits. Thus, negotiators who set high targets and move first will most likely not be able to achieve all of their targets; however, they will probably have higher achievements than what might be reasonably expected. By the end of the negotiation process, they may certainly have achieved their intention points.

4.2. *Opponents' Possible Reaction to Negotiators' Initial High Objectives*

While the *anchoring effect* of the first proposal generates a better outcome for the party who makes the first move, it also has severe limitations.

First, increasing the extremity of the first proposal reduces the probability of receiving a counteroffer. The increased extremity of the initial proposal

---

[11]Van Poucke, D. and Buelens, M. (2002), Predicting the Outcome of a Two-Party Price Negotiation: Contribution of Reservation Price, Aspiration Price and Opening Offer, *Journal of Economic Psychology*, Vol. 23(1), pp. 67–76.

[12]Galinsky, A.D. Ku, G. and Mussweiller, T. (2009), To Start Low or to Start High? The Case of Auctions versus Negotiations, *Current Directions in Psychological Science*, Vol. 18(6), pp. 357–361.

can also offend the opponents to such an extent that they will choose to walk away from the negotiation "table". Negotiators who set high first offers may have high negotiation impasse rates and a low chance of finding a creative final outcome.[13] Moreover, negotiators who set high targets (initial proposals) sometimes tend to experience low levels of satisfaction with regard to negotiation outcomes.[14]

Second, the beneficial effect of anchoring is reduced substantially when the opponents have information, such as market information, which contradicts the negotiators' first proposals. If they have such information, the opponents will probably refuse to take into consideration paying more than others pay in the market. Generally, better information acquired by opponents regarding the negotiator's first proposal, reduces the effectiveness of the first proposal as an anchor.[15] However, in an uncertain situation such as negotiation, higher precision in defining the target (proposal) may increase the proficiency impression the opponents attribute to the negotiator who makes the first proposal. For example, a precise first proposal offered as a quantitative proposal phrased with numerical precision, such as 14,769, rather than a round numerical value such as 15,000, might be perceived as reflecting the true value of the item, and thus facilitate anchor effectiveness, in favor of the negotiator who makes the first move.[16]

Third, the balance of power between the parties involved in the negotiation affects the anchoring effectiveness. The more powerful the negotiators are, the more likely it is that they will be the ones to place the first proposals on the negotiation "table". Low-power negotiators are less likely to propose their targets first and thus have to later adjust their proposals according to the more powerful negotiators. Obviously, since the first high proposal put onto

---

[13]Tasa, K. Celani, A. and Bell, C.M. (2013), Goals in Negotiation Revisited: The Impact of Goal Setting and Implicit Negotiation Beliefs, *Negotiation and Conflict Management Research*, Vol. 6(2), pp. 114–132.

[14]Freshman, C. and Guthrie, C. (2009), Managing the Goal Setting Paradox: How to get Better Results from High Goals and Be Happy, *Negotiation Journal*, Vol. 25(2), pp. 217–231.

[15]Galinsky, A.D. and Mussweiller, T. (2001), First Offers as Anchors: The Role of Perspective Taking and Negotiator Focus, *Journal of Personality and Social Psychology*, Vol. 81(4), pp. 657–669.

[16]Loschelder, D.D. Stuppi, J. and Trotschel, R. (2014), €14,875?!: Precision Boots the Anchoring Potency of First Offers, *Social Psychological and Personality Science*, Vol. 5(4), pp. 491–499.

the negotiation "table" produces benefits, high-power negotiators are more likely to enjoy this advantage.[17]

Fourth, when a negotiator's first high proposals are immediately accepted by their opponents, the negotiators are more likely to be dissatisfied. They may even walk away from the negotiation "table", despite the objective fact that this is the best outcome they could expect. An immediate acceptance of a first proposal may cause negotiators to experience bad feelings about their own performance, believing that they could have done better.[18] This decrease in satisfaction emerges even when the target (the maximum initial proposal) has been achieved. This is exactly what happened to a married couple who advertised their house for sale, asking about 15% more as an initial proposal than the evaluated price of the house. The first potential buyer immediately offered them the exact price they had asked for (the evaluation price plus the 15%). The couple's objective outcome was extremely good; however, they were not satisfied. They sent the buyer away, with the intention of waiting for a better offer. They had to wait a long time, about a year, to sell the house for 20% below its evaluated price. Thus, one's subjective bad feeling, due to an immediate acceptance of the first proposal, may bring about the loss of an objectively good deal.

Fifth, high initial proposals (for example, those made by suppliers) and low offers (for example, those made by buyers) are often used tactically to serve as an anchor, affecting the opponents' counteroffers, sometimes even misleading them. When negotiators raise initial unreasonably high proposals, they hope for a positive reaction from their opponents, because a positive reaction may indicate that their initial proposal is within the "positive acceptance zone" or at least within the "positive bargaining zone", and therefore can serve as an anchor for the proceeding discussions. However, opponents who receive a supplier's initial high proposal or a buyer's initials low proposal may be aware that the proposals are too high (too low), and therefore react in a negative way. Thus, negotiators should ask themselves: What if the opponents refuse to adjust their proposals according to the anchor? What if the opponents' response to their initial high proposals is rough and even

---

[17]Magee, J.C. Galinsky, A.D. and Gruenfeld, D.H. (2007), Power, Propensity to Negotiate, and Moving First in Competitive Interactions, *Personality and Social Psychology Bulletin*, Vol. 33(2), pp. 200–212.

[18]Galinsky, A.D. Kim, P.H. and Husted Medvec, V. (2002), The Dissatisfaction of Having Your First Offer Accepted: The Role of Counterfactual Thinking in Negotiations, *Personality and Social Psychology Bulletin*, Vol. 28 (2), pp. 271–283.

insulting — such as a display of shock, disgust or disbelief? Apparently, a rough response to negotiators' high initial proposals is tactically used to contradict the anchoring effect. Of course, this communicates a clear and immediate refusal, which in many cases, is beneficial to the resisting opponents. Opponents who respond roughly have a better probability to receive a higher share of the negotiation "pie" than those who do not respond roughly. Yet, such a rough response may also damage, at least to some extent, the relationship between the involved parties.[19]

5. Multiple Objectives and Issues

Each objective (position) is usually related to an issue. When negotiators negotiate only one objective issue — for example, price — each concession made by one of the parties is automatically a loss of money; and an equivalent gain of money for the other party (also known as a *"zero sum game"*, in which the loss of one party is an equivalent gain for the other). However, in most negotiations the involved parties have multiple divergent objectives/issues, which are interchangeable. Each objective/issue contains a target, intention point and resistance point, all of which affect the negotiation process and outcome as previously described. In a multiple-objectives (issues) negotiation, negotiators can concede their target or intention point on one issue in order to receive gains in relation to another objective/issue. When negotiators receive high gains on priority issues, they can even exceed their resistance point in regard to other, less valuable, issues. This means negotiators must prioritize the various objective/issues according to their subjective preferences. Recall that the best agreement negotiators can achieve is the one in which they concede some part of a low priority objective/issue, in exchange for some partial gain of a higher priority objective/issue which, in turn, has a lower priority for their opponents. Thus, when a difference in priorities of objectives/issues exists between the parties, and where a certain objective/issue that is valuable to one party is less valuable to the other, a Win–Win outcome can be achieved through a "trading concession" process. For example, imagine a promotion negotiation between a department manager and her superiors. The manager is the first to place her objectives on the negotiation table, which relates to several issues. Her initial three demands are: A higher salary, additional employees and a larger budget for her new

---

[19]Fassina, N.E. and Whyte, G.R. (2014), I am Disgusted by Your Proposal": The Effect of Strategic Flinch in Negotiations, *Group Decision and Negotiation*, Vol. 23(4), pp. 901–920.

department. Does the manager attribute the same value to all three issues? The answer is usually "no"; there is commonly a ranking order of subjective priorities. The differences between the subjective values attributed by each party to each objective issue, may lead to the so-called "integrative" outcome — an outcome which is satisfactory to both parties. Thus, if the manager attributes less importance to her increased salary and more importance to the other two issues; and if her superiors attribute high importance to the salary issue (they find it very hard to increase her salary, as it might be a precedent for other department managers), and less importance to the other two issues, the manager may make some concessions regarding her salary and receive, in return, additional employees and some sort of budget increase for her new department. Finally, are negotiators' concessions of high priority proposals — made in order to prevent a negotiation impasse — actually appreciated by their opponents? Apparently, negotiators' concessions of their initial demands are usually not judged as very attractive by their opponents. Therefore, they do not necessarily prevent a negotiation impasse and also do not improve mutual relationships.[20] Moreover, how do negotiators themselves feel about their integrative outcome? Despite the significance attributed to integrative outcomes, negotiators who negotiate multiple issues and reach a good integrative agreement sometimes still feel bad about the outcome. Their frustration stems from the concessions they have made and their subjective belief that they could have achieved a better outcome.[21]

6. "Interest-Based Negotiation"

It is impossible to conclude our discussion on interests and objectives in negotiation without referring to the term *"interest-based negotiation"*, which has become popular over the last decades.[22] This term refers to the notion

---

[20]Moran, S. and Ritov, I. (2002), Initial Perception in Negotiations: Evaluation and Response to "Logrolling" Offers, *Journal of Behavioral Decision Making*, Vol. 15(2), pp. 101–124.

[21]Naquin, C.E. (2003), The Agony of Opportunity in Negotiation: Number of Negotiable Issues, Counterfactual Thinking, and Feeling of Satisfaction, *Organizational Behavior and Human Decision Processes*, Vol. 91(1), pp. 97–107.

[22]The notion of "interest-based negotiation" has been popular since Fisher and Uri's best-selling books: Fisher, R. and Uri, W. (1981), *Getting to Yes: Negotiating Agreement Without Giving*, in Houghton Mifflin. The book was reissued in 1991 with an additional author: Fisher, R. Uri, W. and Patton, B. (1991) *Getting to Yes: Negotiating Agreement Without Giving*, 2nd Edition, Penguin Books. These books have been cited since then by numerous books and articles.

that an *integrative* (Win–Win) agreement will be reached if negotiators concentrate on interests rather than positions, i.e. on their *interests* rather than their *objectives*. However, interest-based negotiation does not necessarily end in an integrative agreement. Even if it does end in an integrative outcome, it does not necessarily generate negotiators' satisfaction or improve the understanding of mutual interests. If the parties have extremely opposing interests on many issues, it is doubtful whether concentrating on their interests regarding these issues will lead to reaching an integrative satisfying agreement or any agreement at all.[23] In addition, it is sometimes hard to identify the underlying, often vague, interests of negotiators. For example, what does "being treated with respect" mean, when expressed as a negotiator's interest? How should negotiators behave in order to satisfy such intangible an interest? Does "respect" mean bowing (how low?); does it mean keeping one's distance, or does it mean some other form of compensation? Recall that interests are often vague, whereas objectives are explicit and relatively well defined. Due to their relatively concrete nature, the exchange of objectives can help negotiators reach an agreement, where the exchange of interests cannot. While it is possible to find ways to agree by "trading concessions" about explicit objectives that are on the negotiation "table", it is hard — if not impossible — to renounce interests. Thus, it is the objectives, rather than the interests, that facilitate "trading concessions"; therefore, their importance in reaching a negotiation agreement is of great significance.[24] Thus, in real-world negotiation, setting objectives and their possible modifications are no less important than identifying and understanding interests.

Although objectives are associated with interests, it seems that *objective-based negotiation* may sometimes be more important than *interest-based negotiation*.

---

[23] An interesting discussion of the popular erroneous assumption that the "interest-based negotiation" approach leads to an integrative outcome, can be found in *Giacomantonio, M. De Drew, C.K.W. and Mannetti, L.* (2010), Now You See It, Now You Don't: Interests, Issues, and Psychological Distance in Integrative Negotiation, *Journal of Personality and Social Psychology*, Vol. 98(5), pp. 761–774.

[24] Provis, C. (1996), Interests versus Positions: A Critique of the Distinction, *Negotiation Journal*, Vol. 12(4), pp. 305–323.

Practical Applications

- Despite the common conception that negotiators know their own interests, try to make a quick, systematic list of your own interests. You might be surprised to note how helpful this could be in preparing for the negotiation, and later on during the negotiation process.
- If you lead a group to negotiate with your firm's opponent, remember that each member in your group has his/her own unique interests. Therefore, you must reach a consensus among the group members before beginning the negotiation process. Otherwise, you might find that the negotiation has been interrupted or has even failed — not because of the opponents, but because of your own people.
- Think twice before you sacrifice your short-term interests for long-term interests — you do not know what the future holds.
- It is most important to understand the opponents' interests. Try to put yourself in "their shoes" by using simulation, perspective-taking and empathy. Use a "devil's advocate" approach to oppose all of your own arguments, in order to avoid framing or conception.
- Your initial proposals (targets) should be high and precise. If you move first to put them on the negotiation "table", it may increase your probability of obtaining high results. However, take into consideration the idea that putting an extremely high initial proposal on the "table" may cause your opponents to walk away.
- If your opponents raise highly unreasonable (in your opinion) initial proposals, a rough or even insulting response to contradict these proposals may discourage them and cause them to reduce the initial proposals.
- Always remember that it is better to end the negotiation with no agreement, than to end it with a bad agreement.
- Try not to immediately accept your opponents' proposal, as doing so is likely to make them dissatisfied to such an extent that they might increase or even withdraw their own proposals. In this way you may miss out on a good deal.
- When you negotiate only one objective/issue (such as price) you are "playing a zero sum game" in which your loss is your opponent's gain, and *vice versa*. Consequently, you may end up with a Win–Lose type of outcome. Adding objectives/issues to the negotiation process may

help you to concede something in regard to one objective/issue in order to gain more in relation to other objectives/issues. As a result, you may end up with a Win–Win outcome. Enjoy your outcome; do not feel frustrated due to the concessions you have made during the negotiation process.

Chapter 6

Common Power Sources and the Balance of Power

"You can't go to a negotiating table pointing a gun, but you've got to keep it over your shoulder."

Joe Slovo

During a discussion of negotiation power in class, one of the students expressed herself with an emotional outburst. She argued, almost shouted, that negotiation and power are contradictory conceptions. "It is either power or negotiation that is used in order to resolve conflict", she insisted adamantly, "they can't live together under the same roof". Her outburst provoked an enthusiastic class discussion of the pros and cons of using power in negotiation. This was just one more proof that the conception of "power", in general, and in negotiation, in particular, can stimulate highly emotional reactions.[1] For some people, *power* has a negative connotation; it is perceived as being almost identical to violence, as well as an "unavoidable evil". For others, the concept of power has a positive connotation, and is perceived as a strength, which facilitates influencing others in their "righteous goals". For these individuals, power is not equal to violence, but it promotes a feeling of being in control and serves as a means of persuasion. The class concluded the discussion with this interesting notion: Power is an integral part of negotiation and does not necessarily yield violence or other undesirable behaviors. The limited perception of negotiating power as violence, coercion or the ability to punish is somewhat misleading. While the ability to punish and coercion may, at times, be associated with negotiation, they are only one out of many sources of negotiating power. If power stimulates negative reactions, it is only when it has been unethically or illegally used.

---

[1] Robbins, A. and McClendon III, J. (1997), *Unlimited Power — A Black Choice*, Fireside.

1. What is Negotiating Power?

Negotiating *power* can be defined as the potential ability of negotiators to influence their opponents to agree with them, regardless of the opponents' resistance. Another possible definition of negotiating power is the potential ability to control one's opponents, as well as the negotiation process and outcome.

Accordingly, it can be assumed, at least theoretically, that power in negotiation contains an inherent paradox. Powerful negotiators should not seek to negotiate at all, as they can, in any case, achieve their goals or whatever they wish from their opponents, even despite their resistance. Weaker negotiators, on the other hand, afraid of losing, would try to avoid negotiating with powerful opponents at all costs. Following such reasoning, only negotiators with equal power would seek negotiation. However, in the real world of negotiation, negotiations involving parties that possess asymmetrical power are a daily event. Surprisingly, this type of negotiation sometimes ends with the weaker negotiators achieving much better outcomes than expected. Power, whether symmetrical or asymmetrical, is an integral part of negotiation, which can end in the complete success of one side, a negotiation impasse or some form of mutual agreement. Thus, the way in which each negotiation process is conducted, and the nature of its process and outcome, is highly influenced not only by the negotiators' interests and objectives, but also by the balance of power, determined by the sources of power accumulated on each side.[2]

2. Power Sources

There are many sources upon which negotiating power is dependent. This wide range of various sources may influence the negotiation process and outcome. It is possible to classify *power sources* into three major categories: situational, personal and social power sources.

Obviously, the classified power sources discussed in this chapter are merely examples, and by no means include all of the power sources at the negotiators' disposal. In addition, each negotiation may contain its own unique sources of power, typical to the current situation. For example,

---

[2]Zartman, J.W. and Rubin, J.Z. (eds.), (2002), *Power and Negotiation*, The University of Michigan Press.

in *collective bargaining*, both union and employers' representatives may have customary sources of power, such as employers control over resources (financial resources, human resources, equipment, etc.), on one hand, and the union's coalition and solidarity as sources of power, on the other. However, labor market fluctuations create a unique source of power for either union or employers. Thus, a high employment period serves as a power source for unions, whereas a period of unemployment serves as a unique power source for employers. In addition, employee unions that control essential services, such as medical doctors' unions or port workers' unions, which control import and export operations, have better power sources than less essential unions. Moreover, the sources of power may differ among dissimilar situations. For example, in hostage crisis negotiations, physical might (armed forces) may serve as a source of power, whereas in a business negotiation over buying or selling technological parts, physical power may be irrelevant, while expertise serves as a substantial power.

It is noteworthy that during the negotiation process, if negotiators sense that their potential power is weaker than that of their opponents; they might try to modify it. They may try to change the asymmetrical balance of potential power by using their own sources of power. Some of these sources of power, if used at the right time and in the right way, can neutralize and even overcome their opponents' sources of power. For example, seeking out more alternatives, reducing their interests in their opponents' proposals, creating coalitions or threatening to appeal to court may neutralize some of their opponents' sources of power.

One interesting source of power that some negotiators use, in order to neutralize their opponents' sources of power, is simulating other sources of power, thereby enhancing their *perceived power.*

3. Perceived Power

Perceived power is any source of power that negotiators pretend to have, but do not actually have. They may pretend to have alternatives, levels of expertise, control over financial resources, information, etc.; for example, they may have no alternatives, but pretend to have many. As long as their opponents believe they have many alternatives, they have a significant negotiating source of power. Another example is the influence of expertise power. If negotiators are perceived as experts, they will enjoy this power source, even if they are not genuine experts. Contrariwise, if they are genuine experts, but are not perceived as such, they may lose their potential negotiating power. Thus, negotiators may be intimidated, as they subjectively perceive an opponent as having certain power sources, even if, objectively, they do not. In other words, in negotiation, negotiators do not necessarily need to have objective sources of power; it is enough that opponents believe that they possess such power sources, in order to divert the negotiation process and outcome in the negotiators' favor. However, if a perceived power is revealed, it is then identified as a deception. In this case, the pretender is likely to be punished by the other parties, and the pretence may strike back like a boomerang. The other parties may behave harshly in response, by adding more demands or ignoring previous conclusions. In addition, any motivation towards cooperation may be reduced or even disappear completely.[3]

4. Situational Sources of Negotiating Power

Situational power sources are derived from the internal negotiating situation and substantially affect the negotiators' balance of power; for example, alternatives to the specific negotiation process (the number and importance of the negotiators' Best Alternative to Negotiated Agreements (*BATNA*s)), the commitments made during the negotiation process, and coalitions that change the negotiation power balance.

4.1. *The "Alternative" as a Source of Power*

Negotiators enter the negotiation process because they are interested in certain benefits that their opponents control. If they attribute a high value to achieving these benefits, and if their opponent is the only one who can provide them with such benefits, they have low power and are left with no choice but to "pay" the "price" (which may be high) demanded by their opponents. High-power negotiators are often more persistent, more reluctant to make concessions and, more aggressive in their attempt to reach their targets, than low-power negotiators. One way in which negotiators can, however, compensate for their low power is by seeking out further alternatives.[4]

---

[3]Wolfe, R.J. and McGinn, K.L. (2003), Perceived Relative Power and its Influence on Negotiation, *Group Decision and Negotiation*, Vol. 14(1), pp. 3–20.

[4]An interesting discussion on interchangeable power and choice (in our case *alternatives*) may be found in: Inesi, M.E. Botti, S. Dubois, P. Rucker, D.D. and Galinsky, A.D. (2011), Power and Choice: Their Dynamic Interplay in Quenching the Thirst for Personal Control, *Psychological Science*, Vol. 22(8), pp. 1042–1048.

Negotiators who have many alternatives enhance their negotiation abilities. Moreover, negotiators with many negotiation alternatives may be more than three times as likely to make the first proposal at the negotiation "table", usually a significant contribution in gaining distinct negotiating advantages.[5]

However, the association between many alternatives and power in negotiation is not simple. Indeed, having no alternatives means that negotiators are relatively weak, since they are completely dependent on their opponents. Thus, in facing a monopoly, negotiators are relatively powerless and the asymmetrical power is radical. This is, for example, why being in love may cause lovers to lose while negotiating with their spouses. Imagine a negotiating couple, where one is much more in love than the other. In this case, the one who loves more is more dependent on the other and has fewer alternatives. The more beloved one becomes a "monopoly", and the more powerful one between the two. Thus, the beloved negotiator has a much better chance of achieving the best result out of the negotiation.

Yet, there can be various degrees of power asymmetry,[6] since there are various degrees of alternatives and various degrees of benefits in which the negotiators are interested. Negotiators can be less dependent on their powerful opponents, if they have more alternatives than their opponents, if they are offered fewer benefits than they expected, or both. For example, imagine a scenario in which employment candidates are negotiating with a potential employer. They expect to gain some important benefits from the potential employer; however, they also have alternative job offers (perhaps less beneficial) from other employers. Therefore, they are not completely dependent on the current employer's decision to accept or refuse them as employees. Suppose that during the employment interview they find out that the employer cannot, or does not wish to, provide them with the salary and work conditions they expected. As a result, the candidates may experience reduced interests in the employer's benefits and might turn to their alternatives — the other potential employers. Is the negotiation in this case doomed to end

---

[5]Magee, J.C. Galinsky, A.D. and Gruenfeld, D.H. (2007), Power, Propensity to Negotiate, and Moving First in Competitive Interactions, *Personality and Social Psychology Bulletin*, Vol. 33(2), pp. 200–212.

[6]Casciaro, T. and Piskorski, M.J. (2005), Power Imbalance, Mutual Dependence, and Constraints Absorption: A Closer Look at Resource Dependence Theory, *Administrative Science Quarterly*, Vol. 50(2), pp. 167–169.

in an impasse? The answer depends on the quality of the alternative and the quality of the benefits which the other employers offer. If the alternatives offered by the other employers are not at least equivalent to the current employer's offers, and if the benefits offered by the current employer are within the negotiators' positive "acceptance zone" or at least within their positive "bargaining zone",[7] the power asymmetry is reduced and may not be perceived as an obstacle to reaching an agreement.[8] Thus, symmetrical or asymmetrical "alternative" potential powers are not stable situations, and may easily shift during the negotiation process. Furthermore, while "alternative" potential power may be significant, it is definitely not the only existing *power source*. Other sources of power may be needed to determine the potential power balance between negotiators and opponents.

4.2. *Commitments as the Opponents' Source of Power*

Negotiators sometimes make commitments that may work against their own self-interests. Imagine that during collective bargaining, the employers publically announce that if an agreement is not reached within two weeks, they will take the case to court. Suppose the negotiations have lasted much longer than two weeks, and the employers have still not taken the case to court. How do you think this will affect the employers' perceived power? This may influence the union to conclude that the employers are weak, as they do not have a strong legal "case". Consequently, the union may decide to intensify the struggle by going on strike. Negotiations can be further dragged out during the strike, and if the employers still fail to take the case to court, the union may add payment of the strike's costs as a new settlement requirement. Finally, after the employers suffer a great financial loss and lose several customers, an agreement in favor of the union's demands may be reached.

Thus, making commitments during the negotiation process is risky. Negotiators who make a commitment, but fail to follow through with it, may suffer a loss of at least their perceived potential power. A commitment, especially a publically announced one, which is not carried out, sends a signal of weakness to the other parties, which may be used by them effectively.

---

[7] See Chapter 5 of this book.

[8] Kim, P.H. and Pragale, A.R. (2005), Choosing the Path to Bargaining Power: An Empirical Comparison of the *BATNA*s and Contribution in Negotiation, *Journal of Applied Psychology*, Vol. 90(2), pp. 373–381.

Moreover, negotiators who make commitments which are not carried out, risk losing their potential power — not only to their current opponents, but also to other "outside" parties, such as buyers and suppliers. These "outside" parties, who are completely uninvolved in the current negotiation, may still suffer its consequences. As a result, they may try to take advantage in future negotiations, since they now perceive the negotiators as weak negotiators who cannot fulfill their commitments. They may also simply refuse to negotiate with such negotiators in the future.

However, the worst consequence of making commitments in negotiation may be what has been referred to as "Commitment Escalation". Negotiators who make a commitment may risk having to continue with a particular course of action dictated by their previous commitment, despite the fact that this course of action is risky and has a small probability of ending successfully.[9] The more time, effort and resources invested in this course of action, the more negotiators will adhere to it, with the hope that by the end of the negotiations, they may be able to cover their investments or minimize their losses. Thus, instead of withdrawing their commitment, negotiators increase their risky way of negotiation and continue escalating their risky course of action in a subjective effort to confirm their initial commitment.[10] Objectively, however, commitments may cause a critical loss of potential power.

It should be emphasized that commitments made by opponents can be a source of power to negotiators. In contrast, negotiators' commitments may weaken their negotiation power, which may possibly (but not necessarily) lead to loss after loss, if they stubbornly cling to their initial commitment. In any case, commitments may create power asymmetry.

4.3. *Coalitions as a Source of Power*

Negotiators create a temporary or enduring coalition with other negotiators in order to be able to achieve common negotiation objectives. The forming of coalitions in negotiations often results from power asymmetry between negotiators and their opponents, where the low-power negotiators are motivated to create coalitions in order to achieve a more favorable balance of

---

[9]Bazerman, M. and Neale, M. (1992), Nonrational Escalation of Commitment in Negotiation, *European Management Journal*, Vol. 10(2), pp. 163–168.

[10]Zartman, I.W. and Fure, G.O. (2005), Chapter 1, The Dynamic of Escalation and Negotiation, in Zartman, I.W. and Fure, G.O. (eds.), *Negotiation in International Conflicts*, Cambridge University Press, pp. 3–18.

power. Coalitions can be built around any negotiation issues or any type of negotiation — from individual negotiations, organizational negotiations or negotiation between nations. Once several negotiators create a coalition, they can pool their financial funds, human resources, information, etc., and consequently come to possess more power and negotiation efficiency than any individual or group member in the coalition.[11] However, a coalition — any coalition — may serve as a source of power only as long as its sub-units work together to achieve their mutual negotiating goals. Severe arguments within the coalition may lead to its failure or collapse.

There are several types of negotiation coalitions; the most typical are: Ad-hoc coalitions, solidarity coalitions and durable coalitions.[12]

The *ad hoc* coalition: In an *ad hoc* coalition, all sorts of individuals or organizations cooperate to achieve negotiation-specific objectives. For example, a contemporary social protest can include hundreds of thousands (sometimes millions) of protestors from varying socio–economic, political, and religious backgrounds. All these protestors create an enormous *ad hoc* coalition, which demands social justice from the government. Of course, the breadth of such a sporadic coalition generates power which, in turn, may force even governments to comply with the coalition's demands, at least to a certain extent. However, such sporadic coalitions focused around one issue with such a variety of diverse individuals can usually last only a relatively short period of time, while governments regain their dominant negotiating power. In a very similar way, customers sometimes create a coalition in order to reduce food chain prices. This type of coalition also includes various individuals or groups with no common background, interests or ideology, except their demands that food chains reduce their prices. Such coalitions may be very powerful, as long as they last, and do not split into antagonistic sub-groups. However, their life-span is usually very limited — both in regard to time and relationships among members. In addition, since ad-hoc coalition members are usually not a cohesive group, it is the coalition type most inclined

---

[11]Bennedsen, N. and Wolfenzon, D. (2000), The Balance of Power in Closely Held Corporations, *Journal of Financial Economics*, Vol. 58(1–2), pp. 113–139.

[12]Tattersall describes four types of union coalitions: *Ad hoc* coalitions, support coalitions, mutual support coalitions, and deep coalitions. See Tattersall, A. (2005), There is Power in Coalition: A Framework for Assessing How and When Union-Community Coalitions are Effective and Enhance Union Power, *Labour and Industry: A Journal of the Social and Economic Relations of Work*, Vol. 16(2), pp. 97–112.

to engage in difficult debates among its members regarding the preferable negotiation strategy. The time limitation and the limited relationship among members increase the possibility of debates within the coalition, thus substantially reducing the coalition's power versus that of its opponents.

The solidarity coalition: A solidarity coalition is often formed during a crisis, where the asymmetrical gap of power between the negotiating sides is so wide that the party with less power must request the support of the other party or parties. For example, a private medical center is on the verge of bankruptcy. In order to save the medical center from collapsing, the new management decides to dismiss many of the medical center's employees and pay only half salaries to the others. The union rejects the dismissal policy and demands payment in full. The negotiation — with and without strikes — lasts for a few months, as the management insists on the dismissals and considerable salary reductions. As striking does not seem to help, the union requests and receives the support of all the health unions in the country (the national physicians union, the nurses' national union, paramedical national union and hospitals manual employees union). Due to a country-wide solidarity health strike, the government agrees to cover some of the health center's financial deficits and recruits several private financial organizations to give the hospital loans. As a result, the "decrees" are cancelled. Most employees continued working and their salaries are guaranteed. The only mechanism that helped the health center's union during the crisis was the formation of a solidarity coalition with all the national health unions. Thus, when one organization forms a solidarity coalition with other relevant organizations, it significantly enhances its negotiation power, tipping the balance of power in its own favor. However, solidarity coalitions are based on the negotiation objectives of one party, while the supporting organizations usually do not interfere in the negotiation decision-making process, nor do they receive any benefit for their aid — just hope for reciprocation whenever the need arises.

The durable coalition: The durable coalition differs from the solidarity coalition by exposing coalition members to mutually active participation in repeated negotiation processes. Such active participation translates into mutual resources sharing and mutual decision-making regarding various negotiation objectives (targets, intention and resistance points) which the coalition hopes to achieve; for example, a lasting coalition comprised of a teachers union, parents associations and school principal organizations, to promote a "public education campaign".[13] Such a coalition may, in due time, force the government to negotiate not only salary issues, but a comprehensive reform within the education system. Thus, this type of durable coalition — between unions and other relevant organizations — may achieve not only a wide range of negotiation objectives, but also bring about social change.

5. Personal Sources of Negotiating Power

Personal power sources are derived from the negotiators' unique capabilities or characteristics, such as control over resources, charisma, expertise, personal status, personal authority and reputation.

During negotiation, negotiators are often impressed by their opponents' personal power sources, which can be intimidating. At the same time, they may use their own personal sources of power which, in turn, can neutralize and even overcome their opponents' sources of power. Thus, by using special expertise and reputation, negotiators can neutralize even their opponents' control over financial resources, especially if their opponents are in need of such special expertise and believe the negotiators have it. Nevertheless, negotiators have to be aware of their own personal sources of power. Following are some typical examples.

5.1. *Control over Financial Resources as a Source of Power*

Negotiators who have personal control over resources that their opponents' desire, have negotiating power over their opponents. Gaining resources such as financial resources, budgets or information enhances negotiators' influencing abilities and also reduces their dependencies on others; i.e. enhances their power. However, the importance of negotiators' personal resources to their opponents, and the extent to which the opponents can obtain these resources elsewhere (their possible alternatives), determine the negotiators' genuine amount of power. Negotiators who have control over economic resources, such as their own money, budgets or property, and which are important to their opponents, can afford to be patient during the negotiation process. They may ignore time pressures that usually end in concessions and, with their financial abilities, acquire multiple alternatives. For example, a wealthy person can

---

[13]Tattersall, A. (2010), *Power in Coalition: Strategies for Strong Unions and Social Change*, Cornell University Press.

afford the best experts while negotiating with official authorities, and thus reach at least some objectives, which a poor person could not even dream of achieving. Negotiators who have control over financial resources can also take the risk of setting high objectives (targets and intention points), and making the first proposals, which usually produce remarkable negotiation advantages.[14] For example, a bank negotiating a loan to a small firm can risk putting the first offer at a high interest rate, of course taking into account the firm's possible resistance point.

5.2. *Control over Information as a Source of Power*

Negotiators who control information are also powerful negotiators. Actually, one of the most important negotiating power resources is information. On the one hand, it is easier to justify negotiators' own standpoints with information that provides facts and evidence contradicting the opponents' arguments, thus influencing them to accept the negotiators' demands. On the other hand, just imagine how powerful negotiators can be if they have information regarding their opponents' alternatives, interests, intention points and resistance points. Take, for example, a negotiation between a supplier and a buyer. Information regarding the prices other buyers pay, the supplier's production capacity, the cost of the supplier's products as well as information regarding other customers' complaints and grievances, may give the buyer a fair description of the supplier's strengths and weaknesses, thus enhancing the buyer's power. It can also reveal whether the supplier's proposals are authentic or merely a "make-believe" proposal, made in order to buy time. It is true that in today's open information society, it is possible to obtain a great deal of information regarding one's opponents. However, there are still many unknown types of information; and even the true control over resources is often disguised. Therefore, the possibility to reveal true information and control it, may serve as an important source of power.[15]

5.3. *Position as a Source of Power*

Position is a source of power, which derives from negotiator's personal position, including an individual's rank in the social and/or the organizational

---

[14]See Chapter 5 of this book.

[15]For a more comprehensive discussion of the role of information in negotiation, see Chapter 3 of this book.

hierarchy, negotiator's personal authority and personal status. While these components of personal "position" are not mutually exclusive, each of them have unique qualities or characteristics.

The negotiator's rank or status as a source of power: Negotiator's rank or status in the formal or informal social hierarchy is of great importance. Of course in some societies or organizations, one's rank may be inherited (from birth), while in others, it is based on personal achievement. Whatever the basis of the ranking, in many cases it determines the amount of resources negotiators control or the respect they are accorded by others. For example, a religious leader, with a high rank within his group of believers, has a great deal of influence over them. Through this influence, this leader can exert his power even beyond the specific group. A union leader, who has control over union members, can force managements to change their policies regarding their employees. The higher negotiators' formal or informal rank, the greater is their ability to reward or punish others or, in other words, to influence or coerce others. The higher the negotiators' status, the higher their personal power. Thus, high-ranking is a source of power, especially in face to face negotiations. During e-negotiations or other remote negotiation, this influence may decrease as one's rank is less observable.

Authority as a source of personal power: Authority can be translated into legitimate power — the power that is invested in specific positions in society or specific jobs in organizations. The authoritative power of elected or nominated officials, such as CEOs or school principals, is derived from their formal position within a social structure that grants them a certain amount of authority. Personal authority exists as long as the negotiator holds this position, and diminishes once the negotiator no longer holds it. Negotiators who occupy formal positions usually have the power to reward or punish others, which may make their negotiations relatively easy. However, since the power to reward or punish is granted only within the borders of legitimacy, negotiators with high authoritative power may be judged severely if their activities are perceived as illegitimate. This, for example, was the case of a CEO from an international local subsidiary who was authorized to sell only to local customers. When he tried negotiating a big deal with overseas customers, it was immediately cancelled by the international firm's headquarters. This, in turn, caused the customer to sue for enormous compensation. A few weeks later, the CEO was unfortunately looking for a new job.

At times, due to various developments, such as a change of values or a change in education level, lower-ranking individuals may refuse to accept the large range of demands of a person who possesses legitimate authority. When the target population — be it rank and file, an athletic group, or an orchestral ensemble — choose to no longer recognize the formal authority figure, this figure loses its power.

Since in some societies the obedience of many populations to personal authority is shrinking with various social changes, negotiating processes take place instead. For example, even in extremely formal organizations, such as police forces or armies, the obedience of the rank and file grows smaller as democratic values strengthen and the education level increases. Instead, the role of negotiation increases, as an alternative means of accepting or not accepting the authorities' demands. However, negotiating with authorities is still difficult because, as mentioned earlier, authorities have the power to punish or reward. This means that although personal authority as a source of power may be decreasing, but it is still a strong negotiating power.

Personal status as a source of power[16]: Personal status initially derives from the respect or admiration of others. Sometimes respect is a result of controlling resources, such as respect for a person who controls a financial empire or a professor who has won a Nobel prize. Formal authority can also be a source of status, such as respect for a high government official. Sometimes people respect and even admire informal leaders in various fields, be it a political, academic or cultural field. Whatever the reason, negotiators with high status have power over negotiators with lower status. However, at times one's status is often the result of widely-held stereotypes. For example, men who behave assertively during the negotiation process are treated with respect, whereas the same assertive behavior in women engaged in negotiation is treated with less respect. At times, the current stereotype of negotiating women still reduces their status and, accordingly, their negotiating power.

5.4. *Personal Attributes as a Source of Power*

There are various personal attributes which may provide negotiators with power, depending on the negotiations' characteristics. Four classical examples will be addressed in the following sections: Weakness, charisma,

---

[16]Magee, J.C. and Galinsky, A.D. (2008), 8 Social Hierarchies: The Self-Reinforcing Nature of Power and Status, *The Academy of Management Annals*, Vol. 2(1), pp. 351–398.

expertise and reputation. These attributes are by no mean mutually exclusive, as reputation may be associated with charisma or expertise, while charisma may enhance reputation and all of these attributes may be associated with negotiators' strength or weakness.

Personal weakness as a source of power: Apparently, weakness is the classical contradiction of power. Thus, how can weakness turn into power in negotiation? Sometimes negotiators are so weak that it seems they no longer have anything to lose. Since it is very difficult to change the positions of negotiators who have little or nothing to lose, their weakness turns into a source of power. In addition, weakness often stimulates sympathy. It is easy to sympathize with the weak; it is harder to like the strong, and such sympathy may change the power balance. One easily understood example is that of a little girl negotiating for something (candy, sleeping time) with tears in her eyes — think about how powerful her weakness can be. Another such example is hunger strikers. In some societies, the weaker the strikers get, the stronger their negotiation position. Moreover, sometimes, the surrounding environment expects, or even pressures, the stronger negotiator to behave generously towards the weaker negotiator. In return for the concessions of the stronger negotiators, the weaker side has only gratitude to reciprocate with, nothing else. This is how weakness becomes strength in negotiation.

Charisma as a source of power: Some negotiators have charisma, but most of them do not. Charisma is said to be a "gift of God". Charismatic personalities can arise in any field of life, such as science, art, religion and politics; in each one of these fields they may perform as talented negotiators. Charismatic negotiating power arises from the ability to confound and surpass expectations — to be extraordinary.[17] Charismatic negotiators cause others to perceive them as special; and as someone who can be trusted.[18] What makes such negotiators so special? First, highly charismatic negotiators are surprisingly creative in their proposals and moves during the negotiation process. Second, they are excellent communicators — they can describe their proposals with colorful language, supplemented with humor and intriguing metaphors. Finally, they are emotionally intelligent and create a good

[17]Turner, S. (2003), Charisma Reconsidered, *Journal of Classical Sociology*, Vol. 3(1), pp. 5–26.

[18]Gary, Y. and Falbe, C.M. (1991), The Importance of Different Power Sources in Downward and Lateral Relations, *Journal of Applied Psychology*, Vol. 76(3), pp. 416–423.

atmosphere during the negotiation process. Thus, charismatic negotiators are conceived as having a "magnetic" personality, which gives them an advantage to strongly influence and inspire both their followers and opponents to make decisions or concessions, which will be in their favor.

Expertise as a power source: Expertise power is derived from the recognition of the qualifications, skills and/or knowledge, which are relevant to one or several negotiation issues, as well as one's skill and knowledge in negotiation processes. Negotiators' expertise power exists only to the extent that others — especially their opponents — recognize and need their expert knowledge. As individual's expertise negotiating power is usually limited to a particular area or topic, the expert power is also limited in negotiation. In addition, negotiators are more reluctant to make concessions when negotiating with expert peers, than when negotiating with unknown expert negotiators.

Expert credibility is essential in persuading opponents to reduce their proposals or make substantial concessions. Job candidates endeavoring to negotiate their expertise during negotiation interviews are more likely to impress their interviewers and receive the desired job.[19] Moreover, mediators who are presented as expert negotiators are highly influential, much more than non-expert mediators. They are particularly effective in getting disputants to reduce their negotiation proposals and make concessions, as a result of their recommendations.[20]

Reputation as a source of power: The phenomenon is well-known. People are willing to pay much more for a product made by a well-known company (brand) than what they would pay for the same product made by an unknown company. In the same way, negotiators are more likely to react differently to opponents of various reputations. Reputation is the person's "brand", describing her or his typical nature, and in our case, providing an "image" of the opponent, even though one's reputation is often developed by hearsay, sometimes even inaccurate gossip passed along the social networks. Thus, the importance of reputation in negotiation is due to adding

---

[19]Lipovsky, C. (2008), Candidates' Negotiation of Their Expertise in Job Interviews, *Journal of Pragmatics*, Vol. 38(8), pp. 1147–1174.

[20]Arnold, J.A. and O'Connor, K.M. (1999), Ombudspersons or Peers? The Effect of Third Party Expertise and Recommendations on Negotiation, *Journal of Applied Psychology*, Vol. 84(5), pp. 776–785.

information, be it genuine or false, about opponents. In consequence, reputation reduces negotiators' uncertainty to a certain extent, and influences their behavior and decision-making — before and during the negotiation process. For example, when opponents have a reputation for being tough and competitive, even if it is a false reputation, their threats may be perceived as reliable, causing negotiators to make concessions. In this case, reputation works to the opponents' advantage. However, an opponent's reputation as being tough and competitive may also convince negotiators to prepare themselves to be rigid and competitive negotiators; furthermore, it may also affect their willingness to share information and be cooperative.[21] In this case, the opponent's tough reputation may work to the opponent's disadvantage, as it may create a vicious circle of both parties' tough actions, and eventually lead to a negotiation impasse. Thus, despite the limited — and sometimes even false — information, reputation can provide, it still has powerful effects on both negotiators and opponents' negotiating behavior.

6. Social Power Sources

Social values which are accepted by negotiators, may serve as sources of power. For example, the "written word" (contracts, protocols, etc.), bureaucracy and legitimate procedures may or may not be sources of power, according to the negotiators' values and the norms of the culture.

6.1. *The Written Word*

In some societies, the "written word" is important and binding, while in other societies it is not. In societies where the "written word" is significant, it can serve as a source of power, since negotiators who accept its importance may be convinced by written proceedings, protocols, even e-mails. In other societies, "face" — honor and dignity — influence negotiation much more than the 'written word.

6.2. *Bureaucracy*

In almost all societies, however, negotiators who have access to bureaucracy — or are ready to use it — possess an effective source of power,

---

[21]Tinsley, C.H. O'Connor, K.M. and Sullivan, B.A. (2002), Tough Guys Finish Last: The Perils of a Distributive Reputation, *Organizational Behavior and Human Decision Processes*, Vol. 88(2), pp. 621–642.

compared with their opponents who are reluctant to use bureaucracy or do not have such access. When the alternative to negotiation means involvement with bureaucracy, the opponents' power may become substantially reduced. For example, in some societies if the negotiators' only alternatives are to either reach a relatively poor agreement or be dragged into court, negotiators may choose the relatively poor agreement. This is because a poor agreement may be perceived as a better choice compared to wasting time and money on lawyers, for an unpredictable result at the end of the legal proceedings. In addition, negotiators who do not comply with the legal proceedings might be exposed to formal sanctions. Yet, complying with legal procedures may limit negotiators' potential power, even if no formal enforcement is employed during the negotiation process. For instance, over the past decades some societies have adopted and developed a law referred to as negotiating "in good faith". This law limits disloyal negotiation practices, such as negotiating with several parties simultaneously (limiting the alternative source of power). It also inhibits illegitimate behavior, such as attempts to mislead or acts of deception. Furthermore, this law also requires complete transparency in regard to undesirable information, and the general disclosure of all true information, during the negotiation process. As a result, all parties involved in the negotiation may suffer power limitations, but the party who has relatively more alternatives may suffer a relatively greater limitation of power, due to such social procedures. Thus, various social procedures and regulations may enhance some negotiators' power, while reducing others, depending on the type of procedures, the negotiators' access to such procedures, and the importance with which the negotiators perceive these procedures.

Of course, there are more sources of power which are embedded in social values or norms, such as being "just", "honest" "reliable", etc. All these will be addressed comprehensively, further on in this book.

7. The "Weight" of Negotiation Power Sources

Indeed, there are multiple sources of power. However, some of them "weigh" more heavily than others. The "weight" of each power source is determined by its importance — its ability to provide benefits to negotiators.[22] Yet, the weight of a power source depends on its type as well as the negotiation

---

[22] Kim, P.H. Pinkley, R.L. and Fragale, A.R. (2005), Power Dynamics in Negotiation, *Academy of Management Review*, Vol. 30(4), pp. 799–822.

situation. For example, in a job interview negotiation having alternative job proposals as a source of power often has more "weight" than having a good reputation. Alternatively, in a coercive negotiation situation, violence may have more weight than alternatives as a source of power. Hence, an asymmetrical balance of power is produced by the accumulating number of power sources, as well as their "weight", on one side. An equivalent accumulation of power sources of equal "weight" on all sides may produce a symmetrical balance of power. In order to manipulate a desirable outcome, negotiators have to understand how to obtain a greater number of "weighty" power sources, and how to use these various sources to their advantage.

8. About Powerful Negotiators

In many instances, an asymmetrical power balance works in the favor of the powerful negotiators. Powerful negotiators are those who have many weighty sources of power, whether objective or perceived, including weakness as a strong source of power. Powerful negotiators are not only more aggressive in their negotiation style; they often engage less in "perspective taking", i.e. they are less attentive to what the less powerful opponents think and feel,[23] and generally have a tendency to underestimate their opponents. They also are not concerned with potential risks. Potential gains are usually the powerful main interest. Since they focus more on potential gains than on the risks of being caught, they often tend to cheat and deceive.[24] Moreover, powerful negotiators often have access to formal procedures and make use of these procedures to force their opponents' hand. However, all this may increase impasses, walk-outs from the negotiation "table" and a reluctance to negotiate with the same powerful negotiators in the future.

9. On the Difference between Potential Power and its Realization

It is most important to distinguish between potential power and its use in negotiation. Potential power is the accumulation of "weighty" power sources,

---

[23]Magee, J.C. Galinsky, A.D. Inesl, M.E. and Gruenfeld, D.H. (2006), Power and Perspective not Taken, *Psychological Science*, Vol. 17(12), pp. 1068–1074.

[24]Lammers, J. Stapel, D.A. and Galinsky, A.D. (2010), Power Increases Hypocrisy: Moralizing in Reasoning, Immorality in Behavior, *Psychological Science*, Vol. 21(5), pp. 737–744.

whereas the use of potential power is made through implementing negotiation strategies and tactics. In this chapter, only the characteristics and the sources of potential power have been discussed. The next chapter will address the realization of potential power through strategies and tactics. Yet, some factors mediate between potential and realized negotiating power. These factors are: Familiarity with the various power sources, the motivation to use the potential power and the opportunity to actually use it.

9.1. *Familiarity with Various Power Sources*

Unfortunately, most negotiators are not consciously aware of the many power sources available to them. In order to exercise their power effectively, negotiators have to be familiar with their own various sources of power, as well as their opponents' sources of power. By using their own power sources, negotiators can neutralize at least some of their opponents' power sources.

9.2. *The Motivation to Realize Potential Power*

In many cases the mere existence of potential power generates the temptation to use it. However, even if negotiators are tempted to use their potential power, they do not necessarily wish to use it. At times, they may be reluctant to use their potential power for several reasons, such as: Their belief that using power is unethical, their fear that using power will lead to an impasse, or their concern regarding their future relationship with their current opponents. Whatever the reason is, negotiators do not always have the motivation to realize their potential power.

9.3. *The Opportunity to Use Power*

Long ago, Napoleon Bonaparte referred to the relationship between ability and opportunity by saying: "Ability (in our case the ability to use potential power) is of little account without opportunity." Even the most powerful negotiators do not always have the opportunity to realize their power. First, opportunity is often very difficult to identify. Second, at times, no true opportunity exists; consequently, the realization of negotiators' power may be limited. To illustrate, an employment candidate does not have an opportunity to use his/her reputation (as a source of power) to place high demands on the negotiation table during a period of unemployment, when there is a low demand for job seekers. Another such example is that of a powerful government (especially a democratic government) negotiating with a terrorist group over the release of hostages. In such a case, the government often does not have the opportunity to realize its potential military or political power, and must concede to most of the terrorists' demands. Yet, in cases where negotiators identify an opportunity, such as in the case where they discover that their opponents' financial position is not good, they can execute their power in order to achieve a better outcome for themselves. Moreover, not only can negotiators utilize opportunity, they can actually create opportunities so as to realize their power. One such example is a union initiating a strike during negotiation to create an opportunity to force management to accept most of the employees' demands. It should be noted that a strike is a tactic that is frequently used to create such an opportunity.

To conclude, the mere existence of potential power does not guarantee its implementation during the negotiation process. It is rather familiarity with sources of power, the opportunity to use them and, above all, the negotiators' motivation to use their potential power, which are necessary to close the gap between potential power and its realization.

Practical Applications

- Even if you feel powerful (have substantial sources of negotiating power), it does not mean that you have to realize your power. You have to differentiate between negotiations in which it is worthwhile to exercise your power, and those in which your powerful gains may end up as losses. For example, exercising your power while negotiating with your own children may end up as a loss.
- Become familiar with your own sources of power, as well as those of your opponent. Do not give up easily if you find out that your opponents have more power sources than you do. You now know that some of your power sources, even if they look less influential than your opponent's, can neutralize your opponent's significant sources of power. For example, if you have access to bureaucracy, you can neutralize even the strongest monopolistic power.
- It is not enough to be familiar with both your own power sources and those of your opponent. You have to "weigh" each one of them and decide how important they are — both to you and your opponent. This is the best way to estimate and decide how to confront the balance of power in the negotiation.
- Before you weigh your power against that of your opponents, you should accumulate more relevant sources of power. For example: Try

to find more alternatives, create or join a coalition, try to control as many resources as possible and use your personal "charm". If this does not work for you, try to use your weakness as a source of power, which might be of help.

- Before negotiating with someone you perceive to be both demanding and emotional, even if you do not have many sources of power, pretend you have them. For example, demonstrate strong *BATNAs*, and pretend to have relevant information and other power sources. Generating perceptional power can neutralize your opponents' efforts to put pressure on you.
- Just remember that you do not have to possess real objective sources of power. Pretending you have them may help you to acquire these sources of power. Of course, this only works as long as your opponent believes your pretence. The only problem with "perceived" power is that it is sometimes revealed as such, and identified as a deception. This may be dangerous when facing a powerful opponent.
- Revealing your opponents' perceived sources of power is of the highest importance. This may shift the power balance in your favor, and give you some indication about the value of negotiating with these opponents in the future.
- Think twice before making commitments, especially publically announced commitments, before or during the negotiation process. Making commitments is risky as you may not be able to carry them out, at least in the short run. In this case, unrealized commitments may be perceived by your opponents as a weakness or even as a deception and may be used against you.
- If you have made a commitment and you feel that you cannot stand up to it, do not adhere to it. Withdraw your commitment as soon as possible. Just remember — making commitments is risky. Try to avoid making commitments in your next negotiation.
- Assume that power sources derived from values accepted by you as a member of your social group may not be valid in other social groups. Therefore, negotiating with opponents who belong to another social group, using sources of power which are accepted in your own social group (such as "the written word"), might not impress them. Do your "homework" — learn as much as possible about your opponents' relevant types of power sources and try to overcome them or at least, neutralize them.

Chapter 7

Choosing the Appropriate Strategies and Tactics

"Strategy requires thought; tactics require observation."

Max Euwe

Negotiators' realization of their power sources, if they so desire and should they have an appropriate opportunity, is through strategic and tactical decisions. And yet, what are the main differences between strategy and tactics? *Negotiation strategy* can be defined as the planned sequence of tactics according to which the negotiation goals will be achieved.[1] *Negotiation tactics* can be defined as the means by which the negotiation strategy can be carried out effectively. In other words, tactics are the ways negotiators make the most of their power sources, as a means of carrying out their strategies.

1. The "Negotiator's Dilemma"— Cooperative or Competitive Strategy?

Traditionally, over the last decades, it has become generally accepted to distinguish between two types of negotiation strategies: *competitive* strategy, sometimes called *"distributive strategy"*, and *cooperative strategy*, sometimes referred to as *"integrative strategy"*. The competitive strategy is a hard negotiation plan which, assumedly at the end of the negotiation, yields a winning result for one party and a losing result for the other — a sort of "Win–Lose" negotiation agreement. The cooperative strategy assumedly yields winning results for both parties — a sort of "Win–Win" negotiation agreement. Since cooperative strategy is supposed to yield a Win–Win

---

[1] Adair, W.L. (2008), Go-Go Global: Teaching What We Know of Culture and the Negotiation Dance, *Negotiation and Conflict Management Research*, Vol. 1(4), pp. 363–370.

agreement, it should be the logical choice for both negotiation sides. So, why in reality negotiators do not always cooperate with their opponents? The reason is that negotiators may obtain different results if one side chooses a cooperative strategy, while at the same time the others choose a competitive strategy. If one negotiating party chooses a cooperative strategy and their opponents choose, at the same time, competitive strategy, the first party may lose, while their opponents win. Only if both parties choose a cooperative strategy, they can both benefit from their choice. It is implicit that no negotiator will select a strategy without taking the other side's strategy into account. However, in most cases, a negotiator can only assume the other side's strategy without actually knowing precisely what it may be. Thus, the problematic choice between competitive and cooperative strategies has most often been described as the *"negotiator's dilemma"*. The "negotiator's' dilemma", regardless of who the negotiators are — individuals, firms or governments — depicts the problem of the negotiator's choice between cooperative and competitive strategies, where the opponent's strategic choice is unknown.

1.1. *The Results of the "Negotiator's Dilemma"*

The results of the "negotiator's dilemma" are often based on the classic game theory of the *"prisoner's dilemma"*. Perhaps the best way to explain the "prisoner's dilemma" is by telling the story behind it. The story relates to two suspects in a robbery. The police have suspects, but no evidence whatsoever. Therefore, the suspects are taken to the nearest police station and put into two separate rooms. The police investigator tries to convince each one of them to confess and testify against his friend. The police investigator promises each suspect that if he confesses and becomes a state's witness, he will be free to go. However, his friend, the other suspect, who kept quiet and did not confess, will probably receive the maximum sentence for robbery — 10 years' imprisonment. The police investigator also explains to each suspect that if they both confess, taking their confession into consideration, they will both be sentenced to 5 years in prison. The other alternative is related to the relationship between the two suspects. If they both keep quiet and do not attempt to confess or testify against each other — i.e. cooperate with each other despite their being in separate rooms — they will both be convicted for a lighter crime, for which the police have evidence. In this scenario, each suspect will go to prison for only 2 years. It is clear that the one who does not

Table 1. The "Prisoner's Dilemma": Results of competitive and cooperative strategies

Strategies		Suspect B's strategy	
		Competitive	Cooperative
Suspect A's Strategy	**Competitive**	Suspect A: 5 years Suspect B: 5 Years	Suspect A: Free to go Suspect B: 10 Years
	Cooperative	Suspect A:10 Years Suspect B: Free to go	Suspect A: 2 years Suspect B: 2 years

cooperate with his friend and lets him down by confessing, reaps the highest benefit (he goes free); his friend, who cooperated with him and kept quiet, suffers the greatest loss (he will probably get a 10-year prison sentence). Thus, according to the "prisoner's dilemma", a competitive strategy (in this case, confessing and testifying against your friend) yields the most benefits to the one who chose it, and the worst results for the one who, at the same time, chose the cooperative strategy (in this case, not confessing and refusing to testify against his friend). If they both choose the cooperative strategy (in this case, if they both keep quiet and refuse to confess), their mutual benefits will be reasonable (only 2 years in prison for each one), but not as good as in the case where one chose a competitive strategy and the other — not knowing whether or not his friend betrayed him — chose a cooperative strategy (the competitor goes free, while the cooperative suspect serves 10 years in prison), as can be seen in Table 1.

The "negotiator's dilemma" is based on the "prisoner's dilemma", as negotiators according to this theory have to choose between a competitive strategy and a cooperative strategy in an uncertain environment, since they do not know what kind of alternative their opponents will choose. If the negotiators choose a cooperative strategy, they should be open about their interests and objectives. They should also exchange information, make an offer of friendship or even share their emotions in order to create a better relationship and increase the opponents' motivation to cooperate as well. In this case, if the opponents also choose a cooperative strategy, it may lead to mutually beneficial negotiation results. On the one hand, negotiators who cooperate and reveal vital information to their opponents (such as their true interests, objectives and emotions) may be used by their opponent to achieve better results at their expense. Choosing a cooperative strategy is worthwhile only

Table 2. The "Negotiator's Dilemma": Results of competitive and cooperative strategies

Strategies		Negotiator B's strategy	
		Competitive	Cooperative
Negotiator A's strategy	**Competitive**	Bad/Bad — bad for both parties — Probably leads to a negotiation impasse, in which case both parties lose	Very good for the competitor/very bad for the cooperator
	Cooperative	Very bad for the cooperator/very good for the competitor	Good/good — Probably leads to an integrative agreement, in which case both parties gain

if the opponents are also cooperative; otherwise, the cooperative negotiators are vulnerable to exploitation and their outcome may be very poor. On the other hand, negotiators who choose a competitive strategy, if their opponents *also* choose a competitive strategy, might lead to a negotiation impasse or to a very poor outcome for both negotiating parties. Of course, the best strategy for all negotiating parties is the cooperative strategy; however, as the reactions of the other side are not really known, it may also be the worst strategy (see Table 2).

1.2. *Deliberating on the "Negotiator's Dilemma"*

The "negotiator's dilemma" is based on the assumption that choosing the appropriate strategy is made simultaneously, but separately, by each party involved in the negotiation process. While such a situation may occur only rarely, in reality, negotiation situations are different. In contrast to the "prisoner's dilemma", where the suspects are in separate rooms, negotiators do not usually sit apart from one another, and their decisions regarding an appropriate strategy can be made sequentially over the course of several negotiation sessions. Moreover, the "prisoner's dilemma" is a dichotomous-choice dilemma — each side can either be cooperative or competitive. Negotiation is usually not a dichotomous-choice process, as there are more available strategies to choose from. Moreover, negotiation is held over a number of sessions, one's strategy may be chosen and changed, after the negotiators have observed their opponents' strategy in the previous session or *vice versa*. Knowing the opponent's strategy may give negotiators an advantage: Knowing the best response to this strategy. Yet, by making fast decisions regarding their opponents' strategy, negotiators may misinterpret it, especially if, at the beginning of the negotiation, their opponents try to present a "cooperative" face. Choosing a strategy after their opponents may sometimes put negotiators at a disadvantage in terms of lost time and their ability to be the first party to put proposals on the negotiation "table". If, in the first negotiation session, the opponents choose a cooperative strategy, it is reasonable for the negotiators to choose a competitive strategy, in order to achieve more benefits. However, it is not always easy to know what the best strategy is in regard to the next negotiation session. Suppose the opponents present a competitive strategy in the first session: Would it always be reasonable for the negotiators to then also adopt a competitive strategy? Or perhaps they should adopt a cooperative strategy? By adopting a cooperative strategy after the opponents have chosen their competitive strategy, negotiators may lose a lot, while their opponents may celebrate great achievement. Yet, this would not cause a negotiation impasse or even failure, which is often the outcome when both sides choose a competitive strategy. Assume two children — a son and his younger sister — negotiate splitting their father's inheritance. The son, who used to work in the family business with the father, claims ownership of the business as well as other parts of the family property. The son is a forceful person, has financial resources and many friends in the local administration and finds it natural to use a competitive strategy, while harshly demanding a larger share of the inheritance. If his younger sister does not agree to his first offer/demand, he is willing to take the dispute to court. The younger sister considers which strategy she should use. Should she choose the same tough, competitive strategy as her brother? In this case, the negotiations may take a long time; the case can be dragged into court, and most of her share of the inheritance will be wasted on lawyers. Thus, she may decide to adopt a more cooperative strategy. In doing so, she knows she will get a smaller share of the inheritance, but she will get it right away and, more importantly, she would not lose it all.

The "negotiator's dilemma" may be repeated in many negotiation sessions, where the parties may change their strategy in each session as a response to the other party's strategy. Such a negotiation might end up with the worst results for one side and excellent results for the other, unless all sides choose cooperative strategies, at least during the final negotiation sessions, if not at all of them. However, observation of real-life negotiations often indicates the opposite. The negotiating sides may begin the negotiation sessions with cooperative strategies, but change their strategies during the final sessions to competitive pressuring strategies. Also it has been found that a competitive strategy yields different outcomes than a cooperative strategy. While a competitive strategy enhances the highest economic gains, a cooperative strategy yields the highest socio–emotional outcomes.[2]

Finally, the concept of the "negotiator's dilemma" provides important insight into the negotiators' behavior, but it is not a comprehensive description of the entire range of the negotiators' dilemmas and possible strategies.

First, negotiators do not really have to choose between competitive and cooperative strategies. They can use a combination of both strategies at the same time. A typical example is the good negotiator/bad negotiator tactic (based on the "good cop/bad cop" model), in which both good and bad negotiators act together or one good negotiator acts/immediately after the other, bad negotiator, or *vice versa*.

Second, the emotional aspects of choosing a strategy are also of importance. Hate and revenge or friendship and love may play an important role in choosing a strategy.

Third, competitive and cooperative strategies are not the only alternatives negotiators possess when trying to achieve the best results. There are other strategies that do not fall precisely into these categories, such as the "reciprocation" strategy, the "pretence" negotiation strategy and the "beat around the bush" strategy.

2. Other Possible Strategies

Negotiators sometimes choose a strategy that is not exactly either competitive or cooperative. Some of these strategies are discussed as follows:

2.1. *The Disengagement Strategy*

The "negotiators dilemma" depicts a situation where negotiators choose their strategy separately but try to anticipate their opponents' strategy — whether it be competitive or cooperative. For example, negotiators chose a cooperative strategy by anticipating that the other party will be cooperative, in order

---

[2]Huffmeier, J. Freund, P.A. Zerres, A. Backhaus, K. and Hertel, G. (2014), Being Tough or Being Nice? A Meta-Analysis on the Impact of Hard- and Soft-Line Strategies in Distributive Negotiations, *Journal of Management*, Vol. 40(3), pp. 866–862.

to gain an integrative outcome. The disengagement strategy is different in that the negotiators' strategic choice is completely independent, and thus is applied without considering the opponents' strategic choice. For example, it does not matter whether the opponents choose to be competitive or cooperative. The negotiators' decision is to be continuously competitive, regardless of what the opponent does. The decision is made independently, without any attempt to assume knowledge of the opponents' strategic choice, taking into consideration only the negotiators' interests, objectives and pre-determined decisions. This strategic choice indicates a complete disengagement from the opponents' strategies, and may yield unpredictable results or a negotiation impasse.

2.2. *The Reciprocating Strategy*

The best way to describe this strategy is by the saying *"no concession without reciprocation"*. The reciprocity strategy's intention is to prevent negotiators from making one-sided concessions at any time during the negotiation process, without receiving some compensation for the concession they have made in return from their opponents. Since the negotiation process is often perceived as a "trading concession" process, the reciprocation strategy may be perceived as a natural process. It may also prevent opponents' misconceptions about the negotiation balance of power — perceiving negotiators' concessions as an expression of weakness and subject to exploitation. Accordingly, the reciprocating strategy is a way to maintain actual or perceived symmetrical power. Furthermore, the reciprocating strategy may serve as a means by which to preserve trust between negotiators and their opponents, since negotiators' concessions without reciprocation may be perceived as an attempt to deceive their opponents.

Thus, according to the reciprocation strategy negotiators' concessions should be matched by opponents' reciprocation. However, the strategy does not specify the time and extent of the reciprocation. The reciprocation does not have to be immediate, nor must it be a "value-for-value" matching reciprocation. At times, the reciprocation can be smaller than the concession, in order to present a powerful position; alternatively, the reciprocation can be larger than the concession, in order to show generosity and encourage cooperation. The extent of the reciprocation is usually decided according to the negotiators' evaluation of the opponents' behavior, the negotiators' culture and the nature of the negotiation. For example, one-issue negotiation is not similar to multi-issue negotiation. In one-issue negotiation, it is possible that the demanded reciprocation may be "value-for-value". However, in multi-issue negotiation the importance ascribed to each issue by the negotiators may determine the size of the reciprocation.[3]

2.3. *The Pretence Negotiation Strategy*

"Pretence negotiation" is used in order to avoid reaching a final agreement. By using this strategy, negotiators take measures to continue negotiating without any intention of finalizing the negotiation with an actual agreement.[4] There are several reasons for choosing this strategy:

First, negotiators believe that they can benefit by keeping the negotiations alive until some unexpected change occurs and significantly improves their negotiation power. For example, a union knows that the CEO is leaving shortly and expects that the new CEO will have different attitudes towards the union's demands to improve working conditions. Second, the negotiators would like to receive information that may only be obtained during the negotiation process. For example, a business firm that wants to obtain information about a new technology or product may negotiate with the firm that controls the technology, pretending interest in buying the new technology or product. By the time the negotiation reaches an impasse, the first business firm has already obtained essential information regarding the new technology or product. Third, negotiators would like to give the impression that they have other alternatives, thus causing opponents to accept their negotiation demands. For example, to improve a negotiator's current employment conditions, an employee might negotiate with another employer — not to actually reach an agreement, but in order to impress upon the current employer that other alternatives exist. Such pretence negotiation is conducted in order to pressure the current employer into improving the employee's working conditions. Fourth, negotiators would like to buy enough time to establish certain facts. Once these facts have been established, reaching a negotiation agreement is

---

[3]An interesting discussion of considerations related to the reciprocation size can be found in Parks, C.D. and Komorita, S.S. (1998), Reciprocity Research and Its Implication for the Negotiation Process, *International Negotiation*, Vol. 3(2), pp. 151–169.

[4]Glozman, E. Barak-Corren, N. and Yaniv, I. (2014), "False" Negotiation: The Art and Science of not Reaching an Agreement, *Journal of Conflict Resolution*, pp.1–27.

irrelevant. Fifth, at times negotiators purposely cause a negotiation impasse, in order to show their constituents how hard they are working to try and achieve their goals. Finally, the pretence strategy is sometimes used to avoid external pressure. At times, a third party exerts pressure on negotiators in an attempt to change the current situation. In order to avoid the pressure, nego-tiators may continue negotiating, with the hope of alleviating the pressure, at least for the time being; for example, government pressures on both unions and employers to reach a new "package deal" in which both parties may lose. Employers may have to pay increased salaries, while the union may have to undertake a commitment not to strike over the next couple of years. Both parties have no intention of reaching such an agreement; however, keeping the negotiation alive may give them some extra time, until a new government is elected or appointed.

2.4. *The Beating Around the Bush Strategy*[5]

The "*beating around the bush*" strategy aims at exhausting the opponents as much as possible, before and during the negotiation process. It also attempts to cover up information underlying the negotiators' decisions. It differs from the "pretence" negotiation strategy in that it does not try to avoid agreement. On the contrary, it is used to help negotiators achieve an agreement but one which, of course, is in their own favor. Negotiators who use the "beating around the bush" strategy would not start out the negotiation process by actually addressing "the main points", nor would they put a direct offer on the negotiation "table". Instead, they may present their moral principals in negotiations, and then justify them through arguments of justice and fairness. Furthermore, negotiators often begin the negotiation by using proverbs or metaphors, usually with a lesson to be learned. Later, they may use various arguments that are not directly relevant to the negotiation issues or express their arguments in an intentionally unclear manner, so as to confuse their opponents.

There are several reasons for choosing this strategy: First, to play for time as much as possible, putting opponents under time pressures, until they are exhausted and ready to make concessions; second, to examine the opponents' patience in the face of time delays and their resistance to time pressure;

[5]Harinck, F. (2004), Persuasive Arguments and Beating around the Bush in Negotiation, *Group Processes and Intergroup Relations*, Vol. 7(1), pp. 5–18.

third, to avoid revealing information about negotiators' true intentions in this particular negotiation by using persuasive arguments that do not reflect the negotiator' real intentions; and fourth, to learn as much as possible from the exhausted opponents regarding their interests and objectives by carefully observing their reactions to the metaphors, irrelevant arguments and time delays.

3. Tactics

It has already been mentioned that tactics are "the means by which a strategy is carried out". Tactics are also a means of implementing potential power and a means in which to achieve negotiators' interests and objectives. All these make tactics a very important element in the negotiation process. However, tactics are usually short-term actions used to achieve specific ends. In addition, some tactics are more effective than others; therefore, it may be less effective to use each one of the tactics separately than to use a combination of tactics, such as a soft tactic together with a hard tactic.[6]

During the negotiation process, it is most important to identify each tactic and especially evaluate its implications on both the process and the outcome. Unfortunately, most negotiators do not choose tactics because they are aware of their implications, but due to their preferences, beliefs, perceived power or culture.

In this framework, there is no possibility of describing all the tactics that can be used during all kinds of negotiations. Only a few "classic" examples of tactics and their possible implications are described. These tactics can be classified into several general categories: Agenda tactics, hard tactics, soft tactics, time tactics, tension-relief tactics and persuasion tactics. All these tactics are by no means mutually exclusive and can be used either simultaneously or one after the other.

3.1. *Agenda Tactics*

Agenda tactics can be useful for planning the timetable, context and negotiation place. In the agenda framework, the negotiations issues are usually

---

[6]Falbe, C.M. and Yukl, G. (1992), Consequences for Mangers of Using Single Influence Tactics and a Combination of Tactics, *Academy of Management Journal*, Vol. 35(3), pp. 638–652.

decided upon, as well as the timetable for each and every issue. In the agenda framework, the negotiators can also decide when and where each negotiation will take place. These have a significant impact on the negotiation process and outcome.

Agenda and time pressure: A one-sided determination of the agenda timetable can limit the opponents' time for discussion, thus creating time pressure, which may result in the making of hasty decisions in the negotiators' favor. For example, two firms decided to negotiate a business deal. In order to avoid negotiation about the site (my place — your place), they decided on a neutral place — a hotel beyond the city limits. They agreed in advance that the negotiation will not last more than one day. However, they could not decide when the negotiations should begin. Firm A proposed 8:00 am, while Firm B insisted on 11:00 am. The negotiation over the time issue took a long time, and Firm B did not agree to any compromise, such as 9:00 am or 9:30 am, which Firm A suggested. Finally, Firm A gave up and notified Firm B that the negotiations would begin at 11:00 am. Firm B's reply was brief: "As you wish".

An analysis of this short agenda negotiation is interesting. First, a delay tactic is played out by Firm B, which shortens the negotiation time, enabling Firm B to put pressure on Firm A at the end of a shorter negotiation day. Furthermore, the insistence tactic was helpful for Firm B as Firm A conceded without asking for any reciprocation in exchange for its concession; meaning, it might have lost some perceived power and reliability in the eyes' of Firm B. However, the most interesting tactic was Firm B's reply: "As you wish." Such a reply means that you (Firm A) have asked for the opening time and we (Firm B) have graciously accepted. As a result, we are not obliged to reciprocate or give up anything in exchange for your concession.

Informal negotiation agenda: Agenda tactic used before the negotiation begins can be meaningful later on during the formal negotiation. Demanding an informal agenda is a tactic used to reveal the opponents' targets and intentions in advance. Informal pre-negotiations, especially negotiations on the subsequent agenda, can also generate and analyze possible alternatives for reaching an agreement.[7] However, there is also the risk that it is a tactic taken to intentionally misinterpret negotiators' intentions later on in the formal

---

[7]Martinez, J. and Susskind, L. (2000), Parallel Informal Negotiation: An Alternative Second Track Diplomacy, *International Relations*, Vol. 5(3), pp. 569–586.

negotiation, or to cause negotiators to make commitments which are binding, and can even generate a vicious circle of "commitment escalation".

Deciding on the issues: When deciding on the agenda issues, negotiators can decide to exclude some of the issues on the agenda. This can be used as a tactic to avoid problematic issues, which can act to the disadvantage of the negotiators. However, such an exclusion of issues on the agenda might raise opponents' objections[8] and become a new source of disagreement.

The order in which the issues are presented: Another tactic related to the agenda deals with the sequence of issues to be discussed. The kinds of issues discussed first and the kinds of issues discussed later may have a great impact on the negotiation's final results. One well-known tactic is to postpone the most important issues till the end of the process. It is assumed that issues of low importance appearing early in the agenda receive proportionately greater attention and consume more time and energy than more important issues presented later on, and therefore less time and energy remain to discuss the more important issues. Thus, it can be expected that after a very long and tiring process, the exhausted opponents may concede on the important issues. Of course, such agenda tactics incorporate the risk or the advantage — depending on the negotiators' point of view — of exhausting both parties, which will yield trading concessions (sometimes in an integrative process) on both sides regarding important issues. Another consideration regarding the order of issues proposed in the agenda relates to the asymmetrical power of the negotiating sides. It has been argued that low-power negotiators are more interested in negotiating their most important issues first, whereas high-power negotiators are more interested in delaying the most important issues to the end of the negotiation. This is because low-power negotiators would like to encourage a potential change in the *status quo*, while high-power negotiators would like to postpone the negotiation of important issues in order to maintain the *status quo*.[9] Of course, the exact opposite might just as easily be the case. High-power negotiators would like to change the *status quo*, whereas low-power negotiators seek to maintain it. Thus, the sequential

---

[8]An interesting review of agenda tactics can be found in Pendergast, W.R. (1990), Managing the Negotiation Agenda, *Negotiation Journal*, Vol. 6(2), pp. 135–145.
[9]Kteily, N. Saguy, T. Sidanius, J. and Taylor, D.M. (2013), Negotiating Power: Agenda Ordering and the Willingness to Negotiate in Asymmetric Intergroup Conflicts, *Journal of Personality and Social Psychology*, Vol. 105(6), pp. 978–995.

order of the agenda issues is derived from the parties' power balance, as well as their desire to exhaust each other's patience.

3.2. *Hard Tactics*

Hard tactics are usually associated with competitive strategy. The purpose of using hard tactics is to pressure the opponents in order to extract concessions. On the one hand, the more negotiators feel unfairly treated during the negotiation process and the less they are dependent on their opponents, the more often they tend to use hard tactics in order to gain concessions. On the other hand, the better the rapport between negotiators and their opponents, the less frequently negotiators tend to use hard tactics.[10] Tactics such as threats — whether real or false — expressions of anger, ultimatums (such as "take it or leave it"), and opting out of the negotiation, are just a few "classic" examples of hard tactics.

Threats: Threats convey the negotiators' intentions — real or false — to hurt their opponents in the future, unless they fulfill the negotiators' requirements. There are two types of threat: Verbal and non-verbal — both indicate the negotiators' intentions to cause future damage, and often also describe the nature of this potential damage. Some threats are meant to deter opponents from executing some undesirable action (such as a strike); other threats attempt to force opponents to do things they would not otherwise do (make concessions). Threats may also serve as signals regarding the negotiators' preferences. One can assume that negotiators only make threats in certain situations — when it is very important to them to prevent an action from occurring or cause the opponents to take a certain action. For example, negotiators threaten to walk away from the negotiation "table" if the opponents reject one of their proposals. In this case, it is possible to deduce that this proposal is of significant importance to the negotiators. Thus, a careful observation of the issues subject to threats, as well as their frequency and timing, can provide a good representation of the negotiators' preferences.

Threats may be real or false. When negotiators have the capability to cause future damage to their opponents, their threats are real. However, sometimes negotiators use threats without actually having the capability to hurt their

---

[10]Van Knippenberg, B. Van Knippenberg, D. Blaauw, E. and Vermunt, R. (1999), Relational Consideration in the Use of Influence Tactics, *Journal of Applied Psychology*, Vol. 29(4), pp. 806–819.

opponents or without having any intention to execute the threats. These are false threats, which can serve the same purpose as real threats — an attempt to put pressure on the opponents. False threats are effective, as long as the opponents believe in the negotiators' intentions and their capabilities to cause them real harm. Thus, on the one hand, the effectiveness of both real and false threats results from the perceived power of the threatening negotiators. On the other hand, both real and false threats enhance the perceived power of the threatening negotiators,[11] when negotiators who have made false threats are caught and exposed as deceivers, they may be punished by their opponents. Among other punishments, their opponents may increase their demands, offend the negotiators' reputation or refuse to continue negotiating with them currently or in the future.

The effectiveness of threats can be increased by intimidation and/or visible preparation to execute the threat. Intimidation is only a small example of what can happen to opponents if negotiators' threats are executed. Opponents do not suffer immediately from threats. However, intimidation can cause an immediate effect in that it exemplifies what the future might be like on a large scale. For example, the national union of a hospital's medical staff, while negotiating with the Ministry of Finance, may threaten a nationwide work break of all medical staffs. As an intimidation measure, the union stops medical staff operations in only one regional hospital. Another possible way to increase the threat's effectiveness is by visibly and noisily preparing a strike (employee meetings, collecting strike funds, etc.) in order to make sure the opponents have "gotten the hint".

Finally, threats, as an example of all hard tactics, can hardly yield an integrative agreement. By their very nature, threats cannot encourage cooperation; on the contrary, they often cause insult and offense, and lead to a competitive negotiation process. However, threats can cause opponents' concessions and, as a result, help prevent a negotiation impasse and ensure agreement — of course, sometimes not to the opponents' liking.

Expressions of anger: Angry negotiators are perceived as tough, dominant negotiators. An expression of anger may be different from feeling angry. It is possible to assume that negotiators who feel anger sometimes make the wrong decisions. Furthermore, angry negotiators are not usually the most

---

[11] Shapiro, D.L. and Bies, R.J. (1994), Threats, Bluffs and Disclaimers in Negotiations, *Organization Behavior and Human Decision Processes*, Vol. 60(1), pp. 14–35.

cooperative negotiators, and thus achieve less joint outcomes than negotiators who do not feel angry. However, negotiators do not necessarily have to feel anger in order to express anger during the negotiation process. They can express anger as a manipulative tactic without actually feeling the slightest feeling of anger. Negotiators who display anger at the beginning of the negotiation process, without any provocation from the other side, are probably using anger as a tactic. However, whether negotiators are emotionally angry or simply using anger as a tactic, the negotiation results may be in their favor. Displaying anger — whether as an emotional expression or as a tactic — may induce fear, enhance negotiators' dominance and lead to opponents' concessions.[12] A display of anger can very be beneficial, as it can serve as a signal to opponents, indicating the negotiators' expectations. Such signals may enable opponents to reconsider their behavior and reactions in time to prevent a negotiation impasse. As a matter of fact, signaling by displaying anger may enable negotiators to achieve better outcomes than negotiators who maintain a "poker face" during the negotiation process. However, opponents may respond to negotiators' expressed anger, either by lowering motivation and making concessions which are required to maintain the negotiation process or by reciprocation, generating an angry or nasty response that may lead to an impasse.[13] In fact, by displaying anger, negotiators may achieve good outcomes for themselves, but only if opponents have poor or no alternatives (have poor or no Best Alternative to Negotiated Agreements (*BATNAs*)). If opponents have equivalent or good alternatives, angry negotiators may confront the risk of opponents' reciprocation, cause a negotiation impasse and/or damage the prospects of future negotiations with the same opponents.[14]

Ultimatum: "Take it or leave it" is an ultimatum that gives opponents only two unattractive options and turns the negotiation into a "zero sum game".

---

[12]Van Kleef, G.A. De Dreu, C.K.W. and Manstead, A.S.R. (2004), The Interpersonal Effects of Anger and Happiness in Negotiations, *Journal of Personality and Social Psychology*, Vol. 86(1), pp. 57–76.

[13]Liu, M. (2009), The Intrapersonal and Interpersonal Effects of Anger on Negotiation Strategies: A Cross Cultural Investigation, *Communication Research*, Vol. 35(1), pp. 148–169.

[14]Sinaceur, M. and Tiedens, L.Z. (2006), Get Mad and Get More than Even: When and Why Anger Expression is Effective in Negotiations, *Journal of Experimental Social Psychology*, Vol. 42, pp. 314–322.

Its intention is to "push opponents to the wall", where they can either concede and lose, or leave the negotiation "table". It is noteworthy that a "package deal" offer is a type of ultimatum tactic.

In many cases, the ultimatum tactic is enraging, sometimes insulting and usually causes a lot of resistance. Even if opponents are forced to accept the "take it or leave it" proposal, negotiators can expect reciprocation or other undesirable actions in their future relationship (if there still is one) with the other party or parties. Just like the expression of anger, an ultimatum can signal to the opponents that negotiators have gone as far as they can and wish to end the negotiation, unless the opponents give up at this point. Presenting an ultimatum in the form of "take it or leave it" is apparently a commitment to end the negotiation. If making such a commitment is used to put further pressure on the opponents, without any real intention to end the negotiation, it might be difficult to "get out of the corner". Making an ultimatum commitment without fulfilling it may be perceived as a source of negotiators' weakness, which may cause problems, if they want to carry on negotiating.[15]

Yet, there are situations in which the ultimatum tactic is somewhat less aggravating to the other side. Negotiators who apply the same ultimatum to everyone and do not discriminate among particular opponents are perceived as less offensive. For example, all fixed price stores actually use the "take it or leave it" ultimatum. However, the fact that it applies to everyone generates a sense of "fairness", which usually minimizes customers' resistance. Salespeople who use the "take it or leave it" tactic would not state it as an ultimatum, but will try to convince buyers that it is impossible to change the selling conditions, as they are "fair" and apply to all buyers.

Another way of reducing resistance to the "take it or leave it" ultimatum tactic is to legitimize it through policies or regulations; for example, the published policy of a hotel chain to take a non-refundable deposit for each order. The hotel chain does not use the words "take it or leave it", but this is the practical meaning of its policy. Since asking for a non-refundable deposit is backed up by a published policy, it may be less aggravating. Thus, regulations and policies may be helpful when employing ultimatums.

Opting out: *Opting out* does not always mean walking away from the negotiating "table". For example, negotiators can opt out during the negotiation

---

[15] See Chapter 4 in this book.

process by keeping silent or playing with their cellular phones and not responding during face-to-face negotiations. They can also keep silent for a long time in telephone or media conference negotiations. Negotiators can also avoid replying to e-mail communications for either a short or long time. Being silent and unresponsive often encourages opponents to increase their communications; and sometimes, due to negotiators' silence opponents reveal important information, which would not have been otherwise disclosed.

Another tactic of opting out without walking away from the negotiation "table" is a recess. Whatever the excuse for the recess — resting, consultation or just a short break from the discussions — it sends a signal to the opponents about some type of dissatisfaction — either as regards opponents' behavior, proposals or both. Calling a recess can also be helpful for reevaluating the negotiators' own objectives and their previous, as well as future, decisions.

Walking away from the negotiation "table" is an extremely hard tactic, which marks the end of the negotiations. Negotiators sometimes use this tactic in the hopes that such an act will be perceived by the opponents as a simple protest or severe threat, and that they will soon be called back by their opponents. On the one hand, as a tactic, walking away from the negotiation "table" may be risky, since the opponents may not react as expected and may not call the other negotiating party back to the "table". The fewer alternatives the negotiators have, and the more time and efforts they have already invested in the negotiation, the more risky it is to employ this tactic. On the other hand, if the opponents are not interested in a negotiation impasse, the risk taken by negotiators who "walk away" may prove profitable. In this case, opponents may make significant concessions in order to bring the negotiators back to the "table".

3.3. *Time Tactics*

Time is frequently used as a negotiating tactic. The main three best-known time tactics are: Time delays, time pressure and deadlines. All three tactics are by no means mutually exclusive and can influence each other significantly. For example, a time delay can easily influence the time pressure factor, whereas time pressure can also be influenced by the imposing of a deadline. Time tactics are often considered to be hard tactics. However, time tactics, such as time delays and even deadlines, can also lead to conciliation, cooperation and satisfactory outcomes for all involved parties.

Time delays: A time delay is a tactic involving slowing down the negotiation process as much as possible. It is used by negotiators for various reasons. It is typically used by negotiators who adopt the "pretence" negotiation strategy, which attempts to avoid reaching a final agreement, or the "beating about the bush" tactic, which aims to prolong the negotiation. Negotiators who use time delay tactics believe they can achieve benefits by dragging out the negotiation process until some external or internal change occurs.

Time delays are also used when opponents are not ready to make significant concessions. The use of a time delay tactic may assist negotiators in exhausting their opponents, until they are ready to concede. In this case, time delays are only effective if opponents do not have any alternative at all or any good alternatives (good *BATNAs*).

Time delays are not always used for pressure purposes. They may also be used in order to buy time to evaluate complex situations, search for more information or for consultation purposes, in order to prevent an impasse. In this sense, a time delay may even encourage cooperation between negotiating parties.

The risk in using time delays is losing the object/objects of desire at the center of the negotiation process. The following examples demonstrate just how risky the use of a time delay can be:

An employer negotiating with his employees' union uses a time delay as a means of exhausting the union, and thus gaining concessions. However, meanwhile a strike breaks out, work slows down and the employer cannot honor his commitments to customers and suppliers. Another example is of two partners who have an agreement to buy each other's stock (buy me-buy you), but have a disagreement. By delaying the negotiation time in order to exhaust one another's patience, they discover, to their surprise, that another third party has meanwhile bought a large share of their firms' stocks on the stock exchange — and is attempting to conduct a hostile takeover.

Time Pressure: The effectiveness of time pressure tactics depends on the time availability of each negotiating party and the symmetrical or asymmetrical time at the negotiators' disposal. If negotiating parties has no time limits, while their opponents' time is limited, the asymmetrical time factor turns into a negotiating power. For example, negotiators who identify that their opponents' time limitation is short, due to a cash flow problem, can use this information to create time pressure by shortening the negotiation's duration and causing their opponents to accept hasty and erroneous decisions. Faced with a time pressure, opponents may be forced to reduce their expectations and make significant concessions in order to reach an agreement, which probably would be sub-optimal for them. However, in some situations, the time limitation may be short for both sides. In such situations, the parties often reach an agreement more quickly than negotiators faced with more relaxed timeframes. For example, in acquisition negotiation, when both sides perceive they do not have enough time to reach an agreement (for political or financial reasons) that is crucial for their survival, the experience of having a time pressure increases the desire of both sides to finalize the agreement as soon as possible.[16]

Stretching out negotiation time in order to create time pressure for opponents may also be costly in terms of shifting the negotiators' attention from their other profitable activities and forcing them to focus most of their attention on a long negotiation process. In some cases, where negotiators employ costly consultants, attorneys or other mediating agents, stretching out negotiation time may heavily increase the negotiating costs. However, the cost of the negotiation is not necessarily a cause for limiting the negotiation timeframe, especially as long as negotiators believe that their advantages, as a result of the time pressure, is higher or at least equivalent to the efforts invested in stretching out the negotiation time. It is worthwhile emphasizing that when negotiators confront asymmetrical time costs, the resulting agreement is likely to favor the party under less time pressure.[17] In this case, there is no difference between actual time pressures and perceived time pressures; both can create stress, which leads to inferior outcomes.

Deadline: A deadline means that the possibility of negotiators reaching an agreement ends at a defined time, after which the "window of opportunity" then closes. However, if for some reason reaching an agreement after the deadline is still possible, it would be reached under worse conditions than those available before the deadline. In the case of symmetrical time constraints, deadlines often apply to all sides. The same is true if a deadline is imposed on all negotiating parties by a third party. In these cases, it

---

[16]Saorin-Iborra, M.C. (2008), Time Pressure in Acquisitions: Its Determinates and Effects on Parties' Negotiation Behavior Choice, *International Business Review*, Vol. 17, pp. 285–309.

[17]Stuhlmacher, A.F. Gillespie, T.L. and Champagne, M.V. (1998), The Impact of Time Pressure in Negotiation: A Meta-Analysis, *International Journal of Conflict Management*, Vol. 9(2), pp. 97–115.

may enhance the making of mutual concessions before the final deadline, thus increasing the possibility of reaching an agreement and at times, even encouraging a more integrative agreement.

In some cases, however, only one of the parties has a final deadline, while the other parties do not. The outcome in such cases will probably be in the best interests of the sides that do not have any deadline. Assume a partner in a local firm has signed a contract to work in the near future for another firm. He offers to sell his part in the firm to his partners. In this case, he has a final deadline, while his partners do not have any time limitation to consider. As long as his partners do not know he has a final deadline, a reasonable negotiation process can take place. If his partners know he has a final deadline, they may use time pressure in order to reach an agreement that will be in their favor. In this case, revealing the deadline probably will not be in his best interest.

However, there are times when the revealing of negotiators' own final deadline benefits them because the revelation speeds up the process of reaching an agreement in their favor.[18] For example, negotiators advertise that they are selling all their assets, as they are leaving the country in a few days. In this case, revealing the deadline may give the buyers an indication that they can find a bargain, but only if they rush to buy. The more buyers, the more benefits the selling negotiators receive, due to advertising their own final deadline. This is also the case in end-of-the-season final sales. Announcing an end-of-the-season sale, which usually means a final deadline, gives the sellers a legitimate reason to reduce the prices of items which, otherwise, are hard to sell, as well as encourages buyers to speed up their purchasing process. The results can be satisfactory for both sellers and buyers, since each side achieves the desired outcome.[19]

It is also important to note that a deadline is not always a final deadline. In many cases, determining a deadline opposite opponents is not effective, unless a punishment is associated with a failure to meet the deadline. A hotel check-out time is a sort of final deadline. However, the hotel guests may stay after the check-out hour if the hotel does not charge them a penalty fee for

---

[18]Moore, D.A. (2004), Myopic Prediction: Self-Destructive Secrecy, and the Unexpected Benefits of Revealing Final Deadlines in Negotiation, *Organizational Behavior and Human Decision Processes*, Vol. 94(2), pp. 125–139.

[19]Gino, F. and Moore, D. (2008), Using Final Deadlines Strategically in Negotiation, *Negotiation and Conflict Management Research*, Vol. 1(4), pp. 371–388.

failure to do so. The higher the "punishment" associated with the deadline, the more effective it is to use this tactic.

3.4. *Tension Relief Tactics*

Negotiation is usually associated with tension. It can be assumed, therefore, that *tension relief tactics* are essential for the continuation of the negotiation process. There are several tactics for relieving tension; the most effective one is probably the use of humor. Yet, the use of flattery and small talk are also examples of helpful tactics in reducing cumulative tension.

Despite the assumed important role of tension-relief tactics in negotiation, surprisingly enough it is not often used. For example, it was found that tension-relief tactics are seldom used during negotiating with the help of mediators. Only 6% of the tactics used in these negotiations were tension-relief tactics.[20]

Humor as a tactic: *Humor* can be used as an "ice breaking" tactic, which smoothes interaction between negotiators and their opponents, generating a sense of relaxation in the discussions. As laughing is a natural reaction to humor, laughter is generally considered to be relaxing, especially during tense situations, such as negotiation. However, humorous episodes are usually short and may not have a long-term impact on the negotiation process. Moreover, the use of humor can develop from the "ice breaking" relaxing form to a harsher form like sarcasm or even irony, whose aim is to attack or criticize opponents, albeit indirectly and in a supposedly joking manner. Thus, in addition to the "ice breaking" aim of using humor, it can also serve as a way to criticize opponents and their proposals or to propose a new alternative in a joking, safer way.[21]

Several factors may influence the effectiveness of using humor as a tactic in negotiation processes. First, the importance of the negotiation to the involved parties is a major factor. The more important the negotiation, the less positive the influence of humor tactics on the opponents and the negotiation process and its outcome will be. Second, the effect of the balance of power is also an important factor. The positive influence of humor tactics

---

[20]Galin, A. (2014), What Makes Court — Referred Mediation Effective?, *International Journal of Conflict Management*, Vol. 25(1), pp. 21–37.

[21]Bonaiuto, M. Castellana, E. and Pierro, A. (2003), Arguing and Laughing: The Use of Humor to Negotiate in Group Discussions, *Humor*, Vol. 16(2), pp. 183–223.

on one's opponents and the negotiation outcome is higher when it is used by the relatively more powerful negotiator. Third, the sort of humor used is also a telling factor. Using humor that criticizes the negotiators themselves may have a more positive influence than humor directed at the opponents. Sarcasm, irony and teasing directed at the opponents may irritate them and negatively affect their reactions, and thus the negotiation process and outcome. Fourth, signals received by the opponents may serve as good feedback for the negotiation prospects. For example, opponents' laughter signals understanding and a willingness to continue the negotiations process.[22] Of course, cultures affect both the use of humor and its effectiveness in negotiation.[23]

Flattery as a tactic: Flattery can be used by complimenting the other side's capabilities, showing respect or a high level of appreciation. Negotiators, being human, usually react positively to being highly appreciated by others. Thus, simple flattery may reduce tension instantly. It can also affect the opponents' intentions, behavior and as a result, influence the negotiation outcome as well. Opponents' behavior is much more cooperative and less competitive when they receive compliments about their behavior and abilities. Alternatively, opponents may become highly competitive if they receive a negative evaluation from other negotiators.[24]

The effect of flattery is highly dependent on the type of evaluation provided, and the ways in which it is provided. Sincere or honest compliments have a great influence on the motivation to continue negotiating with the same partners. Negotiators would even tolerate a surplus of compliments, regardless of whether they give high credibility to such compliments. Moreover, if the compliments are accurate, they are usually well received, even if they are not genuine. Yet, if the way in which the compliments are offered is conceived negatively by the opponents — if they are perceived as sarcastic or unflattering in any way — opponents may become highly insulted, causing negotiations to reach an impasse.

---

[22]Norrick, N.R. and Spitz, A (2008), Humor as a Resource for Mitigating Conflict in Interaction, *Journal of Pragmatics*, Vol. 40(10), pp.1661–1686.

[23]See Chapter 9 of this book.

[24]Kim, P.H. Diekmann, K.A. and Tenbrunse, A.E. (2003), Flattery May Get you Somewhere: The Strategic Implication of Providing Positive versus Negative Feedback About Ability vs. Ethicality in Negotiation, *Organizational Behavior and Human Decision Processes*, Vol. 90(2), pp. 225–243.

Small talk as a tactic: When negotiation becomes stressful and loud, small talk can mitigate the tension. Engaging in small talk causes an informal break, which enables both sides to address issues that are not relevant in any way to the main negotiation process. Negotiators' small talk may relate to informal mutual topics such as the weather, sports, leisure time and family matters. A short conversation on these topics may help all involved parties to feel more comfortable with one another, which may encourage negotiations to proceed more smoothly. Such small talk may serve to temporarily decrease the stressful atmosphere, but it may also encourage negotiators to be more cooperative and make fewer threats than negotiators who skip the small talk.[25] In addition, small talk may encourage relational negotiations, form communicative channels and establish rapport between the parties.[26]

Small talk will not be an effective tension-relief tactic if parties discuss issues that are not easy to agree upon, core issues related to the negotiation, or those that include thinly-veiled insults. The manner and effectiveness of small talk is also highly affected by cultural values.

3.5. *Soft Tactics*

Soft tactics enable negotiators to achieve their opponents' compliance by convincing them, in a rational or friendly manner, to make concessions. They are usually associated with cooperative strategy and can be easily used when there is an equivalent power balance, i.e. negotiators have little or no power advantage over their opponents.[27] Among the soft tactics, it is possible to find rational tactics, consultations, concession and gesture tactics.

Rational tactics: These tactics include rational arguments which aim to convince opponents that the negotiators' proposals are worthwhile, thus influencing the opponents to make concessions. There are actually two

---

[25]Nadler, J. (2004), Legal Negotiation and Communication Technology: How Small Talk can Facilitate E-Mail Deal-Making, *Harvard Negotiation Law Review*, Vol. 9, pp. 223–253.

[26]Yang, W. (2012), Small Talk: A Strategic Interaction in Chinese Interpersonal Business Negotiations, *Discourse & Communication*, Vol. 6(1), pp. 101–124.

[27]Somech, A. and Drach-Zahavy, A. (2002), Relative Power and Influence Strategy: The Effect of Agent/Target Organizational Power on Supervisors' Choices of Influence Strategies, *Journal of Organizational Behavior*, Vol. 23(2), pp. 167–179.

parts to these rational tactics: The first is rational arguments, intended to persuade the opponents that the proposals on the "table" are feasible and relevant to maximizing the expected value of both negotiators and opponents. The second part involves providing hard evidence to support the arguments. If the relationship between the parties happens to be competitive, the rational arguments may encourage contradiction by the opponents, whereas the presentation of evidence may be declined as inaccurate or even incorrect.

In a common course of negotiation the rational tactic, if presented in the correct manner, may be influential. The following example presents a rational tactic and its possible outcome. Imagine a common negotiation between a real estate agent and a potential house buyer. The buyer complains that the house is too expensive. The real estate agent argues that the price of the house is indeed a little bit higher than the buyer expected (a loss argument); however, it is equivalent to the prices of several other houses which have been sold recently in the neighborhood (a rational argument backed by facts). He also claims that the house is compatible with the buyer's expectations (a gain argument), as it has a kindergarten next door, a school close by and a large variety of stores and night clubs nearby (the buyer's utility). Therefore, the buyer's concession regarding the price is worthwhile. Closing the deal at the required price can maximize the expected values of both the buyer — who is going to achieve all of her essential demands — and the real estate agent, whose commission of the house's price would be relatively high — a sort of Win–Win outcome.

The sequence of the rational argument is also noteworthy. In accordance with the "contrast effect", it is possible to gain some insight into the rational argument sequence in negotiation. According to the contrast effect, the difference between two issues is exaggerated, depending on the order in which those issues are presented. To demonstrate, carrying a heavy object after a light one, gives the feeling that the second object is even heavier than it actually is, and *vice versa*. In other words, a gain argument is perceived in a far more positive and influential light when it follows an initial loss argument. Thus, by presenting the buyer with her gains (the great advantages of the house's location), after presenting her loss (the higher price), the real estate agent enhanced the buyer's perception of her gain and increased her readiness to buy the house. The sequential argumentation is important in order to increase the influential impact on the opponents. If the initial argument indicates a slight loss, but is then followed by a more important gain argument, it increases the powerful effect of the gain argument.[28]

Consultation as a tactic: Consultation actually means dialogue between negotiators and their opponents. By using consultation as a tactic, negotiators seek to gain their opponents' participation in decision-making during the negotiation process, and are willing to take into consideration their opponents' concerns and suggestions. Through consultation, negotiators hope to keep their opponents in a good cooperative mood before defining the negotiation dimensions and discussing the pros and cons of both parties' proposals.

Consultation also includes exchanging information, such as both parties' time pressure issues and/or resistance points. On the one hand, consultation may serve as a tool for collecting and evaluating ideas before the parties' decisions are made. Therefore, negotiation decisions made during the consultation process may yield better outcomes for both negotiators and their opponents. On the other hand, it is a dangerous tactic, as the opponents may utilize the negotiators' information disclosure against them. In order to avoid such risks, negotiators must be certain of their opponents' good faith and the genuine good relations between them and their opponents. Moreover, by using consultation, both parties recognize what concessions are needed in order to reach a beneficial outcome. However, if the needed concessions are asymmetrical, where one party — opponents or negotiators — must make more concessions than the other, the consulting parties may face substantial difficulties in reaching an agreement. Of course, negotiators usually take into account the values and costs associated with consultation; the lower the value and higher the costs, the less negotiators will perceive consultation as a useful tactic.

Concession and gesture tactics: Concession and gesture tactics are associated with the reciprocation strategy. Using the tactic of making concession and gestures (unilateral concessions) is based on a belief that negotiators' concessions and/or gestures will encourage opponents to make reciprocal concessions, resulting in additional negotiators' concessions and so on — a circle of concessions and gestures which increases cooperation and hastens

---

[28]Galin, A. (2009). Proposal Sequence and the Endowment Effect in Negotiation, *International Journal of Conflict Management*, Vol. 20(3), pp. 212–227.

integrative agreement. This process may also possibly involve concession-ary gestures. Negotiators are often advised and, at times, even encouraged to make "gestures" in order to induce a "cooperative atmosphere" during negotiation. While in some cases these tactics achieve cooperation and end in an integrative agreement — this is, unfortunately, not always the case. Concession-making and especially gestures are perceived by the opponents as weakness. While the negotiators' first high offers have a significant impact on the opponents' reactions, it is well known that they are also a form of tactical manipulation — a calculated decision, made in advance, so as to be able to make some easy concessions. However, even such intentional concessions can be perceived by the opponents as weakness, which invites pressures in an attempt to achieve more and more important concessions. Moreover, opponents may perceive negotiators' concessions as either an attempt to deceive (according to the logic that if negotiators can concede, it means that they over-evaluated their first offer in order to deceive), or as the negotiators' attempt to give up nothing of value. Negotiators who make gestures that are not reciprocated by the opponents may be perceived by the opponents in an even worse way than negotiators who make concessions. Take, for example, the following scenario: In a negotiation between a buyer and a manufacturer, the buyer was in urgent need of certain parts from the manufacturer. The buyer wanted to receive the parts no later than the coming Friday. However, the manufacturer claimed that he could not supply the parts until the following Wednesday. During the negotiation, the buyer insisted on the coming Friday. The manufacturer gave in a little and promised to have the parts by the following Tuesday. The buyer kept insisting on the coming Friday, so the manufacturer gave in a little more and promised the parts for Monday. After another negotiation session, the manufacturer conceded again and finally agreed to supply the parts on Friday. The buyer's reaction was very harsh. He could not understand why the manufacturer had forced him to negotiate for such a long time when all along, he could supply the required parts on time — the coming Friday. He felt he would been misled by the manufacturer and thus lost trust in him — making him unwilling to engage in future negotiations. If the manufacturer would have asked for some kind of reciprocation for each concession — such as extra hour payments for manpower or money for purchasing new equipment in order to supply the parts on time, the buyer would have probably perceived the scenario differently. The many concessions would have been accepted as reasonable by the buyer, and he would not have had such a harsh reaction.

It is, however, noteworthy that when there is a positive acceptance zone,[29] an agreement may be achieved despite the negative impression left by concessions, and especially in regard to the negotiators' gestures. For example, a buyer may be offended by a seller who over-evaluated the first price of an object. Yet, if the seller's over-evaluation is still within the limits of what the buyer is willing to pay for this object, any concessions or gestures made by the seller may be accepted by the buyer and lead to an agreement. However, it may also yield what is referred to as "buyer's remorse" or the "winners' curse", which relate to the buyer's feelings that he is a sucker who has paid too much for the negotiated object(s).[30] This feeling of remorse may intensify when the rate of the concessions or gestures is large and immediate, i.e. take place early and all at once in the negotiation.

Active listening tactic[31]: *Active listening* is a skill as well as a negotiation tactic. It includes multiple techniques that may pave the way to finding an integrative solution for critical problems discussed during the negotiation process. These techniques include:

Showing a deep understanding for the opponents' feelings, without arguing or judging these feelings. It is always possible to argue with facts, but no one can argue with, or judge, feelings.

Showing sympathy for the opponents' feelings (such as anger) often has a calming effect on the negotiation process; pauses or temporary silences also enable angry opponents to "let off steam". These breaks may be an opportunity to encourage opponents to talk, and possibly reveal more information.

A brief response to opponents' arguments shows them that their arguments are being listened to attentively, and that the negotiators are interested in hearing more about their points. Often, such brief responses encourage opponents to keep on talking. Thus, more information is received and understood by the negotiators.

Paraphrasing, or repeating the opponents' arguments is evidence that the negotiators are trying to understand the essence of the opponents' arguments,

---

[29] See Chapter 5 of this book.

[30] Kwon, S. and Weingart, L.R. (2004), Unilateral Concessions from the Other Party: Concession Behavior, Attributions, and Negotiation Judgment, *Journal of Applied Psychology*, Vol. 89(2), pp. 263–278.

[31] McMains, M.J. (2002), Active Listening: The Aspirin of Negotiation, *Journal of Police Crisis Negotiations*, Vol. 2(2), pp. 69–74.

without necessarily agreeing or accepting these arguments. Paraphrasing can also be used to figure out the precise meaning of the opponents' requirements, "buy" time, enable more information gathering and even increase information exchange.

Asking questions that clarify the opponents' interests and objectives. Raising doubts may serve as an incentive for opponents to further explain their interests and objectives. Furthermore, raising doubts backed by facts regarding the feasibility of the opponents' objectives may undermine the opponents' confidence in their own arguments or demands.

Asking questions and raising doubts may also cause both opponents and negotiators to look for other, maybe better, solutions for resolving the opposing positions. Asking questions and raising doubts are at the heart of active listening.

4. Some Further Comments on Strategies and Tactics

Strategies and tactics are the core of the negotiation process. However, without appropriate preparation, a sophisticated use of the proper strategies and tactics is impossible. Similarly, without understanding the power balance, it is impossible to determine which strategies and tactics will be useful. It is therefore essential for negotiators to do their "homework" before any decision is made regarding strategies and tactics. The tactics discussed in this chapter are only a few classic examples of possible tactics in each main category including: Agenda tactics, hard tactics, time tactics, tension-relief tactics and soft tactics. Of course, in each negotiation there are additional unique possible tactics to be used in each of the earlier categories. Negotiators can probably achieve better results by using a combination of tactics from all categories. There are also various additional factors that may influence the decision and use of the tactics, such as ethics, trust and culture. These factors will be addressed in the following chapters.

Practical Applications

- Choosing a cooperative strategy may lead to a favorable outcome for both you and your opponent, if you both choose the same cooperative strategy. However, be careful not to choose a cooperative strategy, while your opponents choose a competitive strategy. In this case, you will probably end up with a poor outcome, far inferior to what you could have achieved if you yourself had adopted a competitive strategy.

- Remember to be flexible. Whatever strategy you choose can be changed in response to your opponents' strategy in previous or current negotiation sessions. Sometimes, the true nature of your opponents' strategy is unclear, whether it is cooperative, competitive or another kind of strategy. Be patient and careful when interpreting your opponents' real strategy in order to avoid losses for you and perhaps for your opponent as well.

- It is not advisable to decide and insist upon your strategy without first anticipating and taking into consideration your opponents' strategic choice. Such "independent" decision-making may lead to undesirable consequences.

- Remember the rule: "no concession without reciprocation". Each of your concessions should be reciprocated by your opponents. Such reciprocation should be of importance to you.

- Sometimes it is beneficial (even though politically incorrect) to conduct a "false" negotiation with no intention of reaching an agreement. Such a pretence negotiation may be useful if you expect a future change in the objective conditions, which will be in your favor. By such "false" negotiation, you may obtain essential information that you cannot otherwise get, or avoid external third-party pressures.

- "Beating around the bush" strategy, enables you to conceal your real intentions while at the same time discovering at least something about your opponents' interests and objectives. It may also put your opponents under time pressure, thereby exhausting them in order to get some concessions to your benefit.

- Be as creative as possible in generating the negotiation agenda; the agenda includes the negotiation place, the issues to be discussed during the negotiation and the recommended timetable for the discussion. This can be beneficial to you, your opponents or hopefully both. Remember that agenda tactics can also reveal the balance of power between you and your opponents.

- Use threats in order to deter your opponents from making undesirable decisions or to encourage them to do things they would not otherwise do. However, remember that by threatening you create a competitive negotiation atmosphere and give up, at least to a certain extent, the possibility of cooperating with your opponents and reaching an integrative agreement.

- Your opponents may try to make their threats more effective by either intimidating you (through presenting a frightening mini-example of your possible future suffering), or by visibly and noisily preparing to execute their threats. Before you get scared and concede to their undesirable requirements, make sure that their threats are real and check whether they have both the intentions and capabilities to actually harm you if you do not comply with their demands. You may be surprised to discover that, in many cases, your opponents use "false" threats. However, you should act in a way that minimizes your future damages, in case your opponents' threats are realized.
- Facing angry opponents may be a signal that you need to reconsider your behavior in time to prevent a negotiation impasse. However, if you have good alternatives to the current negotiation, an angry display should not deter you from continuing to demand your own objectives, while reciprocating your opponents' actions by displaying anger or another type of nasty response.
- Presenting an ultimatum in the form of "take it or leave it" may be very aggravating and generate an unpleasant response from your opponents. If you decide to use the "take it or leave it" ultimatum, make sure you can justify it by legitimizing it (link the ultimatum up to policies or regulations) or generate a sense of fairness (the offers applies to everyone or the prices have not changed over the last few years, etc.).
- Opting out of the negotiation does not mean that you have to physically walk away from the negotiation "table". For example, maintaining silence or playing with your cellular phone, during the process is a sort of opting out, and may even encourage your opponents to reveal important information. However, physically walking away from the negotiation "table" with the hopes of being called back is risky, as the opponents' reaction to such extreme behavior cannot be predicted.
- You can use time delay tactics to achieve benefits, future beneficial changes or exhaust your opponents until they concede. However, take into consideration that using time delay tactics is risky, as you may meanwhile lose the object or objects around which the negotiation is centered. For example, it is obvious that in dragging the time out while negotiating on buying a house, someone else may come in

and scoop it up from under your nose. In addition, it is not advisable to use time delay tactics, as doing so may also put you under time pressure.

- When your opponents have time limitations and you do not, imposing a deadline maybe be to your benefit. It is reasonable to assume that your opponents would be inclined to make concessions as the deadline approaches. Try not to reach a situation, however, where the deadline is effective for both you and your opponents. In this case, you will also have to make concessions, which would not be in your favor.

- When the negotiation becomes tense, you may find tension-relief tactics to be of some help. Use humor, small talk and even flattery, in order to "calm the waters" and return to a smoother negotiation process.

- In a cooperative atmosphere, using rational arguments backed by facts may convince your opponents to make desirable concessions. However, rational arguments in a competitive atmosphere may not influence your opponents, as they may contradict your arguments and portray the presented evidence as inaccurate.

- Consulting your opponents may be helpful for you both in defining creative possibilities for an integrative agreement. However, consultation is a helpful tactic only in a cooperative negotiation atmosphere. If your opponents are competitive, they may use the information you provided during the consultation against you.

- In negotiation, making concessions without appropriate reciprocation may depict you as a weak negotiator or even worse — as a deceiver. Be stingy in making concessions. Do not make big concessions early on in the negotiation process, even if such concessions are unimportant to you. Such early concessions may generate feelings of remorse in your opponents.

- Use *active listening*, as it is a very effective tactic. Try to master the techniques of active listening, especially by asking many clarifying questions, such as "What do you want?" and "Why do you want it?" and raising doubts backed by facts. Use active listening techniques as much as possible during the negotiation process.

Chapter 8

Negotiating a Hostage Crisis
with a Terrorist Group

"If I should ever be captured, I want no negotiation — and if I should request a negotiation from captivity they should consider that a sign of duress."

Anonymous

Imagine you have always believed in the policy of "no negotiation with terrorists". A few hours ago, your friend went to the supermarket to buy some groceries. While she was there, a group of terrorists took over the supermarket, taking all shoppers — including your friend — hostage. The terrorists have many demands that must be met in exchange for the hostages' release. Unless these demands are fulfilled, they are threatening to kill one hostage every hour, beginning with the female hostages. Now what do you think about the "no negotiation with terrorists" policy?

Hostage-taking is a unique type of terrorism, as it often (but not always) involves negotiation used by the terrorists to achieve various gains such as ransom, prisoners' release, public attention, publicity to encourage new recruits and, to some extent, public recognition. Negotiating with terrorists when hostage-taking is involved is also an extreme type of negotiation; its outcome often means the life or death of the hostages. Although hostage-taking represents only a small fraction of terrorist acts, it attracts enormous attention on the part of both the media and the public. Therefore, hostage-taking incidents are the most dramatic ones among terrorists' acts, and have great international influence. Foreigners, such as tourists, diplomats, employees of international companies as well as officers and soldiers are all considered highly attractive potential hostages, since terrorists can receive high gains for their release. In addition, foreigners — and especially protected foreigners, such as diplomats or high-ranking officers — receive the widest media coverage and impact the widest range of populations. Thus, they have become the most desired targets of terrorists groups. So, globalization has, in fact, enabled the rise in hostage-taking we are currently experiencing today.

1. The Critical Dilemma — To Negotiate or Not to Negotiate

To negotiate or not to negotiate with terrorists — this is the first main question with which authorities must grapple (whoever they may be) when terrorists take hostages.

1.1. *Supporting no Negotiation Policy*

Supporters of the "no negotiation" policy argue that the costs and the risks of negotiating with terrorists on hostage-taking outweigh the possible benefits of such negotiation.[1] Negotiating with terrorists who have taken hostages may, in some cases, turn the terrorist group into a legitimate and more recognized entity. Moreover, concessions made to terrorists due to negotiation will further encourage terrorists to engage in future hostage-taking. Once terrorists understand they can achieve gains by hostage-taking, they will probably have more incentive to use this method again, to achieve further gains. If negotiation with terrorists is forbidden, preferably by law, then no concessions to terrorists can be made, meaning they can gain nothing by hostage-taking. Another argument is that, in any case, negotiation is not effective because it is impossible to trust terrorists' promises and commitments. Thus, there is no guarantee, and usually there is no third party, for example, who can ensure that a terrorist group will fulfill its commitments. Therefore, negotiation with terrorist groups may end in negotiators' embarrassment, as well as a loss of the hostages' lives. This last point is most important, as mass and digital media expose the final fate of the hostages, as well as the authorities' behavior throughout the crisis. Negotiating with terrorists — especially if it fails and costs the hostages their lives — may serve to undermine public confidence in the negotiating authorities. It is noteworthy that the "no negotiation with terrorists" policy can be most effective and credible when a formal law does not allow the authorities any discretion whatsoever regarding the negotiation issue.

---

[1] Shell, G.R. (2010), The Morality of Bargaining: Identity versus Interests in Negotiations with Evil, *Negotiation Journal*, Vol. 26(4), pp. 453–481.

1.2. *Supporting Negotiation Policy*

Skeptics of the "no negotiation" policy argue that it is immoral not to negotiate in order to save lives. Moreover, from a practical perspective, "no negotiation" is on the whole, an inconsistent policy, which is often impossible to uphold. It is evident that even the most fanatical supporters of the "no negotiation" policy often violate their own policy, either publically or through a secret back-door channel of a neutral intermediary. Thus, no negotiation policy is violated, especially in cases of political pressures and public opinion. In addition, it is often argued that a negotiated settlement should be preferable to any other alternative, especially a military alternative, which may escalate the situation and result in further violence.

This dilemma is complicated, since it relates to multiple issues, such as the alternatives available to the authorities that have to confront the hostage-taking crisis. In addition, the type of terrorist organization involved, the situation in which the hostages have been taken, and where the hostages are being held must also be taken into consideration.

2. Negotiation among Possible Alternatives in a Hostage Crisis

The decision to negotiate for a hostage release may take into account the expected losses versus the expected benefits of each available alternative, including but not only negotiations.

Within the framework of such decision-making, it is necessary to systematically consider the best and worst alternatives to a negotiated agreement with the terrorist group (the Best Alternative to Negotiated Agreement (*BATNA*) and the Worst Alternative to Negotiated Agreement (*WATNA*)). This type of analysis is based on evaluating the advantages and disadvantages of each alternative, taking into account not only the possible outcome of the authorities' decision, but also the terrorists' possible response to such a decision. In order to conduct this analysis, it is useful to divide the alternatives into five main broad categories:[2] Coerce, yield, withdraw, defer and negotiate.

---

[2]See Chapter 1 of this book.

2.1. *Coerce*

In order to coerce the terrorist group to free the hostages, sending in a rescue team — such as a military or police task force team — is necessary. Such a decision is highly dependent on the speed of the authorities' reaction. If the reaction is quick enough, before the terrorists can move the hostages to an unknown location and prepare for a counter-attack, the prospect of forcing the terrorists to release their hostages is higher than if the terrorists have successfully moved the hostages to a hidden location and prepared themselves for a counter-attack. Knowledge regarding the hostages' location is critical when choosing the coercive alternative. If the hostages' location is known, it is at least theoretically effective to use armed forces to free the hostages. If their location is unknown, this alternative becomes irrelevant.[3] Assuming the hostages' location is known, a decision to send in armed forces is still problematic, depending on certain pieces of intelligence, such as — how difficult it is to reach the hostages' secured place, the number of guards and how the public and media will react in the case of failure.

2.2. *Yield*

Accept all terrorists' demands with the hope that the hostages will be released. This decision may prevent more violence; yet, it may also cost the hostages their lives and further incur the price of any concessions made to the terrorists. Since in most cases there are no real guarantees (apart from the terrorists' assurances) that the terrorists' promises will be carried out, accepting terrorists' demands may indeed be costly; in addition to the terrible loss of the hostages' lives and the price paid by the concessions made, there is also the heavy loss of the media and the authorities' credibility in the eyes of the public.

2.3. *Withdraw*

No concessions to terrorists should be made. The decision in this case is to ignore the terrorists' demands, even at the cost of the hostages' lives. Such a decision hopefully assures a better future for the current population at risk, as terrorists would not have incentives to take hostages in the

---

[3] Santifort, C. and Sandler, T. (2013), Terrorist Success in Hostage-Taking Missions: 1978–2010, *Public Choice*, Vol. 156(1–2), pp. 125–137.

future. However, such a decision may be harshly criticized if the hostages are executed by the terrorists, which may completely terrify large sectors of the population. Such a decision may also achieve an opposite result in the future. It may enhance public pressure to renounce any kind of withdrawal decisions, and concede to terrorists' demands in the case of future hostage-taking.

2.4. *Defer*

Deferred hostage-taking crises are all about *time*. Time is crucial in hostage situations — for both the terrorists and the authorities. For the terrorists, holding and maintaining the hostages for a long period of time may be particularly risky and costly. For the authorities, on the one hand, the possible gains in deferring their decision are based on the opportunity to "buy time", and gather intelligence regarding the hostages' location and the terrorists' situation. Such intelligence may lead to an attempt to send in rescue forces in to release the hostages or enable an attempt to reduce the terrorists' demands. On the other hand, since holding the hostages for a lengthy period of time may be costly and risky for the terrorists, they may increase their demands or become impatient and simply decide to get rid of the hostages. In this situation, the losses of a deferral decision may greatly outweigh its gains.

2.5. *Negotiate*

For the authorities, the typical expected gains of negotiation may be: Avoiding or even preventing violent actions. Negotiations may also generate media publicity and public support and, above all if possible, save the hostages' lives. However, by negotiating with terrorists authorities may lose public support in the case of great concessions or if the hostages' lives are lost as a result of a negotiation impasse.

Moreover, losses incurred through negotiation may serve as a greater incentive for terrorists to initiate future hostage-taking. For example, assuring terrorists' a free route to safety through negotiation may help them to find a new place where they can plan their next terror attack. In addition, through negotiating with the authorities, terrorists may also receive some form of recognition.

Choosing from among the alternatives involves comparing the gains and losses of each alternative. Since losses are more painful than gains, it is reasonable to assume that authorities — when deciding whether or not to negotiate with the hostage takers — will consider a decision in which their expected gains outweigh, as far as possible, their expected losses. However, a previous publicly-made commitment not to negotiate with terrorists under any circumstances makes it harder to decide on negotiation, even when its gains seem to outweigh its losses. It is noteworthy that authorities dealing with hostage crises often revise their decisions during the crisis (for example, due to updated intelligence) and shift from one course of action to another, for example, from negotiation to coercive action, or *vice versa*. Such decisions often take into consideration, among other things, information regarding the type of terrorist group and the main reasons behind the hostage-taking.

3. Who Takes Hostages?

Different types of terrorist groups: A *terrorist group* can be defined as a group that uses violence in order to obtain achievements, through the intimidation of large populations. Terrorist groups take hostages in order to attract the attention of a wide population to their power (no one can be protected), cause or both. When negotiating a hostage situation, terrorists make high demands and expect the authorities to make weighty concessions.

According to the earlier definition, terrorist groups can be divided into three broad categories: (a) secular groups, such as criminal groups; (b) ideological groups, such as left-wing or right-wing extremist groups; and (c) religious terrorist groups, such as the Islamist terrorists groups.

An important sub-division of all the above categories can be that of domestic and transnational terrorist groups:

Domestic terrorist groups include domestic criminal groups or national separatists groups. Such groups usually emerge within the borders of one country. However, in many cases it is too dangerous, at least for the leaders of domestic terrorist groups, to stay within the borders of their own country. Therefore, they look for safe locations in other countries from which to attack their own country. They also often receive support, ammunition, and training from their host countries, as well as from other various supporting countries, which they make use of when attacking their own country.

Transnational terrorist groups mainly include ideological or religious terrorists groups, and sometimes also criminal groups. These groups are often financed or assisted by an interested country or countries and have active and, at times, also passive cells in many countries. Both active and passive cells in multiple countries usually consist of native participants. These participants may take part in violent acts of terror in the country where they live, after which they then rapidly disappear and assimilate within the regular, normative population.

Taking of hostages by either a domestic or transnational terrorist group is different than other terrorist acts, as it is very "noisy" and often has objectives that can be achieved through negotiation.

4. Why Take Hostages?

Each terrorist group or individual terrorist has its own typical reasons for taking hostages.

4.1. *Domestic Terrorist Groups*

Domestic criminal terrorist groups usually take hostages in order to negotiate a ransom, to instigate the release of their group's members from jail and to secure their safe passage so they can disappear. Domestic ideological groups typically take hostages in order to attract the attention of the media — both public and digital — for propaganda purposes and to familiarize the population with their ideology, activities and demands. Sometimes, just like the domestic criminal groups, domestic ideological groups demand a ransom as a form of financial aid, used to fund their activities and, more importantly, fund the release of their group members and supporters from jail.

4.2. *Transnational Terrorist Groups*

Transnational terrorist groups, such as cross-national religious terrorist groups, have somewhat different reasons for hostage-taking. They are motivated to display their cultural superiority in the face of what they believe to be an inferior culture, ideology and way of life. For religious terrorist groups, killing hostages may be an aim in itself, rather than a means for negotiating other gains. These terrorist groups are more dangerous than domestic secular terrorists. Hostages who belong to or represent other cultures or ideologies may be humiliated and even dehumanized. By doing so, ideological and especially religious terrorists believe they are demonstrating the superiority of their values. They also believe they are illustrating their commitment to these values to their believers, opponents, and the world, in general.[4] They may also use their hostages as slaves and execute them when they no longer need their services. Foreign, especially Western, hostages are publically executed in order to demonstrate the terrorists' strength and draw more of the world's attention to their ideas and values.

4.3. *Individuals*

There are also individuals who are either unknown members of terrorist groups or who are influenced by an ideological or religious terrorist group. These individuals may take hostages in order to emphasize their adherence and devotion to the group's values. Terrorist groups often encourage such individual activities, using social networks and brainwashing by local preachers and friends, who are supporters of such terrorist ideology or religion. Hostage-taking as well as other terrorist acts are sometimes carried out by hired mercenaries, who are paid for their services.

4.4. *The Risk and its Price*

Hostage-takers, whoever they may be, are exposed to great risks as they are under the surveillance of both the media and the authorities. They may also face great expenses as a result of having to hide and maintain the hostages for an extended period of time. In order to compensate for their high risks and costs, terrorist demands during negotiation involving hostages may be especially high and rigid.[5] Their high gains may be used in many ways: To publicize their "high-quality" values, recruitment benefits, money and far reaching concessions — all of which may be sources of embarrassment to the negotiating authorities.

5. Negotiating the Release of Hostages

5.1. *Intelligence Gathering*

Just like in any other negotiation, gathering intelligence in the preparation stage and afterwards is most crucial. Intelligence needs to be collected,

---

[4]Piazza, J.A, (2009), Is Islamist Terrorism More Dangerous? An Empirical Study of Group Ideology, Organization, and Goal Structure, *Terrorism and Political Violence*, Vol. 21(1), pp. 62–88.

[5]Gaibulloev, K. and Sandler, T. (2009), Hostage Taking: Determinates of Terrorist Logistical and Negotiation Success, *Journal of Peace Research*, Vol. 49(6), pp. 739–756.

evaluated and validated in order to assess the crisis situation and make the necessary decisions regarding objectives, strategies and tactics, in addition to considering the possible reactions of the hostage-takers. Intelligence gathering prior to hostage taking, if at all possible, is problematic due to the short and finite time feasible for the authorities' response. This means that most intelligence must be gathered, updated and validated mainly throughout the negotiation progression — a task which is extremely difficult, demanding and challenging. However, there might be a difference in intelligence-gathering capabilities, depending on whether the hostage-taking was initiated by domestic or transnational terrorist groups.

With regard to domestic terrorists (whether criminal, ideological or religious groups), some information regarding their capabilities, strengths, weaknesses, tendencies and human composition might have been previously gathered by the local authorities. However, intelligence-gathering, regarding transnational terrorist groups, is far more complicated.[6] First, it is possible to assume that authorities who decide to negotiate a hostage release situation with a transnational terrorist group have less, if any, previous intelligence and less understanding of the group's nature. In addition, there is often little previous knowledge about the transnational terrorists' possible demands. Another possible problem is the little existing knowledge about with whom, if anyone, it is possible to negotiate a sustainable agreement.[7] In such cases, it is often impossible to access necessary information, prior to the negotiations, owing to time constraints and the immediate high risk of the hostages' lives. It takes more effort and international cooperation to gather intelligence on transnational terrorists groups, especially during hostage-taking crises. The problematic issue of gathering intelligence is also present in situations where an individual, about whom there is no previous information, decides to take hostages.

Both domestic and transnational terrorist groups, on the other hand, are usually well prepared for their hostage-taking. They collect intelligence regarding the weakest and most worthwhile place where a lot of hostages can be taken easily. They also gather information regarding the traditional

---

[6]Nieboer-Martini, H.A. Dolnik, A. and Giebels, E. (2012), Far and Away: Negotiators on Overseas Deployment, *Negotiation and Conflict Management Research*, Vol. 5(3), pp. 307–324.

[7]Andersen-Rodgers, D.R. (2014), No Table Necessary? Foreign Policy Crisis Management Techniques in Non-State Actor-triggered Crises, *Conflict Management and Peace Science*, 2015, Vol. 32(2), pp. 200–221.

training of hostage release teams, and they are well prepared, often employing a team of well-trained hostage-takers that is well-equipped with suitable ammunition. Thus, they significantly precede the authorities in their preparation and knowledge of how to handle the crisis situation, which they themselves have premeditated, planned and initiated.

Supplied with the proper intelligence, authorities can begin the process of applying strategies and tactics in order to attempt to free the hostages. When discussing the uses of the negotiation strategies and tactics of both terrorists and the authorities, it is important to distinguish between the kind of terrorists responsible for the hostage situation — a domestic or transnational terrorist group, as well as the conditions under which the hostages are being held (for example, in a known versus an unknown location).

5.2. *Strategies and Tactics Used by Domestic Terrorist Groups and the Authorities*

Domestic terrorist groups usually take hostages in order to draw attention to their existence and sometimes to their ideology. They also often demand at least partial recognition, a ransom, freeing jailed members of the group and their guaranteed free passage. The more demands they make, the more likely they will get at least some of them. Therefore, domestic terrorist groups usually use the hostages in order to achieve as many demands as possible; thus, they have less incentive to harm the hostages.

The possibilities of the terrorists moving the hostages to an unknown location and taking many hostages — especially if there are protected people or VIPs among the hostages, such as embassy employees — make the negotiation much more difficult for the authorities.

Despite such probable difficulties, there are several negotiation models, created with the aim of reaching an agreement with domestic hostage-taking groups.[8] Most of these models use more cooperative rather than competitive strategies and tactics. In most of these models, the emphasis is on building rapport between the negotiation team and the terrorist group, especially by using the active listening tactic,[9] showing empathy for the terrorists' feelings

---

[8]Grubb, A. (2010), Modern Day Hostage (Crisis) Negotiation: The Evolution of an Art Form within the Policing Arena, *Aggression and Violent Behavior*, Vol. 15(5), pp. 341–348.
[9]See Chapter 7 of this book.

and trying to help the terrorist save face, without compromising the hostages' safety or security. Finally, in the hope of changing the terrorists' attitudes, an agreement is offered, which answers to the terrorists' demands — such as ransom, free passage to safety or the release some of the group's members from jail — in exchange for the hostages. It is worthwhile to remember that authorities have often at least some prior information regarding domestic terrorists, but even in this case, they still need to buy more time in order to gather further information on domestic hostage-takers. Any additional information they can gather during the negotiation process is important as such information may be effectively used later on, during a more advanced stage of the negotiation.

However, even if the strategies employed by the authorities during the negotiation are somewhat cooperative, make no mistake — this is still a highly ruthless negotiation. It is conducted with the lives of the captured hostages hanging in the balance, in exchange for the authorities' concessions to terrorist demands. Thus, reaching an agreement is dependent on the existing power balance between the authorities and the terrorists, and the gap between the terrorists' demands and the willingness or capabilities of the authorities to concede. For example, not knowing the location of the hostages, as well as public and media pressure on the authorities to rescue the hostages, serve to reduce the authorities' negotiation power *vis-à-vis* the terrorists group. Openly gathering a large police or military force around the terrorists, as well as playing for time and exhausting the terrorists — for example, by using the 'beating around the bush strategy'[10] — may reduce the terrorists' demands. Moreover, numerous casualties among the hostages also serve to reduce the terrorists' negotiation power *vis-à-vis* the authorities. Also, when the gap between the terrorists' demands and the authorities' concession "price" is too high, the likelihood of the domestic terrorists achieving their demands is reduced substantially.

5.3. *Strategies and Tactics Used by Transnational Terrorist Groups*

Translational terrorists groups have rigid, high and tough demands, and are well trained, well equipped and well prepared for the negotiation. These terrorists have received comprehensive training on how to deal with hostage

---

[10]See Chapter 7 of this book.

negotiation situations, including the treatment of the hostages and the strategies and tactics to be used during the negotiation process. They are tough negotiators as they believe that the authorities or their negotiation team have few, if any, alternatives to making concessions.

Oftentimes, there is a power imbalance, which tends to be in favor of the terrorists. The terrorists are in control because they are holding the hostages — whether in a known or unknown remote location where, according to their declarations, they supposedly have abundant stores of ammunition and explosives.

The location of the hostages is often in countries that allow for the easy holding of hostages in an unknown location; the location is also unknown to the hostages themselves, to prevent any and all possible leaks.

Typical hard tactics used by transnational terrorist groups negotiating a hostage release include:

Ultimatum: Demands are presented in a "take it or leave it" manner, and are high and difficult to fulfill. Apparently, no compromise is possible; these demands are meant to force the authorities to either concede to the hostage-takers' demands or risk the hostages' lives while searching for another alternative.

Deadline: Setting a deadline for reaching an agreement regarding the hostages, thus forcing the negotiation to end at a certain defined time. The aim of setting a deadline is to achieve the authorities' concessions in the terrorists' favor within a short period of time.

Timing: Negotiating hostages' release as election time approaches. This increases the pressure on the negotiating authorities, especially in real democracies.

Using threats: Especially threatening to kill the hostages.

The use of pressure: Harming or even killing some hostages during the negotiation process as a means of putting pressure on the authorities or their negotiating team, as well as frightening the public. As the hostages are dehumanized, it is easy for their captors to harm or even kill them in the most brutal way. Sometimes, there is a selection process; executions are carried out according to nationality, gender, etc., in order to emphasize the terrorists' agenda and values.

Embarrassing the authorities: Demanding to negotiate or at least talk with an important leader(s) or a leading decision-making persona, as part of making the authorities take actions for which they might be blamed and, later on, "punished" by their constituency. Concessions made by leading decision-making persona to negotiate with terrorists are especially embarrassing for leaders who have already declared in favor of a "non-negotiation" policy, and are now forced to break their word and negotiate with a terrorist group — all of which is publicized — resulting in a significant blow to their reputation and reliability. However, if the authorities do not concede and refuse to negotiate with the hostage-takers, the execution of many hostages may be carried out by the terrorists in order to embarrass the authorities by reflecting the authorities "cruelty", and "merciless" to the world.

It is noteworthy that transnational terrorists prefer to use such tactics; especially when negotiating with real democracies. Leaders of democratic countries are often more sensitive to public opinion and face pressures before, during and after the negotiation. Such pressures are typically employed by the hostages' families, domestic constituency and both the public and digital media. Democratic leaders cannot ignore such pressures.[11] Furthermore, since democracies respect personal liberties and freedom, and cherish human lives, they might be more responsive to terrorist demands in exchange for the hostages' release. Transnational terrorists are well prepared to take advantage of these characteristics, which are typical of democracies.

According to their religious convictions, in many cases terrorists are not concerned about their own security during hostage release negotiations; sometimes, they are even willing to die to prevent any hostage rescue attempt.

5.4. *Strategies and Tactics Used by the Authorities*

Dealing with transnational terrorist groups, especially extreme religious groups, is much more difficult and demanding than dealing with domestic terrorist groups. There are several reasons for authorities' difficulties in such negotiations. For example: Authorities or their negotiation team often have a hard time communicating with the terrorists, as there is no direct line of communication. Moreover, a transnational hostage-taking crisis often demands a multinational anti-terrorist negotiation team. The possible different interests

---

[11] Lee, C.-Y. (2013), Democracy, Civil Liberties, and Hostage-Taking Terrorism, *Journal of Peace Research*, Vol. 50(2), pp. 235–248.

among the team members may cause difficulties in the negotiation with the terrorists.

In some cases, the authorities or a transnational negotiation team have very little intelligence on the terrorists' forthcoming mode of negotiation, whereas the terrorists are often well informed of the various traditional models used by the authorities to train negotiators who deal with hostage-taking. These traditional models are usually relevant to domestic hostage-taking and, in most cases, are not appropriate for dealing with transnational hostage-takers.

This seems to be an almost impossible situation for the authorities who want to conduct the negotiation. However, even religious terrorists are not always as suicidal or irrational as is usually assumed. They, like everyone, act according to their own *subjective rationality*.[12] Thus, when they make a premeditated decision to take hostages (rather than taking them on impulse during some other operation), a certain extent of specific subjective rationality is behind this decision. For example, it may be that the subjective rationality behind the terrorists' decision to take hostages and publically execute some of them is to demonstrate their strength and frighten the general world populations. When this type of subjective rationale is behind the hostage-taking, transnational terrorists often use the *pretence negotiation strategy*,[13] making it almost impossible for any negotiation team to be able to save the hostages from their fate. In such a case, only forcible rescue might save them, even though the chances are very slim. However, there might be another rationale behind a specific hostage-taking situation, such as: Ransom, putting an end to a long-lasting war, the pullout of army troops from an important area, enabling the recruitment of new terrorist members or the release of important group members jailed in several countries around the world. While many religious terrorists regard death for the group's cause as the highest honor, in the case of hostage-taking death becomes a secondary achievement to the potential broader achievements of the group.[14] In these cases, understanding the subjective rationality behind the hostage-taking may lead to an effective negotiation, which may save some, most or all of the hostages' lives.

Possible tactics for authorities while negotiating a hostage release with transnational (especially religious) terrorist groups.

---

[12] See Chapter 3 of this book.

[13] See Chapter 7 of this book.

[14] Dolnik, A. and Fitzgerald, K.M. (2011), Negotiating a Hostage Crisis with the New Terrorists, *Studies in Conflict & Terrorism*, Vol. 34(4), pp. 267–294.

As has already been mentioned, negotiating a hostage release with a transnational, and especially religious, group is very difficult, but not always impossible. However, it is almost impossible to use even somewhat cooperative strategies, since practically the hostage-takers behave in a competitive manner. Thus, the use of competitive negotiating strategies and tactics by the authorities reciprocate the hard strategies and tactics used by the hostage-takers. Such competitive strategies and tactics may include:

Intimidation of individuals: Intimidating individuals involved in the hostage-taking, by threatening to punish their families and other relatives if they refuse to release the hostages, may be an effective tactic. Even individuals ready to die for their group's cause would usually not want their loved ones to experience anguish and agony, as a result of their deeds. In the face of such threats, the individuals who carry out the hostage-taking may reduce their demands and even release the hostages.

Intimidation of the terrorist group:[15] Because hostage-taking is, in most cases, a decision made by a terrorist group, rather than the individuals who carry out the act, intimidation efforts can also be aimed at the group. Most, if not all, terrorist groups are concerned about the opinions and attitudes of the population whose interests they believe they represent, and from which they recruit their members. The extent of this population's support of hostage-taking tactics and the ensuing results seems to affect both the group's motivation to use this tactic, and the relevant population's attitudes towards the group in the future. If this population feels fear as a result of the hostage-taking, its attitude towards the terrorist group might change which, in turn, might result in severe damages to the terrorist group, and even in rare cases — to its collapse. Thus, by threatening the relevant population which, in return, puts pressure on the terrorist group, the power balance can be altered and negotiations can lead to the hostages' release.

Pressure on sponsoring or influential state(s): Terrorist groups are often maintained, accommodated, trained, provided with recruiting facilities, and are even funded by a state or states that support them — either publically or confidentially. This is typical in the case of transnational terrorist groups, but it is often also the case in regard to domestic terrorist groups. During

---

[15]Merari, A. (2005), Social, Organizational and Psychological Factors in Suicide Terrorism. In Bjorgo, T. (ed.), *Roots, Causes of Terrorism: Myths, Reality, and Ways Forward*, Routledge, pp. 70–87.

hostage release negotiations, it is sometimes helpful to put pressure on the sponsoring country, as this may influence the terrorist group, and thus the negotiation may tend to favor a hostage release.

In addition, in many cases authorities are reluctant to negotiate with transnational terrorists groups, since they are not confident that the terrorists are credible negotiation partners. Facing pressures from other state(s), the supporting terrorist state may be able to provide an enforcement mechanism that not only encourages negotiation for the hostages' release, but mainly prevents the terrorists from reneging on their agreed commitments.[16] However, since terrorist groups are autonomous entities in many aspects regarding their activities, there is no guarantee that the sponsoring state(s) could force the terrorist group to moderate their demands or force them to abide by and honor their agreement to release the hostages.

Time delays: In response to the deadlines pronounced by the hostage-takers/terrorists, slowing down the negotiation process is often possible. The deadlines imposed by terrorists are sometimes arbitrary. As a deadline does not always serve the terrorists' desire to achieve objectives through negotiating the hostages' release, the deadline can be breached. However, breaching the deadline may be possible only if authorities indicate they are seriously dealing with at least some of the terrorists' demands, while at the same time providing satisfactory explanations for the delays. Time delays could be supported by the "active listening" tactic, including asking many clarifying questions. Such questions, which are often used to buy time, may also aid in intelligence-gathering during the negotiation. This tactic helps negotiators glean a better understanding of the terrorists' interests and objectives and, most importantly, their motivation for taking the hostages. However, time delays are used not only for gathering immediate, important intelligence, but also in an attempt to exhaust the terrorists, for coordination purposes or, at least, for consultation purposes with other authorities. Moreover, it may also be an attempt to stall for time, in order to organize a rescue operation.

Using interpreters: Using the proper language in a hostage crisis is essential during the negotiation. Being familiar with the proper language means mastering verbal messages as well as being familiar with the culture. This is essential to prevent communication barriers, which may confound the

---

[16]Bapat, N.A. (2006), State Bargaining with Transnational Terrorist Groups, *International Studies Quarterly*, Vol. 50, pp. 213–229.

messages of both authorities and terrorists. In a transnational hostage-taking crisis, individual terrorists often come from various cultures and speak different languages. Because of this common phenomenon, it is essential for the negotiators to recruit translators, who can send accurate messages and correctly understand the hostage-takers' messages. Translators can also buy 'expensive' time for the authorities, as it takes time to interpret the verbal exchanges between the authorities and the hostage-takers. The play for time incurred by the need to interpret can also provide hostage-takers with an opportunity to think of other options besides killing the hostages. In addition, a well-trained and experienced interpreter can provide helpful, practical information regarding the attitudes and moods of the hostage-takers.[17]

A third-party intervention: Involving a third party in the hostages' release negotiation may be possible only if the third party is acceptable in the eyes of the hostage-takers' terrorist group. Such a third party must have some relationship to the hostage-takers and a high level of credibility with them. This type of third-party intervention may sound suspicious and risky. However, in a situation where the balance of power does not tend favorably to the authorities' side, a third party may introduce some opportunities, and even benefits, to the negotiation process. First of all, as in other situations involving a third-party intervention, both sides (the authorities and the terrorists) should not make concessions, but rather consider the third party's suggestions. This way, they can save face and continue negotiating. Second, this may also help to gain time, which is extremely essential to the authorities. Third, notwithstanding how strongly the third party is connected to the hostage-takers, some concessions may be achieved through the negotiation process, such as releasing one or several of the hostages. Fourth, mediation can lead to better communication between the authorities and the hostage–takers and, with some luck, provide, consciously or unconsciously, some information regarding the hostage-takers' situation and perhaps even their location. Finally, a third party may manage to lower the terrorists' expectations, explaining the constraints (legal and others) of both the third party and the authorities. Thus, even if the third party is not the best choice for the authorities, and even if an agreement cannot be reached through such a process, a third party is still better than giving up completely.

---

[17]Matusits, J. (2013), Interpersonal Communication Perspectives in Hostage Negotiation, *Journal of Applied Security Research*, Vol. 8(1), pp. 24–37.

Practical Applications

This chapter is unique in the sense that, while it unfortunately may be relevant to each of us, everywhere in the world, it is not usually a situation we will ever personally need to negotiate. As was mentioned, this is an extreme kind of negotiation, one which often involves life and death. Negotiating a hostage crisis with a terrorist group usually requires more than we, as individuals, can do. However, if the worst comes to the worst, we might find ourselves involved in one way or another in a hostage crisis. In this case, we must decide whether it is possible for us to negotiate with the terrorists or leave it to the authorities, who will probably deal with it in due time. Hopefully, this chapter has provided readers with a glimpse into the problematic issue of negotiating a hostage crisis, as well as the advantages and disadvantages of the available strategies and tactics.

PART THREE

Values and Perceptions — How They Influence the Negotiation Process

Chapter 9

Globalization and Culture: Their Impact on Negotiation

"Globalization means we have to re-examine some of our ideas, and look at ideas from other countries, from other cultures, and open ourselves to them. And that's not comfortable for the average person."

Herbie Hancock

1. On Globalization

The term *globalization* means the ability to transfer resources, money, goods, labor, ideas, information, etc. across national and cultural boundaries. Globalization is not a new phenomenon; the transfer of resources and ideas has been taking place for thousands of years. However, the use of new, fast-paced modes of transportation, such as trains and airplanes, has shortened distances and our sense of time, enabling rapid transformations from the most remote parts of the world. Many companies have become multinational companies, establishing partnerships and mergers, and purchasing firms with various cultural backgrounds. In this sense, the world has become "a small village", in which rapid exchanges of various types and interaction between people of diverse areas often require communication and negotiation. For example, high technology products can be developed in Israel, produced in China, Hungary and Canada, and then marketed in more than 70 countries.

Transmission technologies, such as internet, e-mail, mobile smart phones and other telecommunication devices, enable an on-the-spot flow of almost endless information pertaining to various types of issues. However, negotiators in the global world also have several constraints which, at times, may also become advantages, such as legal, political and economic systems that differ from their own system.[1] In global negotiations, it is necessary to consider diverse legal regulations, sometimes political control of the markets (instead of a free market), the ways in which financial resources are handled, and cultural differences. Such conditions frequently play a role at the negotiation "table". In this regard, cultural differences is one of the most influential and noticeable features of global negotiations.[2] Negotiation becomes much more complicated when cross-cultural characteristics must be taken into consideration.

1.1. *Globalization and Culture*

Globalization has changed many things; yet, cultures and cultural identities have not disappeared and, in many cases, they have even become stronger.[3] In fact, the rapid globalization process has not done away with cultural environments and identities. Globalization has brought into sharp focus the influence of diverse cultures on negotiations. Since negotiators are usually people who have undergone a socialization process within either a given culture or a multicultural environment, even the choice of negotiating rather than another type of conflict resolution alternative (such as coercion, withdrawal or deferral) is colored, *inter alia*, by cultural or multicultural values. Therefore, the globalization process has brought about contradictory tendencies in negotiation.

On one hand, there is a general decline of *cultural identities* in multicultural negotiators. These negotiators have received a multicultural education, and are well acquainted with various cultural values and ideas. In addition, even within a relatively homogenous culture, not all negotiators have the same level of identification with cultural values, i.e. not all negotiators behave as expected by members of this unique culture. Due to globalization, there are also negotiators who can be characterized as having "*cultural intelligence*", which enhances their capability to successfully adapt to other cultural settings and enables them to make more accurate judgments regarding other cultures. "Cultural intelligence" often results in more effective cross-cultural

---

[1] Acuff, F.L. (2008), *How to Negotiate Anything with Anyone Anywhere Around the World*, 3rd Edition, Amacom-American Management Association, Amacom Books.

[2] Brett, J.M. (2007), **Negotiation Globally**, 2nd Edition, Jossy-Bass.

[3] Belay, G. (1996), The (Re) Construction and Negotiation of Culture Identities in the Age of Globalization, Chapter 15. In Mokros, H.B. (ed.), *Interaction and Identity, Information and Behavior*, Vol. 5, pp. 319–346, Transaction Publishers.

negotiation.[4] Moreover, due to globalization, differences in values, including negotiation values, are apparent between the older and younger generations in many cultures. Some members of the younger generation have more "cultural intelligence" than their elders.

On the other hand, there is a growing trend among negotiators to identify more with their own cultural rules of conduct. Negotiators often find themselves 'adrift' in the "global village" — in unfamiliar cultural contexts, with only their own cultural perceptions to draw on. In a global world that seems, at times, to be unfamiliar, and even threatening and ambiguous, negotiators' need to identify with their own culture becomes increasingly important.[5] This identification provides them with a certain sense of security and self-assurance. Since the negotiation process, by its very nature, often creates a sense of uncertainty and ambiguity, it is not surprising that many negotiators feel safer when identifying with their own cultural values and norms of conduct. Consequently, even some multicultural negotiators are seeking ways to strengthen their relations to their cultural origins, returning to their original values and norms of behavior. Some fundamentalist cultures have a growing influence on their members' cultural identification and behavior, and thus on their negotiators.

1.2. *Culture as a Cause for Negotiation Problems*

Despite the growing experience with various cultures, cultural differences are still among the main obstacles in global negotiations. Cultural divergence may result in an incorrect interpretation of the way opponents behave while negotiating. Naturally, diverse values can generate misunderstandings in perceptions and interpretations about opponents' intentions, behavior and ways of communication. Moreover, negotiators who identify with different cultures take diverse paths to accomplish their goals and achievements during the negotiation process.[6] Lacking a clear understanding of their opponents'

---

[4]Imai, L. and Gelfand, M.J. (2010), The Culturally Intelligent Negotiator: The Impact of Cultural Intelligence (CQ) on Negotiation Sequence and Outcomes, *Organizational Behavior and Human Decision Processes*, Vol. 112, pp. 83–98.

[5]Bulow, A.M. and Kumar, R. (2011), Culture and Negotiation, *International Negotiation*, Vol. 16, pp. 349–359.

[6]Liu, M. and Wilson, S.R. (2011), The Effects of Interaction Goals on Negotiation Tactics and Outcomes: A Dyad-Level Analysis across Two Cultures, *Communication Research*, Vol. 38(2), pp. 248–277.

cultural behaviors, negotiators may not know what to expect at the negotiation table or how their opponents will react and make decisions. As a result, negotiators often encounter severe problems and experience misunderstandings, suspicion and anger.[7] Negotiators' cultural differences may complicate, delay and interrupt the negotiation process.

2. Traditional Classifications of Cultures

In order to gain some insight into cross-cultural influences on negotiation, it is essential to classify cultures into several categories. Taking into consideration that the core of each culture is comprised of its shared values, norms of behavior and rules of conduct it is, of course, impossible to describe the typical negotiation style of each culture in our global world. Therefore, it is necessary to classify cultures into several broad categories. Such a classification necessarily involves generalizations about large groups of cultures. Admittedly, despite the differences between and within these broad cultural groups, and the possible limitations of such generalizations, it is necessary to acknowledge that there are widely shared sets of values, norms and rules of conduct between broad categories of cultures. In other words, besides the diversity between cultures, there are also many similarities among cultural categories. It is therefore possible to describe typical core values shared by several cultural groups and, as a result, to classify them into broad categories. The benefit of such a classification is that it makes it possible to anticipate, at least in broad strokes, the behavior and conduct of negotiators who identify with one of these cultural categories.

Cross-cultural study has offered various classifications of cultures.[8] The main traditional classification can be separated into two broad categories:

---

[7]Sieck, W.R. Smith, J.L. and Rasmussen, L.J. (2013), Meta Cognitive Strategies for Making Sense of Cross-Cultural Encounters, *Journal of Cross-Cultural Psychology*, Vol. 44(6), pp. 1007–1023.

[8]E.T. Hall, (1976), *Beyond Culture*, Garden City: Anchor/Doubleday.

Triandis, H.C. McCusker, C. and Hui, C.H. (1990), Multimethod Probes of Individualism and Collectivism, *Journal of Personality and Social Psychology*, Vol. 59(5), pp. 1006–1020.

Hofstede, G. and Bond, M.H. (1988), Confucius and Economic Growth: New Trends in Culture's Consequences, *Organizational Dynamics*, Vol. 16(4), pp. 4–21.

Trompenaars, F. and C. Hampden-Turner (1997), *Riding the Waves of Culture: Understanding Cultural Diversity in Business*, 2nd Edition, Nicholas Brealey Publishing Ltd.

(a) collectivist versus individualist cultures; and (b) low-context versus high-context cultures.

2.1. *Collectivist versus Individualist Cultures*

Basically, the main difference between individualistic and collectivistic cultures relates to the relationship between the individuals and their group.[9] In other words, it is the difference between I-preference cultures and We-preference cultures. For members of collectivistic cultures, the priority is the group interests, whereas for members of individualistic cultures the priority is, of course, the individual interests.

It is possible to relate to individualistic cultures versus collectivistic cultures as a bipolar construct: At one end of the scale, there is a "pure" individualist culture while, on the other end, there is a "pure" collectivist culture. Obviously, most cultures are *hybrid cultures* — ranged somewhere along this scale. Some of these hybrid cultures are closer to the individualistic culture (such as some North American cultures), while others are closer to the collectivistic culture (such as some East Asian cultures or Arabic cultures). Still others are ranged somewhere in the middle — between collectivistic and individualistic cultures, as described in Figure 1.

2.2. *Low-Context versus High-Context Cultures*

The concept of low-context and high-context cultures relates to a culture's communication characteristics. Communication characteristics are especially important, since negotiation is usually based on communication exchange. The description of cultural communication can be depicted on a bipolar scale where, at one end, we have low-context communication cultures while, at the other end, we have high-context communication

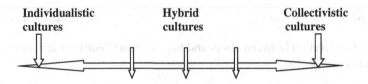

Figure 1: Individualistic, collectivistic and hybrid cultures

---

[9]Hui, C.A. and Triandis, C.H. (1986), Individualism — Collectivism: A Study of Cross-Cultural Researchers, *Journal of Cross-Cultural Psychology*, Vol. 17(2), pp. 225–248.

cultures. Low-context cultures exhibit relatively clear, direct and accurate communication. Messages in low-context cultures are explicit — the meaning of a communication is clearly expressed in the words of the message. Thus, the receiver-negotiator of low-context messages only has to understand the words in the message. In contrast, in high-context cultures, communication is implicit, somewhat vague, usually indirect and can only be understood within the framework of its culture. Since the meaning of the messages conveyed by high-context cultures is embedded in the context, rather than the words of the message, the receiver-negotiator should know that an accurate interpretation of the words in the message is only possible within the context in which they were communicated.

2.3. *"Low/High-Context" Individualistic/Collectivistic Cultures*

High-context cultures are often also collectivistic cultures, in which members share common values that enable them to understand the cultural shared contexts. In low-context cultures, in which the communication is clear and direct, there is also a smaller need for mutual shared contexts when interpreting messages. Low-context cultures are also often individualistic cultures.

Accordingly, there is a correlation between individualistic cultures and low-context cultures, and a correlation between collectivistic cultures and high-context cultures, as can be seen in Figure 2.

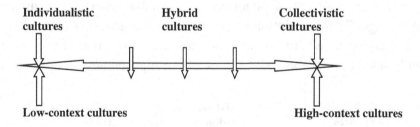

Figure 2:   Correlation between "low- and high-context" cultures and individualistic/ collectivistic cultures[10]

---

[10]Singelis, T.M. Triandis, H.C. Bhawuk, D.P.S. and Gelfand, M.J. (1995), Horizontal and Vertical Dimensions of Individualism and Collectivism: A Theoretical and Measurement Refinement, *Cross-Cultural Research*, Vol. 29(3), pp. 241–275. In this article, Singelis *et al.* expanded on *the distinctions between the categories of individualism and collectivism, dividing them into four categories*: *Vertical Collectivism* (VC) refers to the complete

Some classifications of cultures tend to distinguish between Western cultures and Eastern cultures. Low-context individualistic cultures are often identified with Western countries, whereas collectivist high-context cultures are often identified with Eastern countries. This tendency to identify culture with country or a region should be approached with great caution. A diversity of cultures exists, in many cases, both among and within Western and Eastern countries. For example, there is a strong representation of Latino cultures within some U.S. states, or strong representatives of Arab cultures within Western European countries, and so on. Thus, in many cases, it is possible that differences along individualistic/low-context and collectivistic/high-context dimensions within a country are greater than between countries.[11]

3. Cultural Characteristics and Negotiation

There are several differences between negotiators of individualistic cultures and those of collectivistic cultures. Collectivist negotiators cherish interpersonal relations and are highly dependent on their group and group members. Individualistic negotiators value autonomy and individual independence.[12]

3.1. *Collectivist Negotiators*

In collectivistic cultures, negotiators see themselves as part of the collective (be it community, tribe or even nation). The collective's goals are given priority over the negotiators' own individual interests and goals. The commitment

---

subordination of individuals to their collective. *The individuals are required to accept inequalities and hierarchies within their group. Horizontal Collectivism (HC) refers to individuals as a part of their collective, but all members of the collective are perceived as more or less equals. Vertical Individualism (VI) refers to individuals who are autonomous, but accept inequality and hierarchy within their group. Horizontal Individualism (HI) refers to individuals who are autonomous, independent entities, and where equality exists between all the group members. Horizontal Individualists are focused on their intrinsic identity, self-development and personal achievements, rather than on group interests. Since most collective cultures are vertical (VC) and most individual cultures are horizontal (HI), we will use only two categories — collectivist and individualist — in our discussion.*

[11] Schaffer, B.S. and Riordan, C.M. (2003), A Review of Cross-Cultural Methodologies for Organizational Research: A Best Practices Approach, *Organization Research Methods*, Vol. 6(2), pp. 169–215.

[12] Triandis, H.C. (1995), *Individualism and Collectivism*, Westview Press, Boulder, Colorado.

to collective values and norms are more powerful than the negotiator's own opinions or desires. Furthermore, collectivist negotiators react differently to in-group than to out-group negotiation.

Most collectivist cultures (but definitely not all of them) are hierarchical in nature, characterized by superior–subordinate relations within the negotiation group. In these cultures, negotiators are expected to obey their superiors and almost no decision can be made without the authorization of senior members, who do not necessarily participate at the negotiation "table". There is a high level of internal uniformity within the negotiating group, which is achieved by complying with their superiors' instructions.

3.2. *Individualist Negotiators*

Negotiators of individualist cultures are loosely linked and relatively detached from the group to which they belong. They feel independent and give priority to their own interests and goals over the goals of others. They have independent opinions, and there might be a difference between the negotiators' attitudes and the attitudes of the other group members.

Since individualistic cultures are relatively egalitarian, negotiators can make decisions with a relatively fair degree of independence. Although negotiators of individualistic cultures may also be subordinate to decisions made by higher-level decision-makers, who do not participate in the negotiation process, (such as boards of directors in business companies, or governments in diplomacy negotiations), negotiators perceive themselves as being relatively equal to their superiors as well as to other negotiators on their team. The differences of opinion that frequently appear among members of individualist negotiating teams may be more difficult to resolve than disagreements with the opponents.

4. Some Additional Cultural Differences in Negotiation

Since there might be great diversity between collectivist high-context negotiators and individualist low-context negotiators as described earlier, it is necessary to gain insight into several additional dimensions of these differences. These dimensions include: Differences in communication aspects, both as regards online and traditional communication; differences in interpersonal relations; differences related to "*face*" and *honor* concerns; and *time perception* differences.

4.1. *Online Communication*

The use of electronic communications, in general, and in cross-cultural nego-tiation, in particular, provides active, global negotiation — accessible over distances and time — something no previous form of communication tech-nologies could offer. The existence of friendly software, personal comput-ers, tablets, smart cellular phones and multi-user networks, for example, enable cross-cultural negotiation between negotiators of all levels — indi-viduals, organizations and at the national level. The speed at which extensive information is available online and can be retrieved and transferred allows negotiators to quickly gather essential information, and compare alterna-tives, thus enabling negotiators of different cultures to make better and more information-based decisions. This, in turn, also enables the sending and receiving of immediate messages from various parts of the world, i.e. various cultures. Moreover, on-line negotiation, in contrast to face-to-face negotia-tions may reduce the presence of others who are involved in the negotiation, thus reducing, to a certain extent, the strong impact of cultural influences. E-mail communication is shorter and the negotiators are perceived as more equal than in face-to-face communication. In this sense, online negotiation also tends to eliminate some typical differences between cultures. By nego-tiating on-line, negotiators can make deals all over the world, saving both time and money. However, they are also likely to confront significant com-munication problems.

Despite the many virtues of online communication and its use as a quick and useful tool, it also tends to create great problems. Problems arise during the encoding (writing the message) and decoding (interpreting the message) stages, including some "noise" (communication barriers) when messages pass through the web (such as messages going astray). The interpretation of written messages, which are short in nature and usually decoded (interpreted) according to the cultural perceptions of the receiver, is a frequent source of misunderstandings. Such short on-line message can distort the original intention of the sender, who is used to other cultural conceptions. For exam-ple, the vice president of an American high technology firm (a low-context individualistic culture) explains his experience with his Japanese opponent (a high-context collectivistic culture) as follows: "During the negotiation, I sent a short description of a new technological item to my Japanese oppo-nent (high-context culture)". The response of the Japanese opponent was "please explain further". "I explained further," the vice president continues," but the third response's reply was another request for more information", "Only after several such 'rounds', I finally understood that my Japanese opponent had understood my description of the technological item very well from the beginning. He did not really need any more explanations. He simply believed that my description of the item was incorrect, but did not want to insult me by saying it directly." Let us look at another example: What does the following brief statement — "we'll be in touch shortly" — mean for dissimilar cultural negotiators? Low-context individualistic negotiators can interpret it as "in a few days", while high-context collectivist negotiators may understand the meaning as "some indefinable period of time" (weeks, months, etc.). In addition, low-context individualistic negotiators are heavily engaged (more than usual), when negotiating on-line, in self-interest behavior and the use of hard tactics. Since using e-mail media also obscures social status, high-context collectivist negotiators, who are used to hierarchical status relationships, may feel relatively "free" and at ease via more equal media, such as e-mail. Furthermore, the limiting ability of collectivist negotiators to use emotions and establish rapport via email also may encourage them to use hard tactics more than usual.[13] For example, high-context collectivist negotiators tend to present the first proposals via e-mail, than is typical for their culture, therefore obtaining higher outcomes than low-context individualist negotiators.[14] The use of smart phones for sending and receiving cross-cultural negotiation messages is similar in many ways to cross-cultural e-mailing. However, since smart phones are highly "mobile", sending and receiving messages can often "catch" the negotiators in bizarre places and create time pressures. This may result in further misunderstandings of the messages, or the sending of erroneous short messages. The use of smart phones during face-to-face negotiation can be an intentional opting out tactic — an attempt to leave the negotiation without actually slamming the "negotiating door". However, when a negotiator unintentionally uses a smart phone during negotiation (such as checking messages or texting) it

---

[13]Barsness, Z.I. and Bhappu, A.D. (2004), At the Crossroads of Culture and Technology: Social Influences and Information Sharing Processes During Negotiation, in Gelfand, M.J. and Brett, J.M. (eds.), *The Handbook of Negotiation and Culture*, Chapter 17, pp. 350–373, Stanford Business Books.

[14]Rosette, A.S. Brett. J.M. Barsness, Z.I. and Lytle, A.L. (2012), When Cultures Clash Electronically: The Impact of Email and Social Norms on Negotiation Behavior and Outcomes. *Journal of Cross-Cultural Psychology*, Vol. 43(4), pp. 628–643.

may disrupt the negotiation process, especially in cross-cultural negotiation. Such behavior may be wrongly perceived, especially by collectivist opponents, as a non-verbal cue reflecting lack of respect or a wish to opt out. Thus, the opponents' reaction may be negative, even harsh, significantly reducing their trust and satisfaction with the negotiation process and outcome. Such behavior may also interrupt the natural sequence of the process and divert the negotiator's attention from the negotiation issues.[15] Overall, online negotiation, despite its many advantages, may suffer from cross-cultural disruptions and does not always yield benefits and satisfaction.

4.2. *Traditional Face-to-face Communication*

Traditional communication is mainly based on verbal and non-verbal cues in *face-to-face* negotiation. The way negotiators experience the same phenomena often differs from culture to culture. Furthermore, negotiators from different cultures differ in the way they express themselves, select information, and in regard to the weight they give to such information. The following are just a few examples: Negotiators with a collectivist high-context approach have a tendency to use indirect signals during the face-to-face negotiation process.[16] The conveying of messages relies on cautious implicit communication, often veiled in courtesy and respect. For high-context collectivistic negotiators (such as some East Asian negotiators), it is often important to maintain harmony, and therefore circumvent problems so as to avoid direct confrontation with their face-to-face opponents. At the beginning of the formal negotiations, high-context collectivistic negotiators will often present general principles, as well as engage in general discussion, rather than approach the specific issues on the "table". For them, in face-to-face negotiation, it is more important to silently "read" the opponents' mind during the negotiation, by studying non-verbal cues, such as facial expressions or body language, than it is for individualist negotiators.

In contrast, for low-context individualistic negotiators (for example, some North American individualistic negotiators) communication tends to be

---

[15]Krisbnan, A. Kurtzberg, T.R. and Naquin, C.E. (2014), The Curse of the Smartphone: Electronic Multitasking in Negotiation, *Negotiation Journal*, Vol. 30(2), pp. 191–208.

[16]Galin, A. and Avraham, S. (2009) Cross-Cultural Perspective on Aggressiveness in the Workplace: A Comparison between Jews and Arabs in Israel, *Cross-Cultural Research*, Vol. 43(1), pp. 30–45.,

instrumental, clear and direct.[17] Here, the emphasis is on straightforward and immediate dealing with the issues at hand. According to individualistic negotiators' perception, beginning negotiations with a discussion of general principals or philosophical proverbs, typical to collectivist negotiators, is an attempt to use the "beating around the bush" strategy. Such an approach to negotiations is time-consuming — time that the individualist negotiators would rather not invest in the negotiation. Expressions typical to individualistic negotiators, such as: "talk to the point" designate impatience and a need for decisiveness. These individualist negotiators have an interest in closing the deal as quickly as possible, and getting on to their next activity. Expressing opposition is not perceived as insulting, as it is frequently perceived by collectivist negotiators. On the contrary, direct argumentation, even strong arguments, is perceived as a legitimate tool for resolving differences of opinion. Moreover, the verbal meaning of the words exchanged between the parties during the negotiation is taken very seriously and less attention is paid to non-verbal cues in face-to face negotiation.

Language, both verbal and non-verbal, is not simply a set of words or mannerisms, but an expression of values and norms of conduct. Despite the existence of some kind of an international verbal language (which changes over time), the meaning of the same word does not always have an equivalent in other cultures.[18] For example, in some cultures, negotiators who use the English word "perhaps" mean that something might be possible. For negotiators in other cultures the same "perhaps" means impossible. In some collectivist high-context cultures (such as for some Japanese negotiators), it is undignified to say "no" and negotiators often refrain from using it, whereas saying "yes" is common, even when there is no intention to perform.[19] Negotiators from high-context collectivistic cultures (such as from some Arab cultures) may use rhetoric and hypotheses, metaphors and repetitions, whereas to some individualistic low-context negotiators such rhetoric is irrelevant, sometimes annoying and even unacceptable. Even some

---

[17]Bovee, C.L. Thill, J.V. and Schatzman, B.E. (2003), *Business Communication Today*, 7th Edition, Prentice Hall.

[18]Triandis, H.C. (2006), Cultural Intelligence in Organizations, *Group and Organizational Management*, Vol. 31(1), pp. 20–26.

[19]Miike. Y. (2002), Theorizing Culture and Communication in the Asian Context: An Assumptive Foundation, *Intercultural Communicative Studies*, Vol. 11(1), pp. 1–21. This article addresses communication in the Asian context.

English negotiators negotiating in Australia may find that using some English words have totally different meanings than they do in the England. For example, for Australians, an informal meeting at "tea time" means the meeting will take place at dinner.

In addition, in face-to-face communication, non-verbal cues often differ from culture to culture. The same non-verbal behavior, such as direct eye contact, can be perceived by negotiators in one culture — mainly individualistic low-context cultures — as reflecting honesty and trustworthiness, whereas by negotiators of other cultures — mainly high-context collectivistic cultures — they may be perceived as signs of disrespect, inappropriateness and even rudeness. Thus, cross-cultural negotiators should be aware of the verbal and non-verbal connotations, which vary widely among cultures.[20]

Despite these differences and probably due to globalization, high-context collectivistic culture has become more flexible in adapting to the direct explicit communication typical to low-context individual cultures. High-context collectivist cultures are able to switch from one form of communication to the other with relative ease, as if they have more "cultural intelligence". Conversely, low-context individualist negotiators may find it hard to use and interpret the implicit, non-direct negotiation typical to high-context collectivist communication.[21]

Finally, off-the-record *informal communication* or "*side communication meetings*" often take place before and during the formal negotiations. Such communication is more problematic for online negotiation than for face-to-face negotiation, as online written messages may appear as commitments or promises which, if misconstrued, may be difficult to change without losing face. However, informal face-to-face communications provide good opportunities for information-gathering, which may be useful during the negotiation process. Such informal communication and informal meetings are accepted by negotiators of both individualistic and collectivistic cultures, but with a greater emphasis and need on the part of collectivist negotiators.

To conclude, while the use of online communication increases negotiators' ability to negotiate quickly and conveniently across cultures, it does

---

[20]Okoro, E. (2012), Cross-Cultural Etiquette and Communication in Global Business: Toward Managing Corporate Expansion, *International Journal of Business and Management*, Vol. 7(16), pp. 130–138.

[21]Adair, W.L. and Brett, M.J. (2005), The Negotiation Dance: Time, Culture and Behavioral Sequences in Negotiation, *Organization Science*, Vol. 16(1), pp. 33–51.

not eliminate — and sometimes even enhances — the problems arising from culturally diverse perceptions and attitudes. If negotiators ignore such differences, they may face negative reactions. While it might be easier for some cultures (mainly high-context collectivist) to interpret messages sent by other cultures (even by low-context individualist), culture is still an obstacle in cross-cultural negotiation. Face-to-face negotiation may also be problematic due to the difficulties in interpreting the behavior of other cultural negotiators. However, face-to-face negotiation may give negotiators better insight into opponents' cultural values and rules of conduct. Thus, probably the combined use of cross-cultural face-to-face communication with online negotiation can yield better cross-cultural negotiation outcomes.

4.3. *Interpersonal Relations*

One central tendency of high-context collectivistic negotiators is to build a personal relationship with their opponents. In contrast, developing a personal relationship with opponents is often perceived by individualistic negotiators as inappropriate to "business", an aspect that is separate from — and which should not influence — the negotiation process. Individualistic low-context negotiators' emphasis is on achieving their economic — or other tangible and intangible — gains, and especially concluding the negotiation at hand with no further involvements.[22] Since they believe that developing a personal relationship may get in the way of achieving their goals, they prefer to keep their familiarity with the other party to a minimum and "get down to business". For example, while U.S. individualistic negotiators talk business in a negotiating meeting, their neighboring Mexican collectivistic negotiators may talk about family and trust, in addition to business. In any case low-context individuals believe that, at the end of the negotiation, the obligations of individualistic negotiators will be determined by a legally binding agreement, rather than by interpersonal or social relations.

For collectivist high-context negotiators the emphasis on personal relationships is important, since familiarity reduces uncertainty and increases trust. The personal relationship between the parties is no less important than achieving the negotiation goals. High-context collectivist negotiators

---

[22]Ma, Z. Wang, X. Jaeger, A. Anderson, T. Twng, Y. and Saunders, D. (2002), Individual Perception, Bargaining Behavior, and Negotiation Outcomes — A Comparison across Two Countries, *International Journal of Cross-Cultural Management*, Vol. 2(2), pp. 171–184.

are very sensitive to the differences between foreign negotiators and those they are familiar with. While negotiating with strangers, agonizing surprises may occur, such as submission to pressures or unintended compromises. Such fears of unexpected events while negotiating with strangers result in the tendency to use intermediaries, who can provide essential information on the strangers, or to demand guarantees and commitments from reliable intermediaries. Collectivist negotiators often have a higher appreciation for the people with whom they are negotiating than the organizations which these negotiators represent, or even more than the final achieved agreement. Therefore, the replacement/substitution of negotiators during the negotiation process is somewhat upsetting for collectivist negotiators. Personal relationships determine the amount of confidence between negotiators, and the scope in which all parties can make demands on each other during the negotiation process. High-context collectivist negotiators like to perceive other negotiators as reliable friends, rather than negotiation opponents.[23] The tendency during the negotiation process, both online and face-to-face, is to rely more on personal acquaintance and less on the mere negotiating details.

In many high-context collectivistic cultures, relationships are created slowly and entail obligations. The patience necessary to build such relationships is not always the strong point of low-context individualistic negotiators. This lack of patience is often a major weakness of individualistic negotiators during a negotiation process with collectivistic negotiators.

4.4. *"Face" and Honor Concerns*

"Face" concerns relate to the negotiators' sensitivity about their social importance. Negotiators experience two opposing kinds of face or honor concerns — enhancing face or honor, and avoiding the loss of face or honor. The desire to gain face or honor reflects the negotiators' need for approval or recognition of their negotiation performance. The fear of losing face or honor reflects the negotiators' intention to avoid a negative evaluation of their negotiating performance. Thus, negotiators may *"gain face"* when their negotiation performance exceeds social expectations. Negotiators may *"lose face"*

---

[23]Movius, H. Matsuura, M. Yan, J. and Kim, D.Y. (2006), Tailoring the Mutual Gains Approach for Negotiation with Partners in Japan, China and Korea, *Negotiation Journal*, Vol. 22(4), pp. 389–439.

when their negotiation performance is perceived as unsatisfactory and below expectations.

While the negotiators' sensitivity about "face" is more widespread in high-context collectivistic cultures, it is, in many ways, similar to the negotiators' desire to gain honor and a good reputation in low-context individualistic cultures.[24] However, in many collectivist cultures, face is often embedded in ascription and hierarchy, whereas in numerous individualistic cultures honor is often the estimation of negotiators' achievements in the eyes of others. In both cultures, negotiators have face or honor, according to the expectations of their own cultural members.[25] Thus, both individualist and collectivist negotiators are concerned with gaining face, as all negotiators wish to be respected and honored. However, for negotiators the fear of losing face is sometimes stronger than the desire to gain face. Face may be vulnerable, threatened or even negotiated over, especially under the stress conditions typical to the negotiation process.[26]

While concern over face is, in its very nature, a universal phenomenon, there are several differences in the ways in which cultural characteristics influence negotiators' behavior regarding face concerns, during both intra-cultural negotiation and especially during cross-cultural negotiations. For example, low-context individualist face-enhancing, according to their own cultural perception, is due to the individual's effective management of the negotiation and achieving (at least) most of their immediate negotiation goals. For high-context collectivist negotiators, face-enhancing, according to their specific cultural perceptions, is a result of mutual in-group handling of the negotiations, and achieving long-term interests for their group. The risk of losing face, in high-context collectivist cultures, is more significant than gaining face, as the pain of losing face is often more severe than the pleasure and satisfaction of gaining face. Due to high-context collectivist negotiators' great fear of "losing face", they may try to turn even an objective loss into a

[24]Zhang, X.-A. Cao, Q. and Grigoriou, N. (2011), Consciousness of Social Face: The Development and Validation of Scale Measuring Desire to Gain Face versus Fear of Losing Face, *The Journal of Social Psychology*, Vol. 151(2), pp. 129–149.

[25]Leung, A.K.Y. and Cohen, D. (2011), Within-and Between-Culture Variation: Individual Differences and Cultural Logics of Honor, Face, and Dignity Cultures, *Journal of Personality and Social Psychology*, Vol. 100(3), pp. 507–526.

[26]Liu, L.A. Friedman, R. Barry, B. Gelfand, M.J. and Zhang, Z.-X. (2012), The Dynamic of Consensus Building in Intracultural and Intercultural Negotiations, *Administrative Science Quarterly*, Vol. 57(2), pp. 269–304.

gain. Since different cultures give different interpretations to gaining face and losing face, these differences may complicate behavior during cross-cultural negotiations.[27]

The concept of *facework* refers to the actions negotiators take in order to gain — and especially to avoid — losing face or honor. Facework reflects the negotiators' actions to achieve social "ratings" displaying their competence within their own cultural group and in cross-cultural negotiation. The social sensitivity of negotiators over a high level of face and their greater fear of losing face may create two opposing types of *facework*. On the one hand, the fear of losing face may cause negotiators to become more aggressive and competitive and therefore may create a greater possibility of a negotiation impasse.[28] On the other hand, the threat of losing face may create a relatively more open frame of mind, encouraging a certain extent of adaptation to the other culture, thus making it easier to overcome negotiation problems resulting from cultural differences. As individualistic negotiators are less sensitive to their collectivists opponents' great fear of losing face, which is expressed in their facework, cross-cultural negotiations is more complicated than within-culture negotiation.

4.5. Time Perception

Technology and globalization have accelerated the pace of life all over the world and in all areas — firstly, in the business sector, but also in the arenas of labor, diplomacy and many others. Substantial changes are continuously occurring at break-neck speed, including changes related to time perceptions. Yet, the perception of time is still an area closely linked to cultural differences, and its impact on negotiation is of importance. Negotiations are conducted within the framework of time, whereas time itself is an object for negotiation. Therefore, differences in time perceptions may be an obstacle in cross-cultural negotiations.

It is possible to distinguish between "faster" and "slower" cultures. Some cultures, usually low-context individualistic cultures, are "faster" cultures,

---

[27]Ting-Toomey, S. and Kurogi, A. (1998), Facework Competence in Intercultural Conflict: An Updated Face-Negotiation Theory, *International Journal of Intercultural Relations*, Vol. 22(2), pp. 187–225.

[28]White, J.B. Tynan, R. Galinsky, A.D. and Thompson, L. (2004), Face Threat Sensitivity in Negotiation: Roadblock to Agreement and Joint Gain, *Organization Behavior and Human Decision Processes*, Vol. 94(2), pp. 102–124.

whereas others, usually high-context collectivistic cultures, are "slower" cultures.[29] In "fast" cultures (just as in fast food "cultures") negotiators would like to reach an agreement today, if not yesterday or the day before. There is little patience in low-context individualistic cultures. Almost in contrast, for high-context collectivistic negotiators patience is of great importance. They are ready to negotiate in order to reach an agreement tomorrow and if not tomorrow, then the next day or the one after that. These time pace differences in negotiations are neither a strategy nor a temporary tactic, but rather an issue that is well-rooted in the cultural rules of conduct.

These rules of conduct may vary from *monochronic* (or sequential) at one end of the scale to *polychronic* (or synchronic) at the other end of the scale. According to the monochronic rules of conduct, typical to low-context individualistic cultures, one thing is done per each unit of time. Precision and the efficient exploitation of time are of importance to individualist monochronic negotiators, since time is scarce or "time is money". According to polychromic rules of conduct, typical to high-context collectivist cultures, several actions may be performed simultaneously. Precision is often of little importance, schedules are of modest significance and the efficient usage of time is a minor consideration.

The perception of time in various cultures affects negotiations in several ways.

In individualistic cultures, where monochronic rules of conduct are salient, there is a defined time for the beginning, the process, and for the end of negotiations. The negotiation agenda is lucid and deals with complex negotiation issues sequentially — settling each issue, one at a time. The negotiators often operate under a time pressure in order to end the negotiation on schedule, with or without reaching an agreement. The efficiency of negotiations is measured by "cost-effectiveness" calculations — which in practical terms, means that negotiators balance their financial gains against the price they pay by losing time, as well as other expenditures due to the negotiation process.

In collectivistic cultures, where the polychronic rules of conduct are salient, there is often no definite timeframe for the negotiation's beginning and end — negotiations can proceed even after an agreement has been

---

[29]Macduff, I. (2006), Your Pace or Mine? Culture, Time and Negotiation, *Negotiation Journal*, Vol. 22(1), pp. 31–45.

achieved, since the past, present and future are firmly intertwined. Extending the negotiation process is perceived by collectivist negotiators as the price paid for the opportunity to collect information, and sometimes in order to establish trust and create a relationship with their opponents. There is also the belief held by many collectivist negotiators that "time is on their side"; therefore, there is no hurry to complete and finalize the negotiations. Patience is a very important virtue, as it deters collectivist negotiators from making concessions, even under time pressures. Yet, deadlines and ultimatums are frequently used by collectivist negotiators in order to impose concessions on their opponents.[30] Moreover, collectivist negotiators tend to discuss multiple issues at the same time, so as to accomplish several tasks during the negotiation process, including negotiations with other competing parties on the same issues.

Another difference between the negotiators of different cultures is timing, when it comes to reciprocating the opponents' offers during the negotiation process. It was found[31] that high-context collectivist negotiators tend to frequently reciprocate opponents' offers during the negotiation process, whereas low-context individualistic negotiators tend to reciprocate opponents' offers only towards the end of the negotiation. It seems that high-context collectivist negotiators use the act of reciprocation to offers throughout the entire negotiation process, in order to search for immediate information. In contrast, low-context individualistic negotiators delay reciprocation of offers towards the end of the negotiations, probably in order to better understand and integrate all the information collected during the negotiation process, before reaching their final decisions.

4.6. *The Final Agreement*

The difference between high-context collectivist negotiators and low-context individualistic negotiators is also reflected in relation to the *final agreement*. Individualistic negotiators are used to highly litigious cultures, with concepts of legal codes of behavior. Every simple negotiation may entail pages of written contract, complete with details and sub-details. When a

---

[30]Alon, I. and Brett, J.M. (2007), Perceptions of Time and Their Impact on Negotiation in the Arabic-Speaking Islamic World, *Negotiation Journal*, Vol. 23(1), pp. 55–73.

[31]Adair, W.L. Weingart, L. and Brett, J. (2007), The Timing and Function of Offers in U.S. and Japanese Negotiations, *Journal of Applied Psychology*, Vol. 92(4), pp. 1056–1066.

contract is signed at the end of the negotiation, compliance with all its obligations is mandatory. If a party to the agreement does not comply with all or part of it, the legal system is expected to enforce it. Agreement in the eyes of individualist negotiators is a set of rules of conduct, rights and obligations, to which the parties must adhere as long as the agreement is in force.

In contrast, high-context collectivistic negotiators have some aversion to written agreements, especially if signed during public ceremonies. Every written document contains an inherent risk of a potential loss of face. A written agreement may cause collectivist negotiators' embarrassment or shame, because it may reveal concessions that they had to make during the negotiation process in order to reach the agreement. In any case, the emphasis of collective negotiators is mainly on interpersonal relations and understanding; therefore, it is not necessary to put everything in writing. An informal agreement is sufficient. If there must be a written document, high-context collectivistic negotiators prefer a memorandum of understanding, written in ambiguous terms, whose articles can be interpreted in various ways. If possible, the agreement should be short and vague, and contain no obligations. If the agreement is short and ambiguous, it is possible to make revisions and even major changes after it has been signed. Collectivist negotiators may draw up an agreement to please their individualistic opponents; however they may also wish to change the terms of the agreement immediately after it has been signed. In accordance with collectivist negotiators' perceptions, compliance with the agreement should be achieved through trust relationships, rather than by a legal system.[32] Lacking trust and a relationship, a third party or parties must provide guarantees that the opponents will comply with what the collectivist negotiators believe has been agreed upon, not necessarily in writing.

Attitudes towards the written agreement also symbolize cultural differences. Low-context individual negotiators recognize the written agreement as the natural binding end of the negotiation. For collectivist negotiators, the agreement is only the beginning of developing a relationship, which may change over time, along with their interests in the agreement. They will comply with an agreement — even an informal agreement — as long as it fulfills

---

[32]Hooker, J. (2012), Cultural Differences in Business Communication, Chapter 19, in C. Bratt, S.F. Paulston, Kiesling and Rangel, E.S. (eds.), *The Handbook of International Discourse and Communication*, Wiley-Blackwell.

their interests, if there is a good, working relationship or a strong third-party entity forcing them to comply.

5. Concluding Remarks

The globalization process and the experience gained by negotiators of all cultures via the expansion of cross-cultural negotiation practices in many parts of the world, has probably increased their ability to identify tension areas between collectivistic and individualistic cultures.[33] Thus, due to negotiators' sensitivity to areas such as communication, face and honor, relationships, time conceptions and formal agreements, the very nature of negotiation is slowly changing over time. Individualistic negotiators take into account the unique problems of collectivistic cultures, while collectivistic negotiators try to adjust to and, at times, even please individualistic negotiators. Thus, there is more experience in anticipating the other party's way of negotiation, as well as efforts to untangle the existing contradictions between negotiators' cultural styles. This does not mean that differences between the negotiation styles of various cultures have completely disappeared, nor should this be expected. Yet, the growing knowledge, understanding and sensitivity to these differences may help, at least in increasing attempts to bridge the gaps.

Practical Applications

- When negotiating with negotiators of other cultures, do not draw on your own cultural perceptions. Incorrect interpretations of the opponent's behavior while negotiating, guided by a different value system, may lead to problems. Invest more time than usual in preparing for the negotiation. Try to understand as far as possible the difference between your way of negotiation and that of your opponents.
- It may be extremely helpful to consult a colleague or friend who has experience with your opponents' culture. Once you know more about this culture, try to draw on similarities as much as possible. In the absence of similarities, do not fall into the trap of using another culture's mannerisms or body language, such as giving your business

---

[33]Metcaff, L.E. Bird, A. Peterson, M.F. Shankarmahesh, M. and Lituchy, T.R. (2007). Cultural Influences in Negotiations: A Four-Country Comparative Analysis, *International Journal of Cross-Cultural Management*, Vol. 7(2), pp. 147–168.

card to someone with two hands while negotiating with one culture, or patting your opponent's shoulder in a friendly way while negotiating with another culture. What you really want and need to understand is the different perceptions of interests and objectives held by your opponent, who identifies with another culture. Mannerisms are of less importance. Once you understand your opponents' cultural perceptions, you can concentrate on the best way to negotiate your own interests and objectives.

- If you cannot obtain enough information, relevant to the particular culture of your opponents, you can at least use the traditional classification between low-context individualistic cultures and high-context collectivistic cultures. By using this classification, you can roughly anticipate your opponents' behavior during the negotiations. You can anticipate that low-context individualistic negotiators will talk to the point; their presentations will be explicit, and they will try to achieve their objectives in the shortest possible time. In this case, try to behave in a "business-like" manner, but remember that you can use time pressure tactics on your opponents. If your opponents are high-context collectivists, they will try to avoid negotiation; their communications will be implicit and difficult to interpret. They may have many questions that are not directly related to the negotiations (but apparently are of importance to them). They will probably be the first to put their offers on the "table", but they would not rush the negotiations. In this case, try to correctly and accurately understand your opponents' messages. Moreover, be patient and flexible; otherwise, time pressures will increase your own concession-making decisions.

- Do not decide on your opponents' culture, according to country affiliation. Diverse cultures exist within many countries, sometimes even more than between countries. While preparing for the negotiation, find out to which culture your opponents belong, according to your knowledge as well as their behavior, without using the country as the main frame of reference.

- Be cautious when intercepting cross-cultural short messages via online communication. Try to interpret such messages in terms of your opponents' cultural conceptions, not your own. Of course this is easy to say, but hard to do. However, understanding short messages according to their original intentions is essential for making the correct decisions and taking proper action during on-line negotiation processes.

- Remember that there is more of a tendency to use hard tactics in cross-cultural negotiations via online communication. This may not contribute to a convenient process. However, if you are aware of it, it should not make much difference. Be prepared to put the first offer on the negotiation "table". This might increase your gains.

- Please note that in face-to-face negotiation, the same verbal cue, such as a certain word, may have different meanings in different cultures. Similarly, non-verbal cues, such as direct eye contact, may be perceived as expressing honesty in one culture, while expressing disrespect in another. In preparing for a specific negotiation, try to learn as much as possible about the meaning of verbal and non-verbal behavior — both for you and your opponents.

- Take into consideration that on-line negotiation, even if it is informal, is more obliging than face-to-face informal negotiation. The written word is hard to change, especially in cross-cultural negotiation, where different perceptions and sometime distrust exist.

- Face-to-face negotiation may give you better insight into opponents' cultural values and rules of conduct, than online negotiation. Thus, probably the combined use of cross-cultural face-to-face communication with online negotiation can help you achieve better cross-cultural negotiation outcomes.

- Building a good personal relationship is very helpful, at least for extending your knowledge and information about your opponents. In cross-cultural negotiations, personal relationships may help you to acquire more accurate information about the conceptions of the other negotiators' culture. Be patient — personal relationships take time to establish and develop.

- Try to save your opponents' "face". Remember, the fear of losing face may create undesirable consequences, such as more aggressive behavior during the negotiation process .At the same time, do not let your opponents make you lose your own "face", even if you believe that it is less important than economic or other material gains. Losing face may harm you in future negotiations with the same opponents and may also have a negative impact on negotiations with other opponents — both within your own cultural group and in cross-cultural negotiations.

- Whatever your own conceptions of the negotiation time and pace, do not rush the negotiation process. Negotiations, especially cross-cultural negotiation, take time to prepare and understand. Compare alternatives and do not make rash decisions or act impulsively (when, for example, building personal relationships or establishing trust). Rushing the process would not be to your benefit.
- In a cross-cultural negotiation between collectivist negotiators and individualist negotiators writing a long written agreement with many articles and sub-articles is frequently useless. Why should you waste time and money to please your opponents by drawing up a long written agreement if it can all be changed before the "ink is dry"?

Chapter 10
Ethical Behavior

"Being good is easy, what is difficult is being just."

Victor Hugo

1. Ethical Behavior

Ethics is a somewhat vague term, which relates to norms of conduct based on perceptions about what is good or bad, right or wrong. In this sense, the essence of ethics is in the "eyes of the beholder", in our case, the eyes of the negotiator. Ethical behavior is ambiguous and depends on negotiators' perceptions, attitudes and beliefs, which change according to negotiators' cultural or ethnic identity and their conceptions of appropriate norms of conduct.[1] For example, setting very high objectives at the beginning of a negotiation may be perceived as part of the fair rules of conduct by some negotiators, and as unfair by others. Some negotiators also believe that lying and deceiving during negotiations are acceptable, while others strongly reject these behaviors. Furthermore, negotiators' perceptions of ethical or unethical behavior may be based on whether they initiate this somewhat questionable behavior or if they are the victims of such behavior.[2]

---

[1] Ho, J.A. (2010), Ethical Perception: Are Differences Between Ethnic Groups Situation-dependent? *Business Ethics: A European Review*, Vol. 19(2), pp. 154–182.

[2] Tsay, C.-J. and Bazerman, M.H. (2009), Decision-Making Perspective to Negotiation: A Review of the Past and a Look to the Future, *Negotiation Journal*, Vol. 25(4), pp. 467–480.

2. The Many Faces of Ethical Behavior

Perceptions about ethical behavior in negotiation have several "faces",[3] each of which may influence negotiators' behaviors, especially as regards their perceptions about the other parties' behavior. Thus, it is important to mention at least seven main possible causes that create negotiators' perceptions of ethical behavior.

2.1. *The Perception of Ethical Behavior According to the Negotiation Outcome*

The perception of the negotiation as an ethical process greatly depends on individuals' perception of its outcome. If the negotiation outcome is perceived as "good", then the negotiation process is perceived as ethical, and *vice versa*. The perception of a "good" negotiation outcome depends on the relative proportion between two factors: The negotiators' expectations of the outcome, multiplied by the value they ascribe to it. In a scenario in which negotiators expect to receive a large slice of the negotiation "pie", and assign a high value to this "slice", an outcome that is lower than their expectations may be accompanied by a strong sense of unethical behavior. Of course, in a scenario in which the negotiators have low expectations and assign a low value to the negotiation outcome, no feelings of unethical behavior will likely be experienced, even if their outcome is, indeed, low.

2.2. *The Perception of Ethical Behavior According to the Negotiators' Investments*

The evaluation of an ethical process may also be comparative. The negotiation outcome is compared to one's investment in the process, in terms of time, financial resources, emotional resources, etc. If the investment is low and the outcome is higher than expected, the process may be perceived as ethical. Conversely, if the investment is high and the outcome is lower than expected, the process may be conceived as unethical. Moreover, negotiators tend to compare their outcomes with others who have negotiated similar or

---

[3]Cropanzano, R. Byrne, Z.S. Bobocel, R. and Rupp, D.E. (2001), Moral Virtues, Fairness Heuristics, Social Entities and other Denizens of Organizational Justice, *Journal of Vocational Behavior*, Vol. 58(2), pp. 164–209.

identical negotiations.[4] If other negotiators achieved worse outcomes with higher investments, the negotiators may then perceive their own negotiation as ethical, and *vice versa*.

2.3. *The Perception of Ethical Behavior According to the Negotiation Process*

The perception of ethical behavior is sometimes based on the evaluation of strategies and tactics used during the negotiation process. The use of cooperative strategies and tactics on all sides — such as the reciprocating strategy, consultation or gestures tactics — may cause all involved parties to perceive the negotiation as ethical. Actually, much depends on the opponents' cooperation approach. If the opponents are cooperative, using collaborative strategies and tactics, the process may be perceived by the negotiators as ethical. However, if the negotiators use aggressive strategies and tactics and the opponents use cooperative tactics, in the negotiators' eyes the negotiation process may be definitely accepted as ethical. Conversely, if the opponents use aggressive strategies and tactics — such as threats, displays of anger or ultimatums — the whole process may be perceived by the negotiators as unethical, especially if their own behavior is cooperative.

2.4. *The Perception of Ethical Behavior According to the Negotiators' Social Needs*

Negotiators, like all human beings, have social needs. During the negotiation process, the main needs include: The need for a good relationship, the need to control the negotiation process, and the need for appraisal and compensation.

The need for a good relationship. A good relationship with the other parties may yield rewards during the negotiation, outside of the negotiation process or rewards in future negotiations with the same parties. Thus, when relationships are of importance negotiators will probably choose to act ethically. The more significant the relationship with the other parties, the more ethical behavior on the part of the negotiators may be expected. The less significant the relationship is, the higher the probability of unethical behavior, on the part of the negotiators. Moreover, when the relationship with the other

---

[4]Blount, S. (2000), Whoever Said that Markets Were Fair? *Negotiation Journal*, Vol. 16(3), pp. 237–250.

parties is of importance, the negotiation process may be perceived as ethical, even when the negotiators suffer some tangible economic losses as an outcome.

The need to control the negotiation process. The need to direct the negotiation process towards the negotiators' preferred course requires the ability to predict the negotiation developments. When it seems that the negotiators can predict the course of the negotiation process, it gives them a sense of controlling the situation. For example, some "inside" information attained by the negotiators, whether true or false, gives them a feeling (albeit illusionary) that they can predict the negotiation's course. In light of such information, they may feel that they are in a position of controlling the situation. As long as they believe they are controlling the process, negotiators may perceive the process as ethical, despite any surprising and problematic issues that arise during the negotiation process.

The need for appraisal. The need for appraisal is expressed by being honored and respected by other parties. This need for "face" and respect is so significant that negotiators are ready to exaggerate their own successes and minimize their failures in order to gain respect, at least not lose "face". Therefore, negotiators who gain respect and honor from other parties may perceive the negotiation process as being ethical, even if the outcome is not as good as they might have expected.

The need for compensation. Lacking one or more of the earlier social needs can be compensated for with others. In this regard, it is important to mention the Compensation Effect:[5] For example, a high appraisal of the negotiators can compensate for the lack of their (actual or perceived) control over the situation. In this case, the negotiation may be perceived as ethical, due to the negotiators being compensated with appraisal. Moreover, concern for the negotiators' social needs may compensate for tangible losses. Thus, even if the negotiation tangible outcome is lower than expected, a good relationship with the other parties or a sense of being respected and highly evaluated by the other parties, may result in the perception of an ethical negotiation process, despite its low actual economic outcome. On the other hand, if the relationship with the other parties is not important to the negotiators,

---

[5] Kwong, J.Y.Y. and Leung, K. (2002), A Moderator of the Interaction Effect of Procedural Justice and Outcome Favorability Importance of the Relationship, *Organizational Behavior and Human Decision Process*, Vol. 87(2), pp. 278–299.

if they do not sense any control over the process, and if they do not feel respected, even a higher-than-expected outcome will be perceived by them as unethical.

2.5. *The Perception of Negotiators' Ethical Behavior According to Moral and Cultural Codes*

Moral codes describe acceptable or inacceptable, right or wrong, rules of conduct during the negotiation process. Moral codes are the result of shared social values, as well as cultural and legal norms that are supposed to determine the appropriate negotiating behavior in various possible negotiation situations. However, there are systematic differences when it comes to defining the meaning of right and wrong rules of conduct among and within groups and subgroups. Moreover, sometimes the moral codes of appropriate rules of conduct are the result of the principles, opinions and consciences of individual negotiators. In other words, the perception of ethical moral codes, such as telling the truth, and avoiding the use of threats or coercion, are not in any way universal.

There is an old saying: "Ethics is a matter of geography". Indeed, ethical issues are perceived differently in various parts of the global "village", in accordance with the various cultures.[6] In an extreme individualistic low-context culture, negotiations may be perceived as ethical if their communication is accurate, the decision-making process transparent, and if negotiators consider the other parties' needs. In an extreme collectivistic high-context culture, negotiation is considered ethical if the negotiators achieve their group interests and objectives and manage to maintain their individual and group face. Ethical conceptions, according to the norms of conduct of individualistic cultures, are not the same as those of collectivist cultures, and *vice versa.*[7] Generally, negotiators from different cultures have different conceptions about what is considered appropriate ethical behavior during negotiations. For example, it was found that Greek negotiators (more collectivistic negotiators), evaluate information misrepresentations as being significantly more ethical than British and American negotiators

---

[6]Rivers, C. and Lytle, A.L. (2007), Lying, Cheating Foreigners!! Negotiation Ethics across Cultures, *International Negotiation*, Vol. 12(1) pp. 1–28.

[7]Sims, R.L. (2009), Collective versus Individualist National Cultures: Comparing Taiwan and U.S Employee Attitudes Towards Unethical Business Practices, *Business and Society*, Vol. 48(1), pp. 39–59.

(more individualistic negotiators).[8] Brazilian negotiators (more collectivistic negotiators) were found to approve of bluffing during negotiation more than negotiators from the U.S.[9] However, negotiators are not always necessarily even aware of their own cultural rules of conduct. As a result, even negotiators from a certain culture may be unsure about whether their own behavior is ethical or unethical, and may be even more confused when having to judge their opponents' behavior (which obey other cultural codes of conduct) as ethical or unethical. All this is not to say that the ethical codes of negotiation accepted by one culture or individual negotiators are right, while others are wrong. It is simply meant to emphasize that the ethical rules of conduct accepted by one culture, group or by an individual are not necessarily the same as those of other cultures, groups or individual negotiators.

2.6. *The Perception of Ethical Behavior According to Legal Codes*

Negotiators are supposed to take into consideration local legal rules of behavior. However, the legal rules concerning ethical behavior are often vague and subject to interpretation. Take, for example, the rule of negotiating in "good faith". In many legal systems, there is no explicit definition of the term "good faith"; thus, its range of interpretation is wide. Moreover, legal ethical norms are not even completely followed by lawyers who negotiate on behalf of their clients. Many legal negotiators are cooperative and behave ethically when dealing with an expanding negotiation "pie". However, they may also be competitive and behave in an unethical way, such as by misleading the other party or using aggressive strategies and tactics when dealing with the distribution of the expanded "pie". In other words, negotiators may be cooperative in order to enlarge the pie, but then wish to eat all of it by themselves.[10] Thus, even the legal ethical norms are not straightforward and objective, often leaving negotiators' with no definite guidance.

---

[8]Zarkada-Fraser, A. and Fraser, C. (2001), Moral Decision Making in International Sales Negotiations, *Journal of Business & Industrial Marketing*, Vol. 16(4), pp. 274–293.

[9]Volkema, R.J. (1999), Ethicality in Negotiation: An Analysis of Perceptual Similarities and Differences Between Brazil and the United States, *Journal of Business Research*, Vol. 45(1), pp. 59–67.

[10]Kirgis, P. (2012), Hard Bargaining in the Classroom: Realistic Simulated Negotiation and Students Values, *Negotiation Journal*, Vol. 28(1), pp. 93–115.

2.7. The Perception of Ethical Behavior According to the Negotiators' Moral Intensity

A typical example of an ethical problem in accordance with the negotiator's moral intensity is the *"truth dilemma"*. Seemingly, in some cultures, telling the truth is a significant measure of ethical behavior during negotiation. However, even telling the truth is not a uniform measure, and negotiators may decide what the truth means for them. Does ethical behavior require telling the whole truth or just part of it? Is it necessary to tell the truth all the time or does ethical behavior allow negotiators the freedom to avoid telling the truth in certain situations? Is exaggeration still considered ethical behavior? Where do they draw the line?

Furthermore, the "truth dilemma", or generally, the dilemma of ethical behavior, is apparently not a matter of "pure" morality. It is definitely also concerned with beneficial considerations, such as rewards or sanctions due to ethical or unethical behavior.[11] Unethical behavior could lead to economic benefits but, at the same time, may result in revenge, caused by aggressive reactions of opponents. Also, in some cultures, unethical behavior may lead to a lawsuit. Conversely, ethical behavior may yield a useful cooperation between the negotiating parties, and social and individual benefits, such as respect and negotiators' good feelings. At times, the ethical behavior itself serves as a reward without any expectation of external rewards or sanction-related fears. Apparently, negotiators' moral intensity is highly correlated with ethical perceptions and behaviors. However, it may also be related to concern over the possible consequences of unethical behavior, such as feeling guilty or suffering sanctions.[12]

3. Incentives for Unethical Behavior

There are many types of unethical behaviors, among them: Cheating, deception, providing false information, threats and the offering or accepting of illegitimate favors. Negotiators' subjective rationale for unethical behavior

---

[11]Lind, E.A. Kray, L. and Thompson, L. (2001), Primacy Effects in Justice Judgments: Testing Predictions from Fairness Heuristic Theory, *Organizational Behavior and Human Decision Processes*, Vol. 85(2), pp. 189–210.

[12]Lehnert, K. Park, Y.-H. and Singh, N. (2015), Research Note and Review of the Empirical Ethical Decision-Making Literature: Boundary Conditions and Extensions, *Journal of Business Ethics*, Vol. 129, pp. 195–219.

is mixed motives. On the one hand, they may choose to behave in an ethical manner, in order to give their opponents an incentive to also behave ethically, if possible. On the other hand, negotiators choose to behave unethically and mislead their opponents, with the expectation of obtaining better outcomes for themselves. There is a belief among some negotiators, that being more successful means being able to deceive others, but not be deceived. However, deception, of course, is not always beneficial to negotiators. The consequences may be disagreement, loss of future negotiation potential with the deceived opponents and even legal sanctions. Moreover, opponents are more likely to engage in unethical behavior when they feel that negotiators have taken advantage of them by behaving unethically.

The typical triggers for unethical behavior are: The negotiators' first impression of their opponents, lack of public exposure, unbalanced information, power imbalance, the expected benefits of unethical behavior, the ability to avoid or prevent sanctions and personal attributes.

3.1. *The Impact of Negotiators' First Impression*

It is noteworthy that the first impression of one's opponents is highly influential on the rest of the negotiation process. First impressions are especially influential if the opponents are complete strangers and, even more so, if they are foreigners. During the first stages of the negotiation, when negotiators do not know what to expect from their opponents, the negotiators' first impressions take shape. Negotiators' first decisions are often made according to the previous information (true or false) they have about their opponents' typical strategies and tactics, as well as their first impression of the opponents' fairness and ethical behavior. Such first impressions may also influence the negotiators' decision-making and behavior during the later stages of the process. For example, the negotiators' decision to use hard or soft tactics may be influenced by their first impression of their opponents as being ethical or unethical. Furthermore, each communication or meeting with the opponents may be interpreted differently — according to whether the opponents were first perceived as either ethical or unethical. Communication from perceived ethical opponents may be accepted positively, whereas the same communication from perceived unethical opponents may take on negative connotations and be deemed unacceptable. Thus, opponents who are perceived according to their first impression — as unethical — may cause unethical behavior on the part of negotiators.

3.2. *Lack of Public Exposure*

Many negotiations, even those which concern the public, are often conducted in isolation, far away from the public eye. If one or all parties lie or if they deceive one another, there are no other witnesses to warn negotiators or the public, regarding such unethical behavior and its consequences. In such isolation, incentives for unethical behavior may emerge, as ethical codes may be violated quietly with a low probability of these violations being uncovered. It is worth noting that it is always difficult to uncover unethical negotiators' behavior because they will obviously try to conceal it at all times. It becomes particularly difficult when there is no opportunity for outsiders to examine the honesty of the parties' behavior during the negotiation. This may generate an excellent opportunity for the unethical behavior of one or all parties.

3.3. *Unbalanced Information*

Information is crucial in the negotiation process. Unbalanced information can benefit the informed parties and harm the uninformed ones. Negotiators who know that their opponents are unaware of crucial information that they possess, may lie to and deceive their opponents in order to mislead them into making wrong decisions from which the negotiators may benefit; for instance, an investment house that tries to convince new clients to invest their money by promising a high return on their investment. However, the managers of the investment house are aware that, due to the company's problematic economic situation, they will not be able to actually pay such a high return. They also know that once their clients invest their capital, not only the return but also their original fund, are at great risk. However, they try, through misrepresentation, to convince their new, misinformed clients to make the wrong decision and invest their money in the company. Such unethical behavior is encouraged, especially if one party's knowledge or information predicts large profits for the informed negotiator.[13] Moreover, there is also a high probability that informed negotiators would make high specific demands, many promises or intense threats, assuming that their opponents cannot verify their real situation, as they do not have, and cannot get hold of, the relevant information.

---

[13]Boles, T.L. Croson, R.T.A. and Murnighan, J.K. (2000), Deception and Retribution in Repeated Ultimatum Bargaining, *Organizational Behavior and Human Decision Processes*, Vol. 83(2), pp. 235–259.

3.4. *Power Imbalance*

When the negotiation power is distributed unevenly, usually the more power-ful negotiators have more incentives to behave unethically. There are several reasons for such incentives. First, high-power negotiators are inclined to enforce their preferences over their less powerful opponents, just to display their power. They may also use hard strategies and tactics that are unethical, even from their own moral point of view, in order to emphasize this power. Second, powerful negotiators have a sense of control over others, which they would like to maintain for present and future negotiations. In order to main-tain control over their opponents, even unethical behavior seems reasonable. Third, powerful negotiators may assume that they can force their interests and goals upon their opponents, as they have enough power to avoid undesired consequences and punishments for their unethical behavior. They may con-sider themselves invulnerable and try to satisfy their desires in any possible way, including through the use of unethical behavior. Fourth, powerful nego-tiators are usually self-centered negotiators. Their self-serving approach may lead them to achieve their goals, even by deceiving their opponents or using other unethical, unaccepted strategies or tactics.[14] Fifth, powerful negotia-tors may act unethically, if they believe that other powerful negotiators have reached high outcomes by behaving in an unethical manner as well. Further-more, powerful negotiators interpret ethical behavior differently from their less powerful opponents. Due to their powerful position, they feel a sense of overconfidence in their own interpretation of what ethical behavior is. A sense of ambiguity regarding ethical issues does not disturb the clarity of their own unique self-serving perceptions of acceptable moral codes — the only perceptions that shape their actions and behaviors.[15] They do not care much about others' perceptions of acceptable moral codes, especially those of their opponents. Consequently, according to their own point of view they always behave ethically.

Nevertheless, powerful negotiators, despite feelings of invulnerability, are at risk when behaving unethically. They may aggravate their opponents,

---

[14]Pitesa, M. and Thau, S. (2013), Compliant Sinners, Obstinate Saints: How Power and Self-Focus Determine the Effectiveness of Social Influences in Ethical Decision Making, *Academy of Management Journal*, Vol. 56(3), pp. 635–658.

[15]Wiltermuth, S.S. and Flynn, T.F. (2013), Power, Moral Clarity and Punishment in the Workplace, *Academy of Management Journal*, Vol. 56(4), pp. 1002–1023.

which may lead the negotiation to an impasse. Even if they achieve their desired outcome, they may experience retribution and even revenge from their opponents or other parties, such as the public. Unethical behavior can also damage the negotiators' reputation and their future relationships with the same or other opponents. This type of behavior may also lead to damaging lawsuits, where opponents' demand compensation.

Finally, it also must be said that power does not always corrupt. Powerful negotiators can afford to be more generous and less self-serving than weak negotiators. They may have a broader perspective and show more sensitivity to their opponents' needs. It is possible to explain such contrasts through the association between powerful negotiators and their moral intensity. Thus, a high degree of moral intensity may influence even powerful negotiators to be just and honest, whereas a low degree of moral intensity may allow powerful negotiators to behave unethically.[16]

3.5. *Unethical Behavior and the Ability to Prevent Sanctions*

The ability to prevent sanctions, such as damaging the negotiators' reputation or facing a lawsuit, is not the only incentive for unethical behavior. Highly significant benefits can also serve as incentives for unethical behavior. When high benefits are associated with negotiators' behavior, they may feel a conflict of interest between the benefits they want, and the way they should behave. Actually, receiving benefits may be satisfying in the short-term, but the results of unethical behavior are a long-term concern. The greater the possible benefits, the greater the "appetite" for unethical behavior. Take, for example, politicians negotiating a bribe that would allow entrepreneurs forbidden advantages or overlook their illegal performances. The greater the offered bribe, the greater the possibility that the politicians will accept the bribe, despite possible public criticism or even having to face a potential lawsuit, in the event that they are caught. Similarly, salespeople often face ethical dilemmas between the short-term benefits of selling high by using unethical negotiations tactics, and their long-term goal of maintaining a good reputation as honest salespeople. It is also possible that offering material benefits in exchange for ethical behavior may be perceived by the negotiators

---

[16]DeCelles, K.A. DeRue, D.S. Margolis, J.D. and Ceranic, T.L. (2012), Does Power Corrupt or Enable? When and Why Power Facilitates Self-Interested Behavior, *Journal of Applied Psychology*, Vol. 97(3), pp. 681–689.

as an insult, and end in a negotiation impasse.[17] However, sometimes high material benefits may compensate for the "sacrifice" of ethical behavior, and an unethical settlement may be achieved.

If the opponents themselves do not punish the unethical negotiators for their behavior, the possibilities of getting away without public or other punishment are relatively good. This is true for several reasons. First, negotiations are often conducted away from the eyes of others, including the public. Second, unethical behavior is usually considered immoral, but is not perceived as illegal. Third, there are always possible explanations and rationalizations to justify unethical behavior — such as the particular circumstances that induced the behavior or the notion that the ends justify the means: For example, the negotiation outcome contributes to the public. Fourth, the power of the unethical negotiators justifies the behavior itself.

To conclude, both high benefits and the possibility of avoiding sanctions serve as incentives for maintaining and continuing to engage in unethical negotiating behavior.

3.6. *Some Personality Attributes*

Personality attributes reflect the characteristics that influence individuals' ethical perceptions and behavior. The main characteristics are gender, age and locus of control.[18]

Gender — It is often assumed that gender influences negotiation-related ethical behavior, because women negotiators are more sensitive to relationships with others. Thus, women behave in a more ethical manner than men. Men are more likely to be tempted to act unethically because they are less sensitive to relationships, and thus also to moral codes. However, this is not necessarily so. Both men and women's ethical behavior during negotiation depends on various intervening factors, such as their status (for example, there is no difference or very little difference between male and female chief

---

[17]Atran, S. and Axelrod, R. (2008), Reframing Sacred Values, *Negotiation Journal*, Vol. 24(3), pp. 221–246.

[18]The literature includes additional personality attributes that influence the level of ethical behavior, such as Machiavellianism, self-efficacy, self-esteem and religion, among others. However, it is beyond the scope of this chapter to review all of them. For a more detailed review, see: Craft, J.I. (2013), A Review of Empirical Ethical Decision-Making Literature 2004–2011, *Journal of Business Ethics*, Vol. 117(2), pp. 221–259.

executives) or culture, where culture influences ethical behavior more than gender.

Age — Age apparently influences negotiation-related ethical behavior; older negotiators are more inclined to behave ethically than younger negotiators. Perhaps maturity is essential for ethical sensitivity and ethical behavior. However, just as in the case of gender the correlation between age and ethical behavior may be influenced by other, stronger factors, such as culture.

Locus of control — "*Locus of control*" refers to the extent to which negotiators believe they can control the negotiation process and outcome. Negotiators with a strong *internal locus of control* are convinced that it is solely up to them to control the process and negotiation outcome. Negotiators with an *external locus of control* are convinced that external factors or circumstances are responsible for the negotiation outcome. Since it seems easier to behave unethically when it is possible to blame others or circumstances for the negotiation outcome, negotiators with an external locus of control tend to behave less ethically than negotiators with an internal locus of control.

4. Enjoying Unethical Behavior

Normative negotiators who behave unethically often feel anxiety, due to the gap between their actual unethical behavior and their wish to maintain a positive self image, both privately and within the group to which they belong. Such a gap generates *cognitive dissonance*, which is often solved by either overlooking their behavior or by self-justification — convincing themselves that their unethical behavior was the right thing to do under the circumstances. It is believed that negotiators who feel bad (guilty or ashamed) about their unethical behavior are less likely to engage in such behavior a second time.[19] However, some negotiators are attracted to the use of unethical tactics and enjoy using them with no cognitive dissonance at all. On the contrary, they feel good behaving unethically.[20] Some negotiators enjoy their unethical behavior, on the basis that it is "commonly accepted" — all

---

[19]Massi, L.L. (2005), Anticipated Guilt as Behavioral Motivation, *Human Communication Research*, Vol. 31(4), pp. 453–481.

[20]Ruedy, N.E. Moor, C. Gino, F. and Schweitzer, M.E. (2013), The Cheater's High: The Unexpected Affective Benefits of Unethical Behavior, *Journal of Personality and Social Psychology*, Vol. 105(4), pp. 531–548.

negotiators behave in this manner. For instance, it is reasonable to lie during the negotiation process because everybody lies. Other negotiators do not care about either their reputation or self image, whether in the short or long run. As a result, negative feelings are not associated with their unethical behavior; the opposite in fact is true — they enjoy it. Moreover, negotiators sometimes believe that unethical behavior during the process, such as using hard tactics, may make the negotiation more interesting and effective. Finally, the possibility of escaping the negative consequences of unethical behavior may seem challenging and therefore enhance the unethical behavior's attractiveness. Consequently, unethical behavior does not always trigger negative feelings; it can also trigger satisfaction and even pleasure, which are great internal benefits. When unethical behavior in itself serves as a benefit for negotiators, they are more likely to repeat such behavior in their forthcoming negotiations.

5. On Ethics and Trust

Ethical behavior and trust are strongly linked during the negotiation process. On the one hand, as long as negotiators believe in their opponents' ethical behavior, they can also expect and rely on their integrity and moral reactions, i.e. trust their opponents. It is also believed that negotiators who behave ethically can most likely be trusted by their opponents. On the other hand, a high level of trust between the negotiating parties can influence their perception of ethical behavior during the negotiation process and even afterwards. However, if negotiators feel obliged to behave ethically, while the other parties do not, the negotiators' trust in the others may result in serious losses. Hence, since negotiators are not always acquainted with the ethical norms of their opponents or do not suspect these norms, trust may be broken and replaced by mistrust.

Practical Applications

• Since the conception of ethics is somewhat vague and ambiguous, it is important for you, as a negotiator, to understand what is perceived by other negotiators to be ethical or unethical behavior. The sensation of ethical or unethical behavior that negotiators feel during the negotiation may determine the development of the negotiation process and its outcome. If you can understand the differences between you and your opponents' ethical perceptions, and the reason for such differences, you can minimize the emotional problems (such as anger and remorse) elicited by the use of what you believe to be the unethical behavior of your opponents. At the same time, you can avoid behaving unethically in the eyes of your opponents, as it might put the negotiation process and outcome at risk.

- There are various grounds upon which negotiators base their ethical or unethical decision-making. If you understand these factors, you can control at least some of them. For example, if you understand your opponents' need for honor and respect as a basis for perceiving you as an ethical negotiator, you should compliment them and show a high level of appreciation. However, these compliments should be as authentic as possible. Be careful, as false compliments may be perceived as empty flattery, or worse — hypocrisy, and of course as unethical behavior on your part.

- Seemingly, an unsatisfactory negotiation outcome may imply an unethical process. However, your opponents may often consider negotiation as ethical, not only according to its outcome or cost-effectiveness. They may also consider your reaction to their social needs as ethical or unethical behavior. For example, even if the negotiation outcome is lower than your opponents expected, developing a good relationship, may serve as compensation for the less-than-satisfactory low outcome, and the negotiation process would not be perceived by your opponents as unethical. Thus, just remember the compensation effect, which is highly important during the negotiation process.

- Try to understand the rules of conduct of your opponents' culture. You do not have to identify with it or behave according to these moral codes. However, you have to try to understand them in order to avoid erroneous decision-making during the negotiation process.

- Do not let your first impression of your new opponents mislead you. Take your time; get to know them and try to ascertain whether their behavior is ethical or unethical. If, at first, you perceive your opponents' behavior as unethical, you may also interpret their later acts and decisions in a negative manner. If, on the other hand, you perceive their behavior as ethical in the beginning, you may interpret their later acts in a positive way. In both cases, you may be mistaken. First impressions are not the best guide. Moreover, take into account that your opponents may also change their behavior — from ethical to unethical and *vice versa* — during the negotiation process. You must continuously evaluate your opponents' behavior anew during the negotiation process.

- There are many incentives encouraging your opponents' unethical behavior. The first is the belief that negotiators who are more successful are those who have the ability to deceive others, but not be deceived themselves. However, deception is not always a recipe for a high-quality outcome. The consequences of deception and other unethical behaviors may be harsh. If you detect deception, do not hesitate to retaliate with the threat of hard consequences or ending the negotiation process entirely.

- One important incentive for unethical behavior is the desire for benefits. Fear of sanctions is, however, an incentive to avoid unethical behavior. Therefore, it is essential to use both the "stick and the carrot" in order to prevent situations that may produce unethical behavior on your opponents' part.

- Some negotiators simply enjoy behaving unethically. In this case, the "stick and the carrot" will not be of help. Similarly, retribution will not be beneficial either. Just leave the negotiation "table"; otherwise, you will probably face a very unpleasant negotiation process.

Chapter 11

Trust, Suspicion and Distrust

"Love all, trust a few, do wrong to none."

William Shakespeare

There is some misunderstanding regarding the meanings of trust, distrust and suspicion in negotiation. There are many misconceptions about the need, influence and results of these terms within the negotiation framework.

1. Understanding Trust, Distrust and Suspicion

1.1. *Understanding the Meaning of Trust and Distrust*

Trust is the negotiators' reliance on, or confidence in, the integrity, behavior and good faith of their opponents. Negotiators trust their opponents as long as they believe in their opponents' positive motivations and good will and, most importantly, if they believe their opponents are trustworthy.[1] Negotiators expect good intentions, and rewarding behavior to result from trusting their opponents. They also believe (or at least hope) that their opponents will not take advantage of their confidence, even if they have an opportunity to do so. If all negotiating parties believe that the others have good intentions and can be relied upon, trust may become the basis for cooperation during the negotiation process, and even continue after negotiations have been completed. However, it is hard to determine whether trust generates cooperation between parties

---

[1] For an interesting discussion of the importance of trustworthiness, see Tullberg, J. (2008), Trust — The Importance of Trustfulness versus Trustworthiness, *The Journal of Socio-Economics*, Vol. 37(5), pp. 2059–2071.

or is the result of such cooperation.[2] If one of the parties is trusting and the others are not, the consequences may be harmful for one or all parties involved.

Distrust involves negotiators' negative expectations of their opponents, whom are perceived as unreliable and as having malevolent intentions. Negotiators also distrust their opponents when they expect offensive behavior, or when their positive expectations have been violated. If negotiators feel obliged to act with integrity and comply with moral codes of behavior, while their opponents do not, their trust in their opponents becomes risky and may lead to great losses. In this case, trust may easily turn into distrust.

Thus, both trust and distrust are consequences of negotiators' perceptions or expectations about their opponents' intentions and behaviors. Anticipating opponents' creditable intentions may result in negotiators' readiness to accept their opponents' behavior, promises and willingness to cooperate. Conversely, distrust may result in negotiators repelling their opponents, opposing their offers and a lack of desire to cooperate. Negotiators who distrust their opponents may also try to gain as much as possible, even at the expense of misleading their opponents, which could lead to a negotiation impasse. It is therefore possible that distrust may hinder negotiators from achieving beneficial negotiation outcomes.

1.2. *Understanding Suspicion*

Negotiators may make two problematic mistakes. They can either distrust trustworthy opponents, or they can trust opponents who later turn out to be untrustworthy.[3] *Suspicion* is often the result of these problems. Since negotiators are not always acquainted with their opponents' intentions and norms of behavior, they may experience ambiguity regarding their opponents' expected behavior during the negotiation process. Suspicion relates to negotiators' doubts about their opponents' intentions, motives and behaviors. Suspicion is different from attitudes of trust and distrust. Trusting or distrusting negotiators have definite expectations about their opponents' behavior

[2]Ferrin, D.L. Bligh, M.C. and Kohles, J.C. (2007), Can I Trust You to Trust Me? A Theory of Trust, Monitoring and Cooperation in Interpersonal and Intergroup Relationships, *Group & Organization Management*, Vol. 32(4), pp. 465–499.

[3]Fetchenhauer, D. and Dunning, D. (2009), Do People Trust Too Much or Too Little? *Journal of Economic Psychology*, Vol. 30(3), pp. 263–276.

(positive in the case of trust, negative in the case of distrust), whereas being suspicious relates to vague ambiguous feelings and expectations.[4] Suspicion can be considered a stage — located somewhere between trust and distrust, when negotiators still do not really know what they can expect of their opponents.

2. Positive and Negative Aspects of Trust, Distrust and Suspicion in Negotiation

Trust on the one hand, and distrust and suspicion on the other hand, are considered opposites. Trust is perceived positively, as being essential to negotiation processes, whereas distrust and suspicion are perceived negatively as being harmful and damaging.

2.1. *On the Positive and Negative Aspects of Trust*

It is commonly argued that without trust it is hard, if not impossible, to reach a negotiation agreement. Moreover, it is often believed that high trust levels in negotiation can generate cooperation between parties, thus resulting in an integrative agreement, which creates surplus benefits for negotiators as well as their opponents.

However, trust may cause negotiators to accept the information provided by their opponents unquestioningly, due to their confidence in the trustworthiness and good intentions of these opponents. Therefore, trust is likely to decrease the chances of essential intelligence searches before and during the negotiation process, which may lead to negotiators' erroneous decisions. Moreover, trusting negotiators may be vulnerable to their opponents' malicious intentions and behavior during the negotiation process.

2.2. *On the Positive and Negative Aspects of Distrust and Suspicion*

Conversely to trust, distrust and suspicion are often perceived as damaging to the negotiation process and outcome. Distrust and suspicion is sometimes perceived as insulting. Opponents' feelings may be hurt, engendering mutual feelings of counter-distrust and suspicion. In this sense, distrust and suspicion

---

[4]Sinaceur, M. (2010), Suspending Judgment to Create Value: Suspicion and Trust in Negotiation, *Journal of Experimental Social Psychology*, Vol. 46(3), pp. 543–550.

may create a vicious circle, which escalates conflict and increases competition between the negotiators and their opponents, thus further amplifying distrust and suspicion.[5]

However, distrust and suspicion, despite their negative perceptions, are not necessarily harmful, and even serve at times as an important positive role in negotiation. Assuming that opponents have hidden motives that underlie their behavior, distrust and especially suspicion, stimulate negotiators to thoroughly check any offer and information provided by their opponents. They can also collect more essential information, in order to anticipate and cope with any offending behavior on the part of their opponents and protect themselves from such behavior. Practically, distrust and suspicion may create defense mechanisms and coping strategies that protect negotiators from opponents' manipulations and exploitative strategies and tactics.[6] In this sense, distrust and suspicion may produce more value than trust in negotiation.

2.3. *The Role of Trust, Distrust and Suspicion in Reducing Uncertainty*

Negotiation is an uncertain process. Negotiators usually know their opponents' opening positions as well as their own. Afterwards, some extent of uncertainty regarding the negotiation process and outcome takes place, even if the preparation for the negotiation has been rigorous and insightful. Uncertainty is always intimidating and negotiators are motivated to reduce uncertainty as much as possible. One way of reducing uncertainty is through exhibiting trusting behavior. Trusting negotiators expect rewarding and beneficial behavior, and exclude any possibility of unexpected offensive behavior on the part of their opponents. Thus, trust may reduce uncertainty by narrowing the perceived possibility of negative surprises during the negotiation process. Of course, this may turn out to be a mistake.

---

[5]Butler, J.K. (1999), Trust, Expectations, Information Sharing, Climate of Trust, and Negotiation Effectiveness and Efficiency, *Group and Organization Management*, Vol. 24(2), pp. 217–238.

[6]Oza, S.S. Srivastava, J. and Koukova, N.T. (2010), How Suspicion Mitigates the Effect of Influence Tactics, *Organizational Behavior and Human Decision Processes*, Vol. 112(1), pp. 1–10.

Distrust and suspicion may also reduce uncertainty by searching for, and often providing, necessary intelligence about their opponents' possible unexpected and harmful behavior. Such intelligence decreases the opponents' ability to surprise negotiators with unexpected behavior, thus contributing to reduced uncertainty. Distrust and suspicion may also help negotiators' avoid making errors and aid them in making the right decisions, necessary to protect themselves at critical moments during the negotiation process.

Moreover, negotiators, as well as their opponents, may prefer immediate benefits to future uncertain benefits. Trust, followed by cooperation, is not always valuable or profitable in the short-term. In a sense, the desire for immediate benefits is a result of both negotiators and opponents' immediate greediness. Trust can restrain opponents' greediness to a certain extent, but not completely. In contradiction, distrust and suspicion can prevent immediate greediness by providing intelligence, alerting against opponents' damaging intentions, followed by taking precautions, such as reducing negotiators' confidence in their opponents.

3. Factors Affecting Trust, Distrust and Suspicion

Some negotiators prefer to trust their opponents, while others do not. Several factors influence negotiators' inclination to trust, distrust or suspect their opponents. The main factors are: Negotiators' identification with opponents, negotiators' experience, perception of opponents' characteristics, reciprocation tendencies and culture.

3.1. *Negotiators' Identification with Opponents*

High identification with opponents sometimes occurs with charismatic individuals, good friends, family members or close group members. This generates an often-unrealistic inclination to attribute favorable characteristics — such as honesty and credibility — to these individuals. Negotiators' identification with their opponents is a result of attributing such favorable characteristics to them, whereas trust is related to negotiators' identification (at least high identification) with opponents. Moreover, in the case of trust on the basis of identification, there is often an emotional aspect attached to it. Such emotion further enhances trust. Usually, there is no inclination to suspect or distrust opponents with whom negotiators identify.

3.2. *Negotiators' Experience*

To a great extent, negotiators' previous experience with negotiations influences them to trust, distrust or suspect their opponents' intentions and behavior. For example, negotiators who trusted their opponents in the past and were disappointed or hurt will probably find it difficult to trust again — not only as regards their current opponents, but any opponents. Suspecting or even distrusting their opponents may simply become their default behavior.

3.3. *Perception of Opponents' Characteristics*

It seems that opponents' trustworthiness is one important antecedent to negotiators' trust, distrust or suspicion. Negotiators' perception of their opponents' trustworthiness depends on several characteristics, such as perceptions about their integrity, honesty and benevolence.

Perceptions about opponents' integrity are based on the opponents' behavior, according to just or ethical codes of conduct in the long run. It is noteworthy that in order for trust to ensue, it is essential that the ethical codes of conduct, accepted by both negotiators and opponents, are compatible.

Perceptions about opponents' honesty are based on their reliability, even if it means opponents' need to ignore their own self-serving interests — before, during and after the negotiation.

Negotiators' perceptions about opponents' benevolence reflect the opponents' concern for the negotiators' interests and expectations, and their readiness to reward the negotiators generously for their trust.

Other opponents' characteristics that may serve as an antecedent to negotiators' trust, distrust or suspicion are opponents' reputation (good reputation — trust, bad reputation — suspicion or distrust), various skills that are important to negotiators (such as a high level of medical skills), and similarity between opponents and negotiators.

Of course — trust, distrust or suspicion may be a result of one of these characteristics or a combination of several. The more opponents' characteristics are perceived as trustworthy, the more trust may be invested in them. The less trustworthy opponents' characteristics are perceived, the more incentive for suspicion and distrust develops.

3.4. *Reciprocation Tendencies*

The decision to trust may be based upon negotiators' estimation of the likelihood that their opponents will reciprocate by rewarding their trustful behavior, even if such behavior is not in the opponents' self-interest. This type of anticipation for reciprocity may result from previous experience with the opponents. It can also be based on negotiators' belief that their opponents are somehow in their debt, due to their assistance and good will in previous interactions. Moreover, anticipating reciprocity may be due to negotiators' belief that certain concessions on their part will serve as an incentive for at least some concessions on the part of their opponents. In addition, there is an assumption that reciprocity and good will can be expected, as the opponents would not like to violate the trust invested in them.

It is assumed that reciprocation will generate a positive circle of expectations and behavior, where both parties will make concessions, until an integrative agreement is reached. However, such reciprocation assumptions may be unrealistic. It is possible that the negotiators' expectations for reciprocity are not met, as their opponents decide to take advantage of the trust invested in them in order to satisfy their own self-serving interests or for other unknown reasons.

3.5. *Culture*

Another factor that may influence the negotiators' preference for trust, distrust or suspicion is culture and values. Negotiators of different cultures vary in their willingness to trust one another. For example, collectivistic negotiators trust their opponents less and suspect them more than individualistic negotiators. Individualistic negotiators often make impulsive decisions about whether or not to trust their opponents, and sometimes simply trust their opponents until there is a reason not to. In addition, negotiators who identify with collectivist cultures *"tight cultures"* — where the norms of conduct are clearly and strictly defined and usually imposed by social sanctions — differ in their trust inclinations from negotiators who identify with individualistic cultures which are *"loose" cultures*, where the rules of conduct are flexible and informal. Negotiators who identify with "tight", collectivist cultures tend to expect less from their opponents than negotiators who identify with "loose", individualistic cultures.[7] Furthermore, perceptions about the opponents' concessions also differ between negotiators

---

[7]Gunia, B.C. Brett, J.M. Nandkeolyar, A.K. and Kamdar, D. (2011), Paying the Price: Culture, Trust, and Negotiation Consequences, *Journal of Applied Psychology*, Vol. 96(4), pp. 774–789.

of more collectivist cultures and negotiators of more individualistic cultures. For example, negotiators of "loose", individualistic cultures may make concessions and expect their opponents to reciprocate with counter-concessions. However, their opponents, who identify with "tight", collectivist cultures, may perceive concessions as a sort of weakness. As a result, they do not reciprocate with counter-concessions; they simply employ pressure in order to "convince" negotiators to make more and further concessions.

Generally, as far as cultural values are concerned, negotiators would prefer to trust opponents with the same codes of conduct, especially ethical and loyalty codes, rather than opponents with unknown codes of conduct.[8]

4. Trust may be Risky

The inclination to trust is closely correlated with the inclination to take risks, as trustfulness exposes negotiators to vulnerability if their opponents betray and violate their trust. Such a violation of trust may become very costly, as trustfulness may become a source of negotiators' exploitation by their seemingly trustworthy opponents. Seemingly, it does not make sense for negotiators, of their own free will, to make themselves vulnerable to their opponents and put themselves in a risky situation. However, there are several reasons why negotiators trust their opponents, even though they know they are taking a risk.

4.1. *Predicting Abilities*

Negotiators often think they can predict their opponents' behavior, which may convince them to take risks. For example, high risk-taking negotiators may be inclined to trust their suspected opponents, if they predict high benefits from the negotiation in return for their trust. In this case, they may be less concerned about risking the potential betrayal of their opponents.

Trusting opponents on the basis of predicting their trustworthy behavior may be misleading, as the presumed ability to accurately predict one's opponents' behavior is dubious.

---

[8]Jones, G.R. and George, J.M. (1998), The Experience and Evolution of Trust: Implications for Cooperation and Teamwork, *Academy of Management Review*, Vol. 23(3), pp. 531–546.

4.2. *Relationships and Past Experience*

Opponents' trustfulness is often based upon relationships, acquaintanceships, and past successful negotiation with the same opponents as reliable negotiation partners. However, a reputation for being reliable, as well as close relationships or at least good acquaintanceships, do not necessarily guarantee opponents' trustworthiness. On the basis of such attributes, negotiators may convince themselves that they are free to make substantial investments, both emotional and tangible (such as large sums of money), in their opponents, expecting benefits in exchange for their investments.

The end of such stories may be distressing if the predicted reliable, reputable institutions or individuals opponents defraud and deceive negotiators, creating a serious breach of trust, leading to political crisis (such as war) or economic crisis (such as a stock exchange collapse). Thus, it is questionable whether negotiators can base their decisions on relationship when calculating the likelihood of their opponents' integrity or inclination to be trustworthy. Negotiators who base their opponents' trustworthiness upon their past experience or previous relationship, often do not take into consideration the possibility that their opponents may change their behavior, and their trustworthiness may evaporate.

4.3. *Opponents' Reputation*

In the absence of other information regarding the opponents, negotiators are inclined to rely on their opponents' reputation, as an important consideration when making their decisions. Thus, even the mere decision to negotiate (as well as how to negotiate) may be influenced by the opponents' reputation. However, the opponents' reputation in itself may be inaccurate or even completely untrue. Therefore, predicting opponents' behavior and trustworthiness on a reputation basis is risky and may lead negotiators to make erroneous decisions during the negotiation process.

Negotiators who trust their opponents on the basis of reputation may later find themselves negotiating with opponents who are untrustworthy.[9]

To conclude, decisions regarding trusting opponents may be more accurate and less risky after a measure of suspicion leads to a better and more

---

[9]Lewicki, R.J. and Tomlinson, E. (2003), The Effects of Reputation and Post Violation Communication on Trust and Distrust, *SSRN Working Paper Series*, June, 2003.

accurate understanding of the opponents' behavior than prediction, past experience or reputation.

5. Some Insights into the Violation of Trust

Violation of trust is associated with opponents who breach trust — disproving negotiators' expectations about their opponents' behavior and norms of conduct. Thus, it may be assumed that a violation of trust must involve opponents' awareness of both negotiators' expectations and the accepted norms of conduct. In the absence of such awareness, opponents may not be considered as trust violators by negotiators. However, contrary to this assumption, even when opponents are not conscious of negotiators' expectations and the current rules of conduct, if they breach them, they are still engaged in a *violation of trust*. In other words, a violation of trust can exist even when the opponents are not aware of such a violation having taken place.

Violation of negotiators' trust may be harmful — both in terms of material loss and emotional disappointment. The main reasons for opponents' violation of trust can be seen on a continuum scale, from an unintended violation of trust on one side of the scale, to an intentional violation of trust on the other. The scale includes three main patterns of *trust violations*: Unintended violations, circumstantial violations and premeditated and intentional violations of trust.[10]

5.1. *Unintended Violations of Trust*

An unintended violation of trust is accidental; there is no intention on the part of the opponents to breach negotiators' trust, disappoint their expectations or break the accepted rules of conduct. For example, calculation errors — conveying incorrect information which is believed to be true — occasional misunderstandings, mood changes and the *observer effect* may all cause opponents' unintentionally untrustworthy conduct. Mood changes appear randomly — for example, anger, nervousness and frustration. Such random moods may momentarily change the opponents' behavior by shaking up and interfering with their usual trustworthy behavior. The *observer effect*

---

[10]Elangovan, A.R. and Shapiro, D.L. (1988), Betrayal of Trust in Organizations, *Academy of Management Review*, Vol. 23(3) pp. 547–566.

relates to a change in the opponents' behavior as a reaction to their being observed at a certain time, by people who are uninvolved directly in the negotiation (such as family members, researchers, etc.). Such observations may cause a temporary change in the opponents' behavior, making them appear unintentionally untrustworthy. In addition, opponents may exhibit typical unpleasant patterns of behavior, such as impatience or a loss of self-control which may be followed by unintentional and unplanned accidental violations of trust.

It is noteworthy that such unintentional behavior occurs without fore-thought, and with no intention of causing harmful consequences. When violators realize they have unintentionally violated the trust invested in them, they often consider it as unfortunate and regrettable.

Even unintended trust violations by opponents can be painful and frustrating to trusting negotiators, especially in on-going negotiation. However, when negotiators understand that no bad intentions were involved in the violation, it is possible that the pain and frustration will be temporary or, in the best case scenario, completely disregarded.

5.2. *Circumstantial Trust Violations*

In this case, it is possible to assume that at the beginning of the negotiation process, neither party intends to violate the other party's trust. However, maintaining opponents' trustworthiness becomes difficult if an opportunity to achieve a desired goal by violating trust appears. In certain situations, if violating trust seems more profitable than maintaining it, it is very likely that a decision to violate trust will at least be considered, even if it is not actually carried out.

Thus, a worthwhile opportunity for significant gains, which occurs during the negotiation process, may be so tempting as to cause a violation of trust; for example, when a third party offers higher benefits without negotiation or, in general, a better alternative to the negotiated agreement (*BATNA*) turns up. Another possibility of a circumstantial trust violation is when the violation occurs due to unforeseen economic or technological developments, which tempt opponents to change their strategies in an unexpected way, causing them, quite suddenly, to act in an untrustworthy manner.

In cases of circumstantial violations of trust, negotiators may be less sensitive if they find out that their opponents' violation took place due to unforeseen developments, rather than if the violators' opponents were tempted by a *BATNA*.[11]

5.3. *Premeditated Intentional Violations of Trust*

Premeditated intentional trust violations relate to conscious and cognitive decisions to breach negotiators' trust, disappoint their expectations or breach the norms of conduct involved in the negotiation. There are several possible reasons for such premeditated decisions to violate trust, such as:

- **Self-serving motivations**: Self-serving motivation does not exclude causing hurt, damage and harm to trusting negotiators.[12] The need to promote and satisfy self-interests is often naturally more important than maintaining trust relations with the other party, and may cause premeditated trust violations.
- **Pressures**: Difficult pressures, such as a financial crisis or fierce competition, may sometimes lead to premeditated untrustworthy behavior. For example, suppliers who find themselves enmeshed in cash-flow difficulties may be tempted to undertake, in exchange for advanced payment, terms of supply (substance, quality and time), which they know in advance they are unable to fulfill.
- **Exploiting information**: Business or other forms of espionage may be a reason for trust violations. Information-gathering about the other parties' weaknesses — such as time constraints, financial conditions, competitors' and other secrets — may be of great benefit during the negotiation process, with the same or other similar negotiators. This may serve as a temptation to use the "pretence negotiation" strategy,[13] which is often used only to gather maximum information from trusting negotiators, but with no intention of actually reaching a final agreement.
- **Retribution**: Motivation to avenge past real or perceived wrongdoings (such as a previous violation of trust by negotiators), perpetrated by the negotiators, may serve as an incentive for opponents to engage in premeditated, intentional trust violations.

---

[11] Bohnet, I. and Zeckhauser, R. (2004), Trust, Risk and Betrayal, *Journal of Economic Behavior & Organization*, Vol. 55(4), pp. 467–484.

[12] Galdwell, C. Davis, B. and Devine, J.A. (2009), Trust, Faith, and Betrayal: Insights from Management for Wise Behavior, *Journal of Business Ethics*, Vol. 84(1), pp. 103–114.

[13] See Chapter 7 of this book.

- **The shadow of suspicion**: The shadow of suspicion may be a result of the negotiators' bad reputation or bad rumors, whether true or false, spread by their competitors before the negotiation. Such suspicions may serve as a sufficient reason to intentionally violate the expectations of the suspected negotiators.
- **The degree of benefits**: Previous knowledge of possible high benefits due to violating trust may enhance opponents' inclination to engage in premeditated violations of trust.

If premeditated, intentional violations of trust are detected, negotiators may react harshly — either by leaving the negotiation table or by a partial or entire decrease in motivation to continue negotiating with the same opponents in the future.

While intentional violations of trust may not be detected during the current negotiation process, they might be detected afterwards. In this case, it is most likely to cause problems in implementing the negotiation outcome. Intentional violations of trust may also have an unfavorable influence on the future relationship of the parties, expressed by antagonism and resentment towards the violators. Furthermore, these types of intentional acts can tighten the negotiators' surveillance and monitoring of the violator, and may even lead to a desire for revenge.

Detecting trust violations, especially premeditated intentional violations, are emotionally charged events for trusting negotiators.[14] Therefore, the reactions of the injured negotiators may be notably harsh. In addition to other emotions, violations of trust frequently result in negotiators' blaming themselves and feeling foolish: They should have "known better". In this case, the severe reaction is not so much because of the loss they have suffered due to the violation of trust, but rather because of the *"sucker effect"* sensation they experience. Actually, as a result of this *"sucker effect"*, negotiators respond with greater resentment to a loss, due to the trust violation than to otherwise economically identical losses — such as identical losses in the stock exchange market.[15]

---

[14]Schoorman, F. Mayer, R.C. and Davis, J. (2007), An Integrative Model of Organizational Trust: Past, Present, and Future, *Academy of Management Review*, Vol. 32(2), pp. 344–354.

[15]Effron, D. and Miller, D.T. (2011), Reducing Exposure of Trust-Related Risks to Avoid Self-blame, *Personality and Social Psychology Bulletin*, Vol. 37(2), pp. 181–192.

6. Reduced Risk of Trust Violations

As the risk of trust violations is crucial to the negotiation process and outcome, it is important to consider the factors that can reduce such risk.

6.1. *Opponents' Self-Interest*

While at times, self-serving motivations do not exclude causing damage to trusting negotiators' opponents, at other times, self-interest may reduce the risk of trust violations. When it is in the opponents' self-interest to be considered trustworthy,[16] they may think twice before violating negotiators' trust. For example, a department store in which customers like to shop may prefer not to raise its prices with no significant justification. This is not because there is no temptation to raise prices at the customers' expense, but because of the store's self-serving interests. The department store does not want to take advantage of its customers because it prefers to retain them as customers rather than lose them to competitors. Therefore, it is in line with the department store's self-interest to remain trustworthy.

6.2. *Third-party Involvement*

Another reason for opponents' being trustworthy is when it is forced by a third party. For example, in many cases trust in international negotiations is guaranteed by a forceful third party, who has an influence on all parties involved in the negotiation, either because it provides guarantees, or through its power to reward or sanction negotiators who violate the expected trust.

6.3. *Reduced Risk of Trust Violations between Strangers*

An interesting example of how to reduce the risk of trust violations between strangers is that of online markets, where trust is established between negotiators who often have no common social or cultural background, and who are also situated at geographical distances. In such online markets, buyers and sellers interact with limited communication and apparent anonymity. The uncertainty of buying and selling in such markets might be very risky, unless provided with certain mechanisms to guarantee the trustworthiness of both suppliers and buyers. The huge size of the transactions conducted

---

[16]Fetchenhauer, D. and Dunning, D. (2009), Do People Trust Too Much or Too Little? *Journal of Economic Psychology*, Vol. 30(3), pp. 263–276.

through online markets indicates that the risk of trust violations, even between unknown strangers, can be reduced. Besides the cost benefit of the purchase,[17] it is the ratings of the products, the ratings of sellers and buyers as well as the information received through social networks, which enable the transactions to take place with reduced risk.[18]

Ratings and information: At times, it is the self-interests of the sellers to guarantee refunds for offended buyers, which results in good ratings in the social networks, thus enhancing trust in these sellers. In other instances, such as in regard to consumer websites, there are possibilities to receive feedback regarding the trustworthiness of particular sellers and guarantees for buyers' payments. The feedback received for each seller and buyer may influence their trustworthiness, and therefore the probability of the transaction. Thus, reducing the violation of trust is possible even in transactions between complete strangers, provided it is controlled by a mechanism of tracking the trustworthiness of the involved parties.

Deterrence: Monitoring and surveillance are helpful in deterring opponents from violating trust and therefore reducing risk. Early detection of violations, by surveillance, may prevent trust violations and reduce possible damages. Due to changing conditions and uncertainty, in order to reduce risk and guarantee trustworthiness, negotiators may detect, observe and monitor their opponents' activities — either through a third party or by themselves. Such surveillance and monitoring often yields rewards for being trustworthy on the one hand, and punishments for violating trust on the other hand. When trustworthiness is based on surveillance and monitoring, the degree of confidence in the opponents' positive behavior can be relatively high. It is sometimes argued that reducing the risk by monitoring and surveillance should be excluded from the perceptions of trust. However, the perception of trust has two focal points: Expectations of positive intentions of the opponents' behaviors, as well as negotiators' willingness to accept vulnerability.[19]

---

[17]Evans, A.M. and Krueger, J.I. (2011), Elements of Trust: Risk and Perspective-Taking, *Journal of Experimental Social Psychology*, Vol. 47(1), pp. 171–177.

[18]Gau, S. Wang, M. and Leskovec, J. (2011), The Role of Social Networks in Online Shopping: Information Passing, Price of Trust, and Consumer Choice. Published in Proceedings of the ACM 12th Conference on Electronic Commerce, pp. 157–156, ACM, New York, NY.

[19]Fulmer, C.A. and Gelfand, M.J. (2012), At what level (and in Whom) We Trust: Trust across Multiple Organizational Levels, *Journal of Management*, Vol. 38, pp. 1167–1230.

Accordingly, deterrence might be an integral part of maintaining opponents' trustworthiness.

By and large, when deterrence is the reason behind opponents' trustworthiness — such as in the case where trustworthiness is chosen only to avoid being penalized — or where trustworthiness is guaranteed by negotiators' surveillance and monitoring — negotiators can have more confidence in their opponents' trustworthiness than in other cases where negotiators decide to trust their opponents. Based on deterrence, negotiators' decisions to trust their opponents are reasonably made based upon relatively accurate information and evaluations of their opponents' response.

7. Can Trust Violations be Rehabilitated?

It goes without saying that rehabilitation of trust is much more difficult and painful than its violation. In the fable "The Peasant and the Snake", the famous Russian fabulist, Ivan Krilov (1769–1844), describes the following metaphor[20]: A snake once glided up to a peasant's house and said: "Dear neighbor let us live peaceably together on friendly terms. You need not be on your guard against me any longer. You can see for yourself that I have changed my skin this spring and that I have become quite a different creature from what I was." The peasant, however, was not convinced. He seized his cudgel and cried out:

"Though you have got a new skin, your heart is just the same as the old one" and with that, he killed the snake straightway. Krilov adds: "If you have ever violated trust, there is no sense in wearing a new veil. Whatever you wear, you may end up in the same way as the snake".

The metaphor does not assign great likelihood to the rehabilitation of trust, once it has been lost, which is in fact very problematic. Trust, once violated by untrustworthy opponents — especially if the violation was premeditated and intentional — may never be fully rehabilitated.[21] Trust rehabilitation may be risky. It may revive the negotiators' vulnerability, and cause a repeat performance of the harmful strategies and tactics that were previously used by their opponents. Moreover, trust rehabilitation involves confronting and

---

[20] Kalston, W.R.S (1871), Krilof and His Fables, 3rd Edition, Strahan & Co. Publishers.
[21] Schweitzer, M.E. Hershey, J.C. and Bradlow, E.T. (2006), Promises and Lies: Restoring Violated Trust, *Organizational Behavior and Human Decision Processes*, Vol. 101(1), pp. 1–19.

coping with practical and, especially, emotional challenges, which are difficult to overcome. Nevertheless, it is sometimes possible to rehabilitate trust under certain conditions:[22]

7.1. *Toleration*

Toleration implies the offended negotiators' willingness to tolerate and even forgive the violators. Such toleration may be due to negotiators' acknowledgement that their opponents, who violated their trust, are committed to not exploiting their trust again. Such toleration may help to reduce the emotional anxiety of the offended negotiators, who have suffered pain, loss and self-blame. Such toleration and, in some cases, even forgiveness, may change the atmosphere between the parties — from negative to positive — and consequently assist in the rehabilitation of trust.

7.2. *Communication*

Needless to say, communication between parties is essential for trust rehabilitation. In the hopes of rebuilding trust, the violators are often the first to communicate, conveying explanations, apologies, regrets and excuses. If the offended negotiators accept such communications, a process of trust rehabilitation may ensue. However, each of the above communications has its own advantages and constraints:

- Explanations: Drawing from the above metaphor of the "peasant and the snake", the snake's explanation — that now, after changing his skin, he is a new creature — did not help him very much. The perception of the attributes of the explainers, such as their integrity and reliability as well as the substance of the explanation, significantly influences the acknowledgment of the explanation by the offended negotiators, and their readiness to rebuild their relations with the trust violators.
- Apologies and regrets: The timing of apologies and regrets is of importance. The closer they are to the violation incident, the more effective they are in influencing the tolerance and forgiveness of the offended negotiators. Both apologies and regrets are also more influential when they are perceived as truthful, and if they are accompanied by taking personal

---

[22]For a comprehensive interesting discussion, see Kramer, R.M. and Lewicki, R.J. (2010), Repairing and Enhancing Trust: Approaches to Reducing Organizational Trust Deficits, *The Academy of Management Annals*, Vol. 4(1), pp. 245–277.

responsibility for correcting the problems the violation caused. However, sometimes apologies and regrets may have the opposite influence. The offended negotiators may perceive apologies and regrets as an admission of guilt, which may only worsen the degree of distrust between the parties.

- Excuses and justifications: Excuses and justifications are perceived as self-serving mechanisms, intended to reduce the violators' responsibility for failing to fulfill the negotiators' expectations.[23] They are aimed at minimizing the violators' feelings of guilt, as well as reducing possible punishment. Excuses and justifications may be accepted by the offended negotiators if they are strong, i.e. are backed up by facts, and if they are used only once. The repeated use of excuses and justifications may be rejected by the offended negotiators, further weakening the perceived reliability of the trust violators.

Regaining the offended negotiators' trust solely through verbal communication (explanations, apologies, excuses and justifications) is often insufficient. In order to restore trust following its violation, mere verbal expressions do not provide sufficient guarantees to ensure future trustworthiness. Therefore, offended negotiators often seek something more substantial than just talk before they agree to trust their opponents in the future. Apparently, there is a need for a tangible mechanism that will minimize the possibility of a repeated trust violation; for example, policies and procedures for preventing future violations, including monitoring and punishing the violators' opponents.[24] Such procedures may include legal contracts, compensation for the past violation, and "*hostage posting*" — depositing an item which is of importance to the violator and can be confiscated in the case of a repeated violation. In addition, possibilities for monitoring calculations, transparency and cooperation demanded from the violators' opponents, can serve as a foundation for trust rehabilitation. Such mechanisms may have more influence upon trust rehabilitation than explanations, apologies and other verbal attempts to obtain the offended negotiators' agreement to engage in trust rehabilitation.

---

[23]Schlenker, B.R. Pontari, B.A. and Christopher, A.N. (2001), Excuses and Character: Personal and Social Implications of Excuses, *Personality and Social Psychology Bulletin*, Vol. 5(1), pp. 15–32.

[24]Dirks, K.T. Kim, P.H. Ferrin, D.L. and Cooper, C.D. (2011), Understanding the Effects of Substantive Responses on Trust Following a Transgression, *Organization Behavior and Human Decision Processes*, Vol. 114(2), pp. 87–103.

Practical Applications

- Do not assume that trusting your opponents is essential for a proper negotiation process, collaboration and an integrative outcome. Trustfulness may make you vulnerable; thus, your opponents' behavior may become harmful and damaging. Being trusting may also "blind" you to the possible manipulation of your opponents. It is possible that suspicion and distrust may motivate you to search for essential information about your opponents and, at the same time, serve as a defense mechanism and coping strategy against your opponents' potential manipulations. In this sense, suspicions and distrust may be valuable to you before and during the negotiation process. Thus, try to maintain the right balance between a certain amount of trust on one hand, and a certain amount of suspicion — and even distrust — on the other. This way you will benefit from both the advantages of distrust and suspicions, as well as the advantages of trust.

- Trusting your opponents can be risky and even costly. Negotiation, as you know, is an uncertain process. There are many dilemmas which may arise due to this uncertainty. By trusting your opponents, you often consider mainly rewarding and beneficial behavior on their side, which can apparently solve many of your dilemmas. Seemingly, you can make your decisions on "solid ground". This may be one of your biggest illusions. Expecting your opponents to reciprocate your trust may be an erroneous belief. Thus, think twice before you decide to be trusting.

- Deciding who and when to trust may lead you to make mistakes. You can either distrust a trustworthy opponent or place your trust in an opponent who, later on, turns out to be untrustworthy. In order to avoid both mistakes, do not rush when it comes to either trusting or distrusting your opponents. Suspect your opponents and gather as much intelligence as you can. Make decisions about your opponents' trustworthiness on the basis of the data you have collected and analyzed, rather than on the basis of assumptions.

- If you try to discern your opponents' trustworthiness by considering their reputation or through your own past experience with them, you may make erroneous decisions. You may wrongly evaluate your opponents — especially when circumstances have changed. Your opponents may also have changed over time. In addition, they may now have new opportunities and information — enhancing their motivation to violate your trust — which they did not have in the past. Their reputation may be false and rumors may mislead you. Try not to take risks by attempting to predict your opponents' behavior. Instead, reduce your risks by protecting yourself; for example, ask for third-party guarantees and closely observe your opponents' behavior — this way you will make decisions about trust based on relatively solid ground.

- Try to calculate the damages in the event that your opponents choose to violate your trust. The more damages are expected, the more protective measures you should take.

- Being trustful is less risky if it is in your opponents' interests to reciprocate your trust in a favorable manner. The risk is even lower if you have guarantees or if you can observe and monitor your opponents' behavior.

- Violations of trust by opponents can be accidental — with no intention of causing any harm. Such accidental violations of trust may be due to a mistake, which is easily corrected. In this case, you may forgive your opponents and rehabilitate your trust. However, beware of repetitions of such "accidents", which may indicate a pattern of behavior that is far from accidental, but rather intentional.

- Do not forgive too easily if the trust violation is circumstantial, i.e. when an opportunity to gain benefits at your expense arises for your opponents. Despite the fact that, in this case, violating your trust was not premeditated, it still may be harmful. A circumstantial violation of trust is somewhat problematic, as it will probably be repeated should circumstances once more allow for such an occurrence. Therefore, past circumstantial trust violations may raise your demands for compensation, guarantees and other deterrence mechanisms, in order to avoid harmful consequences in both the present and the future.

- The most harmful trust violation is one that is premeditated and intentional. When a trust violation is intentional and premeditated, do not blame yourself for not noticing the harmful intentions in time. Try to break off all dealings with your opponents immediately, and stay away from these opponents in the future. However, if the benefits of the negotiations with these opponents are still in your interest or if the continuance of the negotiations is forced upon you by a third party, applying means — such as guarantees, compensation or "posting a hostage" — is essential to reduce your current and future risks.

PART FOUR
Third Party Intervention
in the Negotiation Process

Chapter 12

Voluntary, Compulsory and International Mediation

"An ounce of mediation is worth a pound of arbitration and a ton of litigation."

Joseph Grynbaum

1. The Traditional Model versus the New Mediation Model

Mediation can be defined as a third-party intervention in negotiation between disputants, conducted in order to help them overcome a conflict. The history of mediation is as old as that of negotiation. Since people of all cultures have always had disputes, mediators emerged to influence, persuade or advise the involved parties, in order to facilitate a reasonable mutual agreement between parties, instead of using force.

1.1. *Traditional Mediation Models: A Few Examples*

Traditional mediation came in different forms and styles among various cultures according to region, class, age and gender differences. For example, traditional Chinese mediators were elder males, respected in their community, who shared social or family ties with the disputants. The mediator's informal intervention concluded with an offer of various options including persuasions which could lead to forming an agreement.[1] Such options often went beyond the disputed issues, and included ethics, sacrificing individual

---

[1] Deng, Y. and Xu, K. (2014), Strategy to Motivate and Facilitate Compromise in Chinese Mediation, *International Journal of Conflict Management*, Vol. 25(1), pp. 4–20.

interests in an attempt to maintain harmony, focusing on the good of the community, as well as other appropriate conducts of behavior.[2]

In ancient Greek society, mediation practices were highly valued and therefore believed to be appropriate not only for humans but also for Gods. The mediators could be either female or male, as long they were able to influence the disputants by acquiring their trust. In addition, the Greek mediators were perceived as ethical individuals with empathic abilities, and the talent of presenting ideas that could help disputants reach an agreement.[3]

In recent decades, mediation has received a "face lift", and is now looked upon as a favorable Alternative Dispute Resolution (ADR) method, which emphasizes the advantages of mediation compared to the litigation process. In many countries, mediation has been institutionalized and accepted as an effective process, which can assist disputing parties to resolve their conflicts and reach a satisfactory agreement.

1.2. *The New Mediation Ideal Model*

The new model has advocated completely voluntary mediation, in which the parties voluntarily choose mediation as the best way to resolve their conflict. The disputants can choose to use mediation at any stage — before negotiation, during negotiation, after negotiation has reached an impasse and even during litigation. The rationale for voluntary mediation is to enable the parties to retain their control of both the mediation process and its outcome — i.e. they not only have the freedom to choose the mediators, but also to either accept or reject their proposals. The chosen mediators are professionals and can be either male or female. They are supposed to be neutral and have no ties to any of the disputants or their relatives. Social relations and personal friendships are also automatically considered a source of favoritism. In addition, the mediators are meant to help the parties reach an agreement by facilitating discussion around their interests, rather than by employing persuasion or pressure and definitely not through coercion. Consequently, the achieved agreements are supposed to result in the disputants' approval and satisfaction.

---

[2]Chia, H.-B. Lee-Partridge, J.E. and Chong, C.-L. (2004), Traditional Mediation Practice: Are We Throwing the Baby Out with the Bath Water?, *Conflict Resolution Quarterly*, Vol. 21(4), pp. 451–462.

[3]Gutierrez, A. (2012), The Seasons of Alternative Dispute Resolution: A Study of Mediation Tactics in the Context of Ancient Greek Mythology, *The American Journal of Mediation*, Vol. 6, pp. 65–84.

It is noteworthy that mediation has always been, and still is, the most prevailing method of third-party intervention in disputes. Therefore, it is essential for retaining stability in many systems, both domestic and international.

2. Some Advantages of the New Mediation Model

Imagine an employee who was sexually harassed by her superior. She would like to receive compensation from the management for her suffering. However, applying to court seems a lengthy and embarrassing process. A friend, who serves as a mediator, suggests a mediation process with the management, as it can be a shorter and less embarrassing procedure. The employee hesitates because she suspects that during mediation she will have to renounce a lot of her demands. Finally, however, she agrees to mediation, since her friend ensures her that if the final mediation results are not to her liking, she can still apply to court. Her friend also assures her she will discover that there are more advantages to the mediation procedure.

2.1. *Justifying and Legitimizing Concessions*

In order to bridge the gaps between the conflicting parties, sometimes at least one of them should renounce its resistance points. Renouncing resistance points is a very painful process. The renouncing parties feel a need to justify their actions — to themselves as well as to the other involved parties in the dispute, including their principals. Mediators can occasionally justify as well as legitimize difficult concessions, which disputants have to make in order to solve a severe conflict. In addition, mediators play an important role when it comes to agreements that have apparently been made by the disputants themselves. Sometimes, the disputants themselves make far-reaching concessions in order to bridge the gap between them and reach an agreement. However, they would not like to admit to making such far-reaching concessions to either their constituencies or their principals. Using a mediator to initiate the agreement at this stage could help justify their concessions. For example, collective bargaining agreements in labor relations are sometimes reached by the union and the employers' representative, without any external intervention. However, once an agreement has been reached, neither the union nor the employers' representative wish to admit to their concessions behind "closed doors" to their constituencies. A made-up designed mediation process is a good solution for such a problem. Both the union and employers can always claim that there was no choice but to make concessions according to the mediators' suggestions.

2.2. Saving Face

Disputants often set high demands and feel they will lose face if considerable concessions are made. Consequently, they often miss an opportunity to achieve an agreement due to their inability to renounce their pride or lose face. Avoiding the loss of face is important in individualistic cultures, and even more so in collectivist cultures. Mediation provides the disputants with a way to make even considerable concessions without losing face. High appreciation of the mediator's suggestions can always serve as an excuse for making concessions without losing face.

2.3. Controlling the Final Decision

According to the mediation new model, choosing mediation as a form of third-party intervention in a conflict leaves the final decision in the hands of the disputants. Consequently, all parties to the dispute may prefer mediation to other forms of external intervention. Disputants are supposed to believe that mediation is better and more just than another external form, which forces the final outcome upon them — such as arbitration or litigation.

2.4. Reducing Risks

In situations of uncertainty, such as negotiation, disputants may find themselves in a risky situation in which they do not have essential information. Therefore, they cannot make the right decisions and acquire at least some control over the situation. The probability of one or more disputants obtaining a favorable outcome is unknown. Mediators can often reduce these risks by providing new general information, as well as information gleaned from other disputants. Such information may help the disputants make better decisions, and therefore reduce their risks.

2.5. Saving Time and Money

Customary alternatives to mediation are negotiation, arbitration and litigation. Negotiation between disputants as a way to resolve their conflict may be both a time-consuming and costly endeavor. In terms of preparation time, long meetings, representatives' costs and even in terms of emotional investments, negotiation is a lengthy, and often expensive, process.

Arbitration may be quicker than negotiation, but it also might be arbitrary and more costly than negotiation. Litigation, as a means of resolving the conflict, may take much more time than both negotiation and arbitration and is more expensive in all aspects, including representatives' costs and emotional investments. Mediation may be much shorter and less expensive than arbitration and litigation. It may also save time, money and emotional anxiety for the disputants. Furthermore, during mediation, the disputants can keep their cards close to their chest and wield some control over the final conflict resolution — which is impossible in the cases of both arbitration and litigation.

2.6. *Changing Disputants' Attitudes*

Disputants are inclined to neither understand nor believe the other sides' view of the conflict. They are more inclined, however, to be convinced by mediators, even if the mediators support the other side's view. In addition, disputants are more willing to accept a suggestion that comes from the mediator compared to the same suggestion coming from the other disputants. As a result, mediators can often alter the disputants' attitudes towards the conflict and the possible conflict resolution. For example, during collective bargaining the management's demand to reduce salaries may cause furious employees' reactions. Such reactions are a product of the employees' belief that the management wishes to increase its profits at their expense. The management sincerely assures the employees that the problematic economic situation is the reason for this demand. However, due to the employees' disbelief, they totally reject the management's demands and the negotiation reaches an impasse. A mediator can convince the employees that the management's demand is truly an objective result of the economic situation, and does not increase the management's profits. At the same time, the mediator can convince the management to promise to later compensate employees for the current salary reduction, once the economic situation improves. In this type of case, the employees' attitudes may change — from furious to understanding — while the management also has a better understanding of its obligations to its employees. Thus, disputants' trust in a mediator's integrity may help mediators to change disputants' attitudes and prevent a negotiation impasse.[4]

---

[4]Gilin, D.A. and Paese, P.W. (2002), Mediation as Persuasion: Central Route Attribution Change as a Conflict Resolution, *SSRN Working Paper Series*, April, 2002.

2.7. *Mediation as "Aspirin"*

If mediators do not succeed in resolving the main issues of the conflict, they can still treat its symptoms. For example, some relief is gained even if, for a short time, there is a break in the disputants' "wrestling". If the mediation process provides the disputants with a brief respite, in which to reevaluate its potential results, they might change their attitudes and behaviors. Therefore, mediation as an "aspirin" or "band-aid" can temporarily ease crisis symptoms, providing an important contribution by allowing disputants' to experience a brief but much-needed "time-out".

2.8. *Reducing the Disputants' Emotional Involvement*

Disputants usually do not take their conflict calmly — they are highly emotionally involved. Their emotional involvement may result in a negative interpretation of the other side's reactions and behaviors. Consequently, there is a great tendency to reject any, and even all, of the other side's proposed suggestions, even if they are of value. This emotional involvement may be especially severe when the disputants know each other well — such as in a divorce conflict. Mediators can reduce disputants' emotional involvement by separating them and preventing contact, at least in the short-run. In addition, the mediation process may serve as a catharsis for the disputants — a way of "letting off emotional steam". All this, however, is possible only if the disputants believe in the mediators' integrity and neutrality, and do not transfer their negative emotions onto the mediators.

3. Some Disadvantages of the Mediation Model

Despite the advantages of the mediation model, from a practical aspect, it does not always work as expected. Apparently, there are some problems with the new mediation model. For example, in some cases it has been difficult to detect any direct effects of the interaction between disputants and mediators on the mediation outcome: Agreement/no agreement.[5] It seems that in such a case, the mediation process and the disputants' relationship with the mediator hardly affect the mediation outcome.[6] Moreover, there has been some

---

[5]Wall Jr., J. and Chan-Serafin (2009), Processes in Civil Case Mediations, *Conflict Resolution Quarterly*, Vol. 26(3), pp. 261–291.

[6]Wissler, R.S. (2004), The Effectiveness of Court-Connected Dispute Resolutions in Civil Cases, *Conflict Resolution Quarterly*, Vol. 22(1–2), pp. 55–88.

evidence that the likelihood of achieving a settlement through mediation is mainly related to the source of the dispute, rather than the mediator or the mediation process.[7] All of the above-mentioned may be due to substantial deviations from the mediation model.

3.1. *The Mediators' Doubtful Neutrality*

According to the mediation model, mediators are supposed to be neutral. However, mediators often have concerns which are beyond the interests of the disputants and do not necessarily fit the perception of them being neutral. For example, in a strike incident government mediators may consider the interests of the public, rather than those of the disputants. In this case, the mediators may be interested in reaching neither a just agreement, nor even a compromise. They may be interested in ending the strike as quickly as possible, whatever it takes, to avoid any damage to the public, due to the risk of the strike's further expansion. Thus, if appointed by the government, the courts or another organization, mediators' agendas may be more focused on pleasing the appointing organization, rather than helping the disputants to reach a fair and mutually satisfactory agreement. Mediators may also be biased, in favor of one of the disputants — most often the more powerful one.

3.2. *Mediators under Pressure*

A distinguished mediator from the U.S. was invited to give a lecture in our faculty. At the end of the lecture, one of the faculty members asked: "How do you guarantee the neutrality and objectivity of your mediators?" "I am very pleased that you asked this question," replied the distinguished visitor, "because it gives me some sense of the prevailing attitudes towards mediators in various countries. For example," he continued "on my way to your faculty, I stopped in another country to give a lecture on mediation. There, I was asked: 'How do you guarantee the lives of your mediators...?'".

Sometimes mediators are exposed to the disputants' pressures, external pressures or both. If one or both of the disputants pressure the mediators, it may influence the mediators' performance. For example, it may cause the mediators to act in favor of the disputants exerting the pressure. Sometimes

---

[7]Posthuma, R.A. Dworkin, J.B. and Swift, M.S. (2002), Mediator Tactics and Sources of Conflict: Facilitating and Inhibiting Effects, *Industrial Relations*, Vol. 41(1), pp. 94–109.

external pressures are put on the mediator, by political, business or other organizations. Such pressure is meant to influence the mediator to solve the dispute in the way that most pleases the external organization. Sometimes mediators are presented with an offer they cannot resist or refuse. All such pressures may distort mediators' performance, in accordance with the mediation model. Thus, whatever the reason may be, it is impossible to assume that even the most professional mediators can always remain completely neutral and impartial.

3.3. *Mediation and Timing*

The mediation model does not take into account the very important element of *timing*. According to this model, mediators' intervention can take place at any stage of the conflict. However, at the beginning of a conflict it is reasonable to assume that the parties believe in resolving the dispute through direct negotiation, without any external intervention. Therefore, at this stage the disputants may have no inclination towards mediation. Hence, mediators' intervention at this stage may be ineffective and unsuccessful. It is only later on — when the disputants are desperate and tired of their own unsuccessful attempts to negotiate — that the time becomes ripe for mediators' intervention. At this final stage, the likelihood of the mediation being effective and ending in a satisfactory agreement is much higher.

3.4. *Mediators' Styles*

There is no consensus on how to classify mediators' practice styles.[8] However, most often mediators' styles are described on a continuum scale — ranging from low to high mediator intervention. At the low end of the scale are the *facilitating* (neutral) styles, where mediators take on a very passive role in the mediation process, mainly supplying and transferring information to and among the disputants. Typical to the *facilitating* (neutral) styles, mediators have only a small influence on the mediation process and its outcome, but they allow disputants complete control over the mediation process and outcome.

---

[8]Charkoudian, L. (2012), Just My Style: The Practical, Ethical, and Empirical Dangers of the Lack of Consensus about Definitions of Mediation Styles, *Negotiation and Conflict Management Research*, Vol. 6(4), pp. 367–383.

Mid-scale are the *formulative* (evaluation) mediation styles, which include addressing the underlying issues of the conflict, identifying options for possible agreement, suggesting alternative solutions, and helping the disputants evaluate the alternatives in order to reach the best agreement. *Formulative* mediation styles allow mediators more influence than the *facilitating* (neutral) styles, allow disputants only partial control over the mediation process and outcome.

At the high end of the scale are the *manipulative* (coercive) mediation styles. These styles advocate mediators' putting pressure on the disputants and using power to force them to reach an agreement, usually in accordance with the mediator's preferences. The *manipulative* mediation styles give mediators almost complete control over both the mediation process and outcome, leaving the disputants little, if any, control over the mediation process and outcome.

According to the ideal mediation model, mediators are meant to be facilitators only; meaning, to help the involved parties reach an agreement by facilitating information and discussion regarding their interests. They are not supposed to employ pressure, and certainly not force the disputants to reach an agreement. However, in practice, both the formulative and manipulative styles are often used, and third-party interventions frequently include mediators' high involvement, as well as powerful, coercive behaviors. In theory, mediators do not have the power to persuade or coerce disputants. Yet, mediators have various options by which to pressure disputants, in order to "push" them towards the mediators' preferred agreement.

3.5. *Mediators' Ways to Pressure Disputants*

Mediators who want to pressure disputants can, on the one hand, use rewards and benefits, such as financial benefits or other tempting payments. On the other hand, they may employ threats and punishments. For example, mediators can threaten to leave the mediation sessions if disputants do not comply with their suggestions. In this case, the disputants will be left to solve their own problems through probably unsuccessful negotiation attempts or by either arbitration or litigation. Another way to pressure disputants is through *face threatening*: A threat to disgrace all or one of the disputants in public. Mediators can also apply pressure if they have the legitimate/legal authority to threaten or punish the disputants who refuse to accept their offers. Such pressures invariably distort the original intention of the mediation model.

Empirical observations of mediators' behavior styles during the process are somewhat varied. Some indicate that facilitating mediators who do not use pressure during the mediation process identify with the perception of fairness and the disputants' satisfaction with the results.[9] However, other observations indicate that the use of mediator pressure during the process often leads to final agreements.[10] It seems that in a highly intensive and difficult conflict, applying pressure and force may be an effective way to resolve the dispute.[11] Alternatively, in an easy, low-intensive dispute putting pressure on the disputants is mostly ineffective. Moreover, it is most likely that in a low-intensive, easy dispute the disputants will reject any mediator intervention.[12]

4. Compulsory Mediation

Imagine a divorce case in which the wife is hurt mentally, but also suffers financially. She demands custody of their children as well as high alimony from her husband. They negotiate their demands but, unfortunately, the negotiation ends in an impasse. The impasse amplifies the conflict and increases the "bad blood" between the couple. At this point, it seems that the wife's last recourse is a court ruling. The wife sues her husband in court, with the hope that the court will rule in her favor. However, instead of litigation, she receives an invitation to participate in a mediation process, under the auspices of the court. She is notified that even though the court does not legally enforce the mediation outcome, it strongly encourages disputants to reach an agreement, and comply with the settlement, according to the results of the mediation process. Since most disputants perceive the mediation outcome as a compromise, such a compromise was not exactly what

---

[9]Albert, J.K. Heisterkamp, B.L. and McPhee, R.M. (2005), Disputants' Perception of and Satisfaction with a Community Mediation Program, *The International Journal of Conflict Management*, Vol. 16(3), pp. 218–244.

[10]Wall, J.A. and Chan-Serfin, S. (2010), Do Mediators Walk Their Talk in Civil Cases? *Conflict Resolution Quarterly*, Vol. 28(1), pp. 3–21.

[11]Wall, J.A. Dunne, T.C. and Chan-Serafin, S. (2011), The Effects of Neutral, Evaluative and Pressing Mediator Strategies, *Conflict Resolution Quarterly*, Vol. 29(2), pp. 127–150.

[12]Salmon, E.D. Gelfand, M.J. Celik, A.B. Kraus, S. Wilkenfeld, J. and Inman, M. (2013), Cultural Contingencies of Mediation: Effectiveness of Mediator Styles in Intercultural Disputes, *Journal of Organizational Behavior*, Vol. 34(6), pp. 887–909.

the wife was looking for. She perceived the mediation process as worthless, as she has already exhausted all possibilities to achieve a reasonable settlement during the negotiation. However, the court insists on mediation previous to litigation, apparently in order to help the court reduce its own litigation load. This type of *compulsory mediation* prolongs the couple's previous negotiation, albeit with the intervention of a third party, before proceeding to trial. For the wife — the plaintiff — the compulsory mediation is perceived as blocking her access to a desired verdict. For her husband — the defendant — the compulsory mediation is perceived as a process that forces him to compromise. Such perceptions may produce negative emotions and the unwillingness of both husband and wife to participate in compulsory mediation.

4.1. *Voluntary versus Compulsory Mediation*

According to the mediation model, mediation is supposed to be a voluntary form of dispute resolution, in which the disputants have the initial freedom to choose mediation as a way to resolve their dispute, as well as choose the mediators. However, quite often, mediation is enforced by law, rather than chosen by the parties. For example, in many countries divorcing couples' disputes — regarding the distribution of property as well as the custody of their children — are forced in accordance with the law to participate in mediation.[13] In other instances, mediation is forced on the disputants by various organizations, such as civil courts, labor courts, governments and domestic and international organizations. Organizational-referred mediations deviate from the original voluntary mediation model, as they are mandatory from the beginning, even if they sometimes become somewhat voluntary towards the end.

4.2. *Experience with Compulsory Mediation*

There are some mixed experiences regarding the effectiveness and results of this type of compulsory mediation.

On the one hand, in some cases disputants, who are forced to participate in mediation, participate unwillingly in the process. The asymmetrical nature of compulsory mediation may even lead disputants to completely

---

[13]Greig, J.M. (2005), Stepping into the Fray: When do Mediators Mediate? *American Journal of Political Science*, Vol. 49(2), pp. 249–266.

oppose it.[14] Under compulsory mediation disputants often refuse to compromise, resulting in a low agreement rate and a low level of satisfaction from the mediation outcome. Moreover, being forced to participate in a mediation process induces disputants' fear of being treated unfairly. In general, it is not clear whether compulsory mediation's effectiveness and efficiency outperforms or performs as well as litigation.[15]

On the other hand, in other cases it is not the *form* of mediation (compulsory or voluntary), which determines the effectiveness of the mediation, but rather the disputants' *subjective perception* of the mediator and mediation process, which influence the mediation's effectiveness. If the disputants perceive the mediation process as unjust, they have less motivation to communicate openly with the mediators, and they may well suspect and doubt the mediators' motives. They may believe that the appointed mediators are making efforts to reach agreements in order to protect their own interests, as well as the interests of those who appointed them. In such cases, even if disputants receive a favorable mediation outcome, they may still be dissatisfied with what they believe is an unfair process. However, when the disputants perceive the mediation process as being fair, even when it is forced upon them, it raises their general satisfaction with both the process and its outcome. When mediators use a high rate of soft tactics, such as consultation and active listening, disputants tend to perceive even compulsory mediation as just and fair. The disputants' perception of the mediators' contribution to solving their problems also leads to a high rate of agreement and disputants' satisfaction, even in compulsory mediation.[16] Therefore, it is not the compulsory versus voluntary mediation which leads to good or bad results, but the type of process and the mediators' behavior. If the effectiveness of the mediation process is measured by the rate of agreement and the disputants' satisfaction with the mediation outcome, both voluntary and compulsory mediation may lead to mediation effectiveness, providing the disputants perceive the mediation (in whatever form) as a fair and just process.

---

[14]Ufkes, E.G. Otten, S. and Van der Zee, K.I. (2012), The Effectiveness of a Mediation Program in Symmetrical versus Asymmetrical Neighbor-to-Neighbor Conflicts, *International Journal of Conflict Management*, Vol. 23(4), pp. 449–457.

[15]Wissler, R.L. (2004), The Effectiveness of Court-Connected Dispute Resolution in Civil Cases, *Conflict Resolution Quarterly*, Vol. 22 (1–2), pp. 55–88.

[16]Galin, A. (2014), What Makes Court-Referred Mediation Effective?, *International Journal of Conflict Management*, Vol. 25(1), pp. 21–37.

5. Mediators as Human Beings

According to the mediation model, mediators are supposed to be not only neutral, but also objective and impartial. However, mediators, like all human beings, have their own interests, prejudices, and subjective rationalities. Consequently, mediators often find it difficult to be objective and impartial. Following are just a few examples.

5.1. *Mediators' Self-Interests*

It is only human that mediators have their own interests, which may be completely different from the disputants' interests or ideas about what constitutes a just agreement. For example, mediators may be interested in enhancing their own reputation. Sometimes mediators become involved in disputes that have little chance of being settled. However, they believe their intervention may yield self-interested benefits — such as recognition and gratitude. If they are being paid by the hour or the day, they can increase their mediation fees by dragging out the process, at the disputants' expense. In some cases, mediators intervene in a dispute because their own interests are at stake. For example, if they believe that the dispute (such as a strike resulting from a union-employers' dispute) threatens their status or their own chances of being reelected for a high political position. In other cases, mediators try to assist the more powerful disputants, in order to establish good relations with them, which may be helpful to their own business.

5.2. *The Impact of Predisposition*

Mediators often have predispositions regarding the disputants' expectations of the process, their attitudes towards each other and towards the mediator. During the mediation process, mediators may encounter different disputants' behaviors and attitudes, which contradict the mediators' predispositions. In this case, there is a high probability that mediators will ignore the contradicting information, and adhere to their previous perceptions. As a result, mediators may perform according to inaccurate perceptions that fit their predispositions, rather than according to the actual behavior and attitudes of the disputants. Take for example, the case where the mediators are predisposed to the idea that there is a lot of "bad blood" between the disputants. They are continually under the impression that the relationship between the disputants is very bad, even though this may not actually be the case. As a result, the mediators might miss the fact that the disputed issues can actually be resolved with relative ease.[17]

5.3. *Escalation of the Mediators' Commitment*

Sometimes mediators continue with the mediation procedure, despite clear evidence that the disputants do not intend to reach an agreement through mediation. A typical expression of mediators' escalated commitment is their efforts to continue the mediation process beyond its time limits and without any reasonable justification. Such an escalation of commitment is the result of mediators' previous investment in the process, and their own or public commitments to resolve the dispute. The greater their investment in the process and the stronger their commitments, the bigger the escalation. Mediators' difficulty to opt out of the process in time often results from their general sense of failure, concern about their principals' reaction, and fear of losing face by damaging their reputation. Therefore, mediators frequently continue trying to bring the mediation to a "happy end", at all costs. Mediators' escalation of commitment may prolong the conflict and sometimes even cause its complete deterioration.

5.4. *Mediators' Subjective Preferences*

Mediators' subjective preferences can be referred to as *mediators' partiality*. It is not a rare phenomenon to find that mediators prefer one of the disputants more than the other, for example, the stronger one. The preference may be a result of a self-serving interest, predisposition, pressure or even identification with the favored disputants. Such preferences may have far-reaching consequences. The preferred disputant usually tends to be demanding, rigid and unwilling to make concessions, which are essential to resolving the dispute. However, sometimes mediators may have an influence over their own favored disputants, and thus be able to persuade them to make concessions in order to reach some kind of an agreement. In other words, the mediators' subjective preferences influence the mediation process and outcome, with no necessary connection to the context of the actual dispute.

---

[17]Thompson, L. and Kim, P.H. (2000), How the Quality of Third Parties' Settlement Solutions is Affected by the Relationship Between Negotiators, *Journal of Experimental Psychology — Applied*, Vol. 6(1), pp. 3–14.

5.5. *Mediators under a Time Pressure*

Pressure to resolve the dispute quickly may be put on mediators by external powers or by the mediators' other commitments. Such pressures may shift the mediators' attention from the dispute context to the timeframe context. Time constraints may reduce the mediators' motivation to delve into the core problems of the dispute, which may result in a small probability of ending the dispute with an agreement. Mediators working under a time pressure may also use hard tactics in order to urge the disputants to reach an agreement within a short time period. Thus, as a result of their time constraints, they may put pressure on the disputants to make far-reaching concessions in order to accept their suggested agreement, without actually resolving the dispute. These actions may cause the disputants to perceive them as unjust mediators. In such cases, even if disputants unwillingly reach the suggested agreement, the likelihood that this agreement will be sustainable is small.

6. International Mediation

Since ancient times, mediation has been accepted in international relations as a useful method to prevent or resolve conflicts, especially aggressive or violent conflicts. International mediation is aimed at resolving disputes, between countries, international companies, and sometimes even between nations and transnational terrorist groups. International mediation is of special importance because for many of these disputants, there is no available litigation channel for solving their conflict. The background for such disputes are tangible issues, such as land, resources, power, security and business conflicts, as well as intangible issues like attitudes, symbols, myths and deep-rooted fears.[18] It is easier for international disputants — and especially for international mediators — to bridge the gaps between the tangible issues, compared to the intangible ones. The intangible issues sometimes make a conflict intractable, often followed by long-enduring violence. However, efforts to bridge the gaps among all of the issues — both tangible and intangible — are continually made by all kinds of international mediators.

International mediators can be friendly states, major power states, international organizations and international companies. Famous individuals, such

---

[18] Kaufman, S.J. (2006), Escaping the Symbolic Politics Trap: Reconciliation Initiatives and Conflict Resolution in Ethnic Wars, *Journal of Peace Research*, Vol. 43(2), pp. 201–218.

as former presidents, famous mediators, business people who have a relationship with the disputants, etc. can also mediate international conflicts.[19] International mediation, just like domestic mediation, can be either voluntary or compulsory.

6.1. *Motivation to Mediate International Conflicts*

The most common motivation of intervening parties, especially powerful countries, to mediate an international conflict is a self-serving motivation. Countries often decide to mediate international conflicts in order to maintain their own interests in conflicted areas. Political interests, interests in resources or business interests are all incentives for intervening in an international conflict. For example, it is sometimes worthwhile to intervene in a conflict as a mediator in order to stop a flood of refugees from entering an area where armed conflict prevails. Other examples are: To avoid damaging, or even completely depleting, essential natural resources, due to war; to prevent trade interference resulting from conflict; to gain influence over one or all disputants or to prevent others from gaining such an influence. There are also some genuine altruistic humanitarian organizations and individuals who wish to mediate between international disputants to stop conflicts and especially wars, so as to prevent the suffering and misery of the involved populations. Such incentives to mediate in an international conflict may serve to either increase or decrease the conflict — due to the nature of both the conflict and the disputants themselves.

The information the mediators have regarding the dispute and the disputants' nature plays an important role in the mediators' motivation to be involved in resolving the dispute. International mediators tend to intervene in cases where, according to their information, they can achieve an agreement. They tend to avoid mediating conflicts in which they expect to be unsuccessful in reaching their self-serving or other desired outcome.[20] However, sometimes due to the information they have, mediators make a wrong decision, i.e. try to mediate a dispute where there is only a small chance of achieving their desired outcome. Other times, despite the difficulties, they

---

[19]Vukovic, S. (2014), International Mediation as a Distinct Form of Conflict Management, *International Journal of Conflict Management*, Vol. 25(1), pp. 61–80.

[20]Iwanami, Y. (2014), The Selection and Signaling Effects of Third Party Intervention, *Journal of Theoretical Politics*, Vol. 26(1), pp. 135–157.

may still continue mediating, due to their escalation of commitment. The mediators' escalation of commitment may then become a vicious circle — the more the mediators try to force an outcome, the less the disputants are interested in such an outcome.

6.2. *Motivation to Accept Mediation*

Several factors may influence international disputants' willingness to accept or reject mediation, including the balance of power between the disputants; the cost of the conflict; as well as the natures and tendencies of the potential mediators.

Conflict intensity and its costs: When the conflict intensity level is high and lengthy, with no promising end on the horizon, disputants may become tired of the prolonged conflict, and seek constructive intervention as a possible solution to the conflict's continuation. Thus, the mediators are accepted by the disputants, not because of their neutrality, but because of their supposed ability to bring about a positive solution. The mediators' ability to provide such a solution is strongly affected by the parties' needs for a practical outcome.[21] In this case, the likelihood of international mediators reaching an agreement is relatively high. However, just like in domestic mediation, when the conflict intensity level is low, the disputants' motivation to seek intervention from some international mediator is substantially reduced, as they can often solve their own problems. Likewise, when the costs of the conflict for all disputants are high (in terms of funds, international problems, causalities, etc.) disputants may seek mediator intervention; contrariwise, they may refuse international intervention when the cost of the conflict is low.

The conflict stages: Sometimes disputants' motivation to accept mediation may depend on the conflict stages. International mediation is often rejected in the early and final stages of the conflict. In the early stages of the conflict, disputants still believe they can win — achieve their objectives. In the final stages of the conflict, despite calculations related to the conflict's high cost, their awareness of the *sunk costs* (including the death rate, in the case of

---

[21]Zartman, I.W. and Touval, S. (1985), International Mediation: Conflict Resolution and Power Politics, *Journal of Social Issues*, Vol. 41(2), pp. 27–45.

war) that have already been invested in the conflict may reduce disputants' motivation to compromise during mediation.[22]

The power balance: Another consideration is that of the power balance between the disputants — which increases or decreases their motivation to use mediation. When the power balance is comparable, for example, when the parties' military abilities are almost equivalent, disputants still have hopes for victory; therefore, they are usually inflexible and reject mediation. If, however, the power balance tends in favor of one or a few of the disputants, the powerful disputants may reject mediation, while the weak disputants may desire it. On the other hand, in cases where there is an overlap of interests between powerful disputants and the mediator, even the powerful disputants may tend to accept mediation. Moreover, mediators who favor one of the sides can also use their power to exert pressure on their favored disputants, forcing them to accept even costly concessions. The disfavored disputants, in this case, may benefit from the intervention of the partial mediators. However, if the disfavored disputants are hesitant to accept the partial and forceful mediators' painful proposals, they may be "convinced" by the mediators' ability to either exert force or withhold benefits. Therefore, in international conflicts a partial mediation process is, at times, more likely to end in an accepted agreement than a neutral mediation process.[23] Yet, sometime such forcible mediation, especially if it favors one of the disputants over the other, may simply prolong the violence.[24] In a different context, a partial mediator is sometimes the only way to communicate between disputants. For example, in a hostage-taking crisis, a partial mediator may be the only non-violent way to communicate with the terrorist group, with the hope of saving at least some of the hostages.[25]

Mediators' reputation and attributes: Reputable and credible mediators, who have managed to successfully mediate many international conflicts, may

---

[22]Greig, J.M. and Regan, P.M. (2008), When Do They Say Yes? An Analysis of the Willingness to Offer and Accept Mediation in Civil Wars, *International Studies Quarterly*, Vol. 52(4), pp. 759–781.

[23]Svensson, I. (2009), Who Brings which Peace? *Journal of Conflict Resolution*, Vol. 53(3), pp. 446–469.

[24]Favretto, K. (2009), Should Peacemakers Take Sides? Major Power Mediation, Coercion and Bias, *American Political Science Review*, Vol. 103(2), pp. 248–263.

[25]See Chapter 8 of this book.

increase the disputants' willingness to accept their mediation advice. High confidence in the mediators' ability to achieve a reasonable agreement may also cause disputants to consider resolving their dispute with the help of these mediators. Shared identity between the mediators and the disputants, be it ethnic, racial, linguistic, religious or related to mutual culture and history, may encourage disputants to accept mediators who can help them achieve a successful conflict resolution. In contrast, differences between the disputants and the mediators' cultures may reduce their motivation to accept mediation.[26]

Pretence mediation: In some situations, disputants may pretend to willingly accept mediation, in spite of their lack of motivation to resolve the conflict through mediation. In these cases, at least some of the disputants use the mediation process as a ploy — in order to play for time. Stalling, through employing the mediation process, may allow disputants more time to prepare and take other measures, which may improve their abilities to confront the conflict from a stronger position, and to possibly end it with a better resolution from their own point of view.

Generally, international disputants are prone to consider mediation if they believe it is the best alternative from among the other alternatives available to them — such as forcing a solution (as in a war victory) or deferring their decision for a certain period of time and meanwhile maintaining the *status quo*.

6.3. *Possible Outcomes of Mediation in International Conflicts*

There are various possible outcomes that may result from mediation in international conflicts. However, the most important result is the outcome's ability to sustain itself over time. Of course, even a short-term outcome may be useful if it provides disputants with some breathing room — a break in which to reevaluate and quietly reconsider future actions and decisions. Yet, an outcome that is sustainable over time is obviously the most beneficial one.

Any type of mediation outcome involves concessions. For some disputants, concessions are painful and may generate an impression of weakness which may, in turn, generate possible pressures by other disputants in the future. Concessions may also be unpopular with the disputants' own

---

[26]Inman, M. Kishi, R. Wilkenfeld, J. Gelfand, M. and Salmon, E. (2014), Cultural Influences on Mediation in International Crisis, *Journal of Conflict Resolution*, Vol. 58(4), pp. 685–712.

constituency and raise the opposition objections. Furthermore, mediation — especially partial mediation — may produce aggravation when disputants believe that the mediation outcome was a "zero sum game"; meaning, the opponents received all the benefits while the disputants had to pay all of the costs. In this case, the mediation agreement may be easily broken. In order for such a mediation outcome to be durable, it should be enforced and carefully monitored by the mediators.[27]

Practically, it seems that the *manipulative* and *formulative* approaches — more active styles of mediation — have a stronger effect on the likelihood of reaching relevant formal agreements.[28] The *manipulative* mediation styles are mostly able to resolve tangible issues, whereas the *formulative styles* are more useful in resolving intangible issues. The *facilitative* style of mediation — the more passive style — is more effective in reducing post-agreement tension, as it enables disputants to realize that a mutually-achieved agreement is preferable to any violent conflict.[29] Consequently, there is no single mediation style that always provides an enduring, sustainable agreement between international disputants. It is most likely a combination of all the different mediation styles that is essential in increasing the probability of a long-term agreement.

Practical Applications

- Do not choose voluntary mediation before you have checked all other alternatives for resolving your dispute. Choose mediation only after you have checked and decided that mediation is your best, current alternative.
- If you are involved in an exhaustive, severe and lengthy dispute, it is most likely that voluntary mediation is one of your best alternatives for achieving a mutual agreement. Most of the other available alternatives for resolving the dispute (such as arbitration and litigation) may end in receiving a dictated enforced outcome.

---

[27]Lefler, V.A. (2015), Strategic Forum Selection and Compliance in Interstate Dispute Resolution, *Conflict Management and Peace Science*, Vol. 32(1), pp. 76–98.

[28]Duursma, A. (2014), A Current Literature Review of International Meditation, *International Journal of Conflict Management*, Vol. 25(1), pp. 81–98.

[29]Wallensteen, P. and Stensson, I. (2014), Talking Peace: International Mediation in Armed Conflicts, Journal of Peace Research, Vol. 51(2), pp. 315–327.

- Before accepting mediation, look for information — try to find out as much as you can about the mediators; for example, their reputation as fair mediators, evidence regarding their rate of achieved resolutions, other disputants' satisfaction with these mediators and the mediators' tendency to favor one of the sides involved in the conflict. The more you know, the more solid your decision to take part in such mediation will be.
- Beware of mediation if you are the weaker side in the dispute; there is some probability that the mediators will prefer the more powerful disputants. In this case, litigation, if possible, is preferable to mediation as a procedure for resolution.
- If you need to justify some of the concession you have made during the negotiation or if you need to save face after yielding some issues to your opponents, expressing a high valuation of the mediators' suggestions may help you to justify your concessions, as well as recover your dignity and face.
- If your involvement in the dispute is highly emotional, it is not advisable to try solving it by negotiating yourself. Mediators can serve you better as a neutral party, and enable a reasonable outcome. However be careful not to transfer your negative emotions onto the mediators.
- Just remember that voluntary mediation means you retain complete control over the mediation process and outcome. If you find the mediators' behavior to be unsatisfactory or unfair, you can always opt out or reject the mediators' suggestions.
- Do not assume that mediators are always objective and impartial. Mediators have their own interests, predispositions and preferences. If there is a contradiction between your interests and those of the mediators, it is more likely that the mediators will try to further their own interests and preferences, neglecting your interests and sometimes even those of your opponents, for the sake of their own interests.
- Try to choose mediators with whom you are familiar. Such familiarity increases your chances to influence both the mediators and the mediation process.
- If you use mediation as a pretence strategy in order to stall for time, take into consideration that your opponents, as well as the mediators, may notice it and try to use it against you.
- Compulsory — or organizational-referred mediation — is not necessarily a bad thing for you. It can be a shorter and less expensive way

to solve the conflict than other possible alternatives (such as litigation or arbitration). At the same time, it may be just as fair and helpful as voluntary mediation. Actually, it is not the *form* of mediation (voluntary or compulsory), which makes the difference between a fair process and outcome and an unfair process and outcome; rather, it is the mediators' *behavior* and their willingness to facilitate the conflict resolution, which really counts. Mediators can be fair and just in compulsory mediation, and unfair and unjust in voluntary mediation — and *vice versa*.

- If you are involved in an international conflict, mediation can prevent violence as well as bring an end to existing violence. However, a fair and sustainable outcome may be achieved if the mediators solve both tangible and intangible issues embedded in the conflict. Yet, even if the mediators achieve only an "aspirin" effect, which relieves the conflict symptoms, but not its source, it can at least provide you with some "breathing room." Whether such a break is worthwhile, in terms of the violence, only time can tell.

- International mediators, just like mediators in other fields, often have their own self-serving interests and agendas. If you are involved in an international conflict or any other substantial conflict, do not hesitate to reject such mediators unless their interests overlap with your own interests.

Chapter 13

Negotiating Representatives

"Do you think when two representatives holding diametrically opposing views get together and shake hands, the contradictions between our systems will simply melt away? What kind of a daydream is that?."

Nikita Khrushchev

1. Expectations versus Actual Representatives' Behavior

Representatives can be defined as individuals appointed by principals in order to negotiate on their behalf in exchange for remuneration. Representatives differ from mediators, as they are supposed to promote the interests of only one side of the dispute, rather than serve as intermediaries. Naturally, there may be some differences between disputants and their representatives, regarding which decisions would best serve to maximize principals' negotiation gains. It is assumed that representatives, motivated by payment or other rewards, are loyal to their principals and thus negotiate to the best of their abilities to achieve an agreement that will satisfy and be acceptable to their principals. However, in practice these assumptions are not always realized. Principals and their representatives often have differences of opinion regarding how the representatives should behave. Moreover, representatives' intervention does not always reduce the conflict's intensity. In fact, the opposite is sometimes true — representatives' behavior and actions may serve to polarize the conflicting interests. It is remarkable how sometimes representatives, negotiating on behalf of their principals — whether they be individuals or groups, can change the course of events for better or worse, given the authority or opportunity. The following story describes, for example, how love ended, due to representatives negotiating on behalf of their principals.

1.1. *Time for a Story*

Guy and Natalie met at Club Med. It was love at first sight. After a few months of love and passion, Guy proposed marriage on a luxurious yacht. Since they were both apparently financially well-to-do, they decided to sign a prenuptial (pre-marital) agreement, which was supposed to help define each one's assets, financial rights and obligations, including what would happen if the marriage unfortunately ended in divorce.

All attempts to reach an agreement by themselves failed, for various reasons. The most important reason was their emotional involvement, which made discussing the agreement details embarrassing. Consequently, they decided to hire lawyers to help them reach an agreement.

Guy called his good friend, Jim, who was a lawyer at the famous *Chen & Sons* legal firm. He asked Jim to take care of the agreement. When Jim asked what kind of agreement Guy was looking for, Guy just laughed and assured Jim that he believed his lawyer's common sense and experience would get him the best agreement. His only specific request from Jim was to make the agreement in the shortest possible time.

Natalie found her lawyer, Gale, on the Internet. During their first meeting, Natalie explained exactly what kind of agreement she was looking for. She repeated, again and again, that the lawyer must report any deviation from her instructions, and that nothing in the agreement would be done without her personal consent and approval.

Both lawyers met in a restaurant to discuss the agreement details. The wedding atmosphere apparently influenced Jim, who represented the future husband. Jim found Gale, who represented the future bride, to be the most attractive woman he had ever met. Jim decided that Gale would become his future beloved wife. During their discussions regarding the prenuptial agreement, Jim tried to amuse and fascinate Gale. Natalie arrived unexpectedly and interrupted the discussion. She apologized and claimed she had forgotten to give Gale some legal documents regarding her financial situation. When she left, Gale told Jim that the documents were from Natalie's bank, confirming a considerable loan she had taken. Gale told Jim that Natalie had taken the loan, due to an unsuccessful deal, which had caused her financial condition to deteriorate. After this discussion, the lawyers reached an interim conclusion by way of a very pleasant conversation. Accordingly, in the event of a divorce, Natalie would receive Guy's expensive car, the house, half of the assets earned during their married life and a diamond necklace that Guy had inherited form his family. The lawyers concluded their meeting and went to inform their principals about the details of their interim conclusion. They also decided to meet again the following day in order to finalize the conclusion.

Gale happily updated Natalie about the details of the interim conclusion. Jim, also happy and in love, went to update Guy. Guy was furious. He threatened Jim, saying he would ruin his reputation as a lawyer, unless he immediately changed the interim agreement. From now on, Guy told Jim he would require a report for "every cup of coffee Jim ordered"....

Jim returned home frustrated. He could not understand what the problem was. From his point of view, his good friend Guy should have understood that he was in love — and why should he have to choose between friendship and love? Moreover, after the unexpected meeting with Natalie, he understood that her financial condition was not as good as Guy believed; thus, she needed more guarantees than Guy. In addition, Jim, feeling angry and frustrated, decided it was all very unfair: Why should he have to do all the dirty work for Guy? In Jim's opinion, Guy, as a future husband, should have made the agreement himself, including all guarantees regarding his bride's future.

Over the next two weeks, furious, angry and frustrating discussions took place between all involved parties. As a result, Guy and Natalie's wedding was canceled, while Jim and Gale found themselves in a conflict they could not resolve. Everybody was miserable.

1.2. *The Story and its Implications*

In the earlier love-lost story, it is possible to trace several elements that often characterize the problematic interaction between principals and their representatives: The principals' expectation that their representatives will protect their interests versus the representatives' possible disloyalty; ambiguous instructions received by representatives versus clear instructions; the delegation of full authority to representatives versus the delegation of partial or non-authority; several complex lines of communication versus one direct line of communication; the supposed secrecy between principals and their representatives versus the representative who leaks the secrets; representatives' self-serving interests versus their need to protect their principals' interests; the reliability versus unreliability of the representatives, as well the representatives' possible emotional or material involvement in the conflict, including their tendency to take the other side's point of view. An additional problem is the representatives' cost.

2. Problems Caused by Representative Intervention

Representatives' intervention in negotiation may have advantages; however, sometimes they create problems that outweigh their advantages.

2.1. *Representatives' Possible Disloyalty*

Representatives' disloyalty to their principals may cause irreparable damage during negotiations. Principals obviously expect their representatives to protect them and their interests during the negotiation. They certainly do not expect their representatives to harm their interests. Thus, when principals feel they are being harmed by their representatives they may experience a sense of betrayal. Such perceived betrayals are usually also accompanied by a sense of the representatives' intention to betray — whether the representative had such an actual intention or not. The principals' emotional experience associated with the representatives' betrayal produces negative feelings, such as a desire to punish the representatives or the principals wanting to distance themselves from the representatives. The emotional reaction is stronger and the desire to punish is even greater when the damages are great or, at least perceived by the principals as such.[1] In the earlier love-lost story, Guy feels betrayed by his good friend, Jim. The very risky interim agreement meant a great deal of potential damage for Guy. Even though Jim had no intention of harming Guy, Guy reacted emotionally by threatening to harm Jim's career and reputation.

2.2. *Ambiguous Instructions*

When principals do not convey clear instructions to their representatives about how to act and what to aim for during the negotiation, the representatives must find their own interpretation for their principals' interests and objectives. A representative confronting expressions such as: "do your best" or "you know what to do; you're more experienced than I am", may be confused regarding their principals' actual intentions. In such cases, representatives have a wide range of possibilities for essential decision-making during the negotiation. They may also negotiate according to their own preferences,

---

[1] Koehler, J.J. and Gershoff, A.D. (2003), Betrayal Aversion: When Agents of Protection Become Agents of Harm, *Organizational Behavior and Human Decision Processes*, Vol. 90(2), pp. 244–261.

which may include gratifying their own self-serving interests. In the earlier love story, Guy's instructions are ambiguous. Jim conducts the negotiation according to his own understanding, including his personal interest in Gale.

Ambiguous instructions is only one reason why representatives sometimes make erroneous decisions. At times, inherent misunderstandings take place between principals and their representatives about the basic negotiation issues. For example, in medical malpractice lawsuits there are often misunderstandings between plaintiffs (the principals) and their lawyers about what the litigation is all about. While plaintiffs may have substantial demands (such as the laying off of the medical doctor in question or the closing of certain medical departments), all their demands are often rapidly translated by their lawyers into only monetary compensation, with no comprehension of the plaintiffs' feelings, attitudes and specific demands.[2] The problem of ambiguous instructions and misunderstandings intensifies even more when the representatives simultaneously represent several principals with incompatible objectives.

2.3. *The Delegation of Authority*

Level of authority delegation can be perceived as a spectrum — beginning with a minimum delegation of authority and ending with a complete delegation of authority. An example of a minimum level of authority is appointing a representative as someone who is supposed to present only the principals' ideas and suggestions to the opponents. An example of a full delegation of authority is delegating power of attorney. Partial delegation of authority can be granted to the representatives in several forms, such as the delegation of authority for only certain subjects; the delegation of authority conditional upon the obligation to report back to the principal after each negotiation session or the delegation of authority solely for the negotiation process, but not the final outcome, to which the principal has to consent. The principals' decision regarding the amount of delegated authority is crucial and often problematic. If principals delegate only limited authority to their representatives, the representatives may reject a profitable agreement, which is outside the limits of their authority, thus causing their principals a loss. Limited authority can cause a similar result if the representatives refuse any

---

[2]Relis, T. (2006), It's Not About the Money: A Theory on Misconceptions of Plaintiffs' Litigation Aims, *University of Pittsburgh Law Review*, Vol. 68(2), pp. 341–386.

suggestion that exceeds their terms of reference. Moreover, low or limited representatives' authority may be perceived by the other side as an indication that the representatives lack credibility.[3] It is noteworthy that the delegation of minimal authority or, at times, even partial authority, accompanied by monitoring and reporting demands, often damages principal-representative relationships.

In the case of the delegation of full authority — as in a power of attorney situation — the representatives may use this authority to further their own inclinations and agendas, including their own self-serving interests. Thus, they may achieve an undesirable outcome for their principals.[4]

In the earlier love-lost story, Guy at first delegates full authority to Jim — his representative, only to discover that he is in danger of losing all his assets in the event of a divorce. Accordingly, in the second stage of the negotiation, he delegates almost no authority to Jim, and demands that Jim account for "each cup of coffee". The sense of betrayal felt by Guy on the one hand, and Jim's frustration on the other, damages the relationships between Guy and Jim (who used to be good friends), making it impossible for Jim to reach any agreement at all.

2.4. *Communication Complexity*

A direct negotiation between disputants involves a single line of communication between negotiators and their opponents. However, even a direct single line is not without communication barriers. The disputants may have problems formulating messages, overcoming barriers related to delivering the messages, and problems decoding and understanding the original meaning of each messages. Furthermore, the communication becomes much more complex when representatives enter the communication circle: First, principals communicate their wishes to their representatives; second, the representatives communicate with each other. In addition, principals can also communicate with one another and, in rare cases, principals may communicate with the other side's representatives. These multiple lines of communication between all of the negotiating participants are highly problematic.

---

[3]Fisher, R. and Davis, W. (1999), Authority of an Agent: When is Less Better? in Mnookin, R.H. and Susskind, L.E. (eds.), *Negotiating on Behalf of Others*, Sage Publications, pp. 59–85.

[4]Fassina, N.E. (2002), Direct and Representative Negotiation: A Principal-Agent Authority Continuum, *SSRN Working Paper Series*, April, 2002.

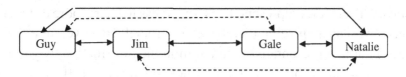

Figure 1:   Six lines of communication — between all parties involved in the story

The communication barriers are magnified; each line has its own specific problems.

At the end of the earlier mentioned love-lost story, furious, angry and frustrating discussions take place between all of the involved parties, resulting in six lines of communications (see Figure 1) — a situation which could not end well. As a result, Guy and Natalie's wedding is canceled and Jim and Gale find themselves in a conflict they cannot resolve. In short, everybody is miserable.

2.5. *Representatives and Information Leaks*

It is questionable how much information should be revealed to representatives. There is always a possibility that representatives will share their principals' confidential information with the opponents, despite their first obligations to their principals. Representatives may share information with the other side in order to make an impression and show their importance, in an attempt to gain some benefits from the opponents, or both.[5] In the above love-lost story, Gale revealed confidential information regarding Natalie's financial situation to Jim, perhaps hoping to convince him to concur with the interim agreement in Natalie's favor.

2.6. *Representatives' Reliability*

When appointing representatives, the principals may become partially, and sometimes even completely, dependent on their representatives' performance and reports. Information asymmetry may emerge, as representatives receive essential information that is unknown to their principals. Frequently, most of the principals' information about the negotiation proceeding, including the representatives' decisions and achievements, comes from the representatives

---

[5] Kurtzberg, T. Moore, D. Valley, K. and Bazerman, M.H. (1999), Agents in Negotiation, in R.H. Mnookin, and LE. Susskind, (eds.), *Negotiating on Behalf of Others*, Sage Publications, pp. 283–298.

themselves. Therefore, representatives' readiness to share more or less information, as well as their reliability, becomes crucial. However, at times even the most reliable representatives tend to limit the information they report on to their principals, in order to avoid principals' criticism. If the principals are unable to monitor the representatives' behavior, they are completely in the hands of the representatives. If their representatives are unreliable, the principals' perceptions about what is truly happening in the negotiation may be wrong. Based on this misconception, principals may well be unable to accurately predict whether the negotiation outcome will be to their benefit. This is certainly an unpleasant feeling, which sometimes calls for criticism. Yet, even reliable representatives who report everything may expect some level of disapproval regarding their behavior and decisions.

In the earlier love-lost story, Jim was a reliable representative and reported all of the information regarding the interim agreement. As a result, he was harshly criticized and humiliated by Guy — his principal.

2.7. *Representatives' Costs and Self-Serving Behavior*

Disputants who wish to employ representatives often take into consideration only the representatives' remuneration. They usually assume that in return for the money they pay in exchange for the representatives' services, the representatives will be loyal and act only in their —the principals' — best interests. Disputants often do not take into account the heavy costs of representatives' erroneous decisions, as well as their self-serving behavior. Representatives frequently have a "split personality": On the one hand, they need to protect and promote their principals' interests. On the other hand, they have their own interests and agendas, apart from their remuneration. If the principals' interests and those of the representatives contradict one another, there is a high probability that representatives will prefer to promote their own interests, even at the expense of neglecting their principals' interests. There are several main types of representatives' self-serving behavior, which act against the principals' interests[6]: An insufficient drive to promote the principals' interests, extravagant behavior (for example, extravagant efforts to amplify the representative's self-image), telling the principals' secrets to the other side in order to present an image of importance, in addition to the

---

[6]Thepot, J. (2015), Negative Agency Costs, *Theory and Decision*, Vol. 78(3), pp. 411–428.

expectation of rewards and benefits from the other side. For example, union delegates may sometimes betray their constituency in exchange for material benefits or promotion.

In the earlier love-lost story, Jim was ready to waive Guy's property in order to gain Gale's love. Thus, representatives' behavior may be much more costly than their remuneration.

3. Possible Advantages of Employing Representatives

Empirical studies have found that the rate of agreements achieved in direct negotiation between disputants is significantly higher than the rate of agreements achieved by negotiating representatives.[7] Thus, from the simple point of view of agreement rates, it is better for disputants to negotiate directly without the problems and the costs of employing representatives. This raises the question of why negotiating with representatives is so prevalent.

Some agreements cannot be reached without representatives. For example, for organized labor, large groups, firms, etc. it is impossible to negotiate without representatives. Yet, usually in negotiations between individuals, disputants can choose between negotiating directly and employing representatives. Even when there is a choice between direct negotiation and negotiation with representatives, disputants are often motivated to employ representatives. In such cases, the negotiators main motivation is the assumption that representatives can better confront the conflict and are more capable of generating an agreement, which will be better than any agreement the negotiators could achieve by negotiating directly. Obviously, there are various advantages to employing representatives.

3.1. *Representatives' Knowledge and Skills*

One important advantage is the representative's knowledge and skills, both in relation to negotiation as well as the conflicting issues at hand. For example, in a conflict regarding a prenuptial agreement or a final business contract, it is reasonable to employ a lawyer as a representative. Lawyers know the laws, regulations, and legal procedures. They are familiar with similar precedents

---

[7] Schotter, A. Zheng, W. and Snyder, B. (2000), Bargaining through Agents: An Experimental Study of Delegation of Commitment, *Games and Economic Behavior*, Vol. 30(2) pp. 248–292.

and may know how to best resolve the conflict.[8] In short, lawyers as representatives may have a significant advantage when the disputed issues demand legal knowledge and experience. In such cases, lawyers may achieve a better agreement for their principals. However, principals without experience and knowledge of legal procedures have no way to accurately evaluate the lawyers' concessions during the negotiation or the final agreement they have achieved for them.

3.2. *Connections and Networking*

Another important advantage in employing representatives is their acquaintanceships, connections, and being part of a network with the "right people". For example, due to representatives' participation in professional networks or by maintaining a central office, they can acquire knowledge that would otherwise be impossible to obtain. Through acquaintanceships with important decision-makers, representatives may find added opportunities to influence the negotiation; as a result, they can better contribute to their principals' final agreement. For example, lawyers may know judges and court commissioners. Other representatives may know politicians and leading businessmen, who can help promote their principals' interests and improve their achievements.

3.3. *Minimizing Emotional Stress*

Negotiators' (principals) emotional stress may create additional communication barriers. Negotiators may refuse to talk directly to their opponents, try to mislead their opponents, and even harm them if possible. Such emotions may divert the negotiation from focusing on the actual negotiation issues, causing the now-emotional disputants to attack each other over completely unrelated issues. For example, an emotional negotiation between a couple that wants to divorce may even develop into a physical argument. Thus, an additional advantage to employing representatives is expanding the physical and social gap between the disputants, thus reducing emotional pressures. Hence, the prevention of principals' direct interaction enables the relaxation of all parties involved in the negotiation, and decreases stress levels during the process. The high emotions accompanying a divorce, when negotiating

---

[8]Roberson, L. (2006), Negotiation Strategies: Civility and Cooperation without Compromising Advocacy, American Journal of Family Law, Vol. 20(1), pp. 7–20.

over mutual property and especially when discussing the child's custody arrangement, may be a good reason to minimize the couple's direct contact with one another and reduce their emotional stress levels by employing representatives.

3.3.1. *Representatives' tactics*

Representatives can be of help in using tactics such as playing for time, shaking off authority and playing the "good negotiator/bad negotiator" game. Representatives can stall for time by requesting time out to urgently consult with their principals regarding the issue/s on the negotiation "table". They can come back to the negotiation "table" after a long period of time, thus delaying unwanted conclusions, in the meantime allowing their principals to look for better alternatives. In addition, representatives can shake off authority by claiming that while they completely understand and accept the opponents' demands, it is their principals who cannot accept such demands or *vice versa*. They can play the tough guys during the negotiation process, enabling their principals to be the good guys and accept some "softened" conclusions or compromises.

4. Representing Organizations

The role of organizations' representatives, whether representing business companies, labor organizations, nations, etc. is both difficult and challenging. Instead of representing one principal, they may represent hundreds to millions of constituencies, as well as complex organizations. Organizations are comprised of many members — individuals, groups, departments, etc. These members often have different interests and objectives, which frequently conflict with one another. In addition to conflicts over other matters, they may also disagree about the manner in which their representatives should conduct their negotiation. For the representatives, this means that there is no one single source from which they may receive instructions, draw authority, receive necessary information and mutually identify the desired objectives. Moreover, organizational representatives may receive conflicting instructions and demands from different organizational departments. To make the situation even more complicated, too often several representatives, with no connection or coordination, represent the same organization, at the same time, during the same negotiation.

4.1. *The Problem of Multiple Principals*

Since organizations are complex entities, they are often unable to reach a unanimous decision about how to conduct and what to aim for in the negotiation. This is a consequence of three levels of conflict within the organization regarding the negotiation. Conflict between the organization's various departments; conflict between organizational levels, such as between superiors and their subordinates; and conflict between the organizational members who are authorized to give instructions to the organizations' representatives. As a result, the representatives often receive opposing and unclear instructions, and have to decide by themselves how to actually manage the negotiation. On the one hand, such conflicts may give the representatives a wide range of discretion, including making self-serving decisions about how to conduct the negotiation. On the other hand, if some or all of their multiple principals are not satisfied with their conduct or the negotiation outcome, the representatives will most likely become the organization's scapegoats. In this situation, the representatives face great difficulties. They must confront their opponents' strategies and tactics, without making mistakes about their principals' preferences. The easiest way for representatives to confront such difficulties is to use aggressive strategies and tactics toward the opponents, in an effort to comply with the norms of the organization's more aggressive department. This is because the more aggressive departments of the organization, even as minorities, are usually the most influential ones in the organization. Furthermore, exhibiting a cooperative attitude towards the opponents can be perceived as risking the organization's interests, as well as disloyalty on the part of the representatives. Therefore, in the absence of clear instructions, organizational representatives tend to negotiate aggressively.[9]

4.2. *The Problem of Multiple Representatives*

Organizations are obviously not homogeneous entities, including individuals and departments with different objectives. When representatives represent two different departments in the same company, which fail to reach a consensus regarding their representatives' instructions, they may receive two

---

[9] Steinel, W. De Dreu, C.K.W. Quwehand, E. and Ramirez-Marin, J.Y. (2009), When Constituencies Speak in Multiple Tongues: The Relative Persuasiveness of Hawkish Minorities in Representative Negotiation, *Organization Behavior and Human Decision Processes*, Vol. 109(1), pp. 67–78.

sets of instructions regarding their expected behavior during the negotiation. For example, one set of instructions from the R&D department and another from the Marketing department. The different sets of instructions from the two departments creates ambiguity in regard to the question of how to best conduct the negotiation. In this case, the representatives have a wide, but problematic, range of decision-making possibilities regarding the best way to conduct the negotiation.

In addition, it is not unusual that different departments within the same organization send their own representatives to negotiate on their behalf, as they do not trust the representative sent by the other departments. Consequently, in addition to multiple principals, there are also multiple representatives. If all of these representatives work together as a team, in the form of a delegation, disturbing disagreements may arise among them regarding the best way to negotiate. As there is no consensus among the multiple principals on the desirable strategies and tactics to be used during the negotiation, achieving consensus among the delegation of representatives is very difficult, if not impossible. Taking into account the different self-interests of each delegation member, it is more than likely that the negotiation will reach an impasse. However, representatives do not always work together as a delegation and each department sends its own individual representative to the negotiation. This is the worst scenario, as the opponents are approached by different strategies used by different representatives of the same organization. In this case, opponents will most likely be bewildered, and not really understand with whom they should negotiate. This undermines the trustworthiness and reliability of both the organization and some or all of their representatives during the negotiation process.[10] Consensus among both principals and representative is therefore essential, but often hard to achieve, for efficient negotiation with opponents.

4.3. *The Influence of the Organization versus the Influence of the Representatives*

Though there is no doubt that representatives' attitudes and relationships influence the negotiation process and outcome, organizations, despite their heterogeneity, are often much more influential than their representatives.

---

[10]Rabbitt, E.F. (1999), Challenges for International Diplomatic Agents, in Mnookin, R.H. and Susskind, E.L. (eds.), *Negotiating on Behalf of Others*, Sage Publications, pp. 135–150.

When representatives negotiate on behalf of their organizations, their individual attitudes and relationships are often put aside in face of the organization's demands.[11] There are some major reasons for the greater power and influence of organizations compared to their representatives.

First, organizations usually remain stable over time, while their representatives are changeable. The attitudes of their former representatives may not resemble those of the newly appointed representatives, who may think and behave differently than those who preceded them. In addition, representatives' attitudes prevail mainly on the personal level and it is often hard for representatives to change their organization's attitudes. For example, good relationships between both sides' representatives, in most cases, will not necessarily lead to good relations between the disputing organizations. However, when there is a change — for better or worse — in the relations between the disputing organizations, the representatives' attitudes might also be affected. Good relations between organizations may generate a positive rapport between their representatives, and *vice versa*.

Second, during the negotiation, representatives may identify with the opponents, either because they believe the opponents' demands are just, or because of some beneficial rewards offered to them by the opponents. Such identification may lead to a possibility of far-reaching concessions to the opponents during the negotiations. In such cases, the organizations may decide to step in and take control — either by persuading the representatives to adopt another approach or simply by replacing them with other representatives.

Third, in many typical situations during the negotiation, the representatives are often more extreme than their organizations — an attitude which is supposed to protect them from allegations of being disloyal. In these cases, the principals are usually able to force their representatives to use more favorable attitudes towards their opponents. In general, as far as negotiation between organizations is concerned — and despite their possible intrinsic problems — organizations are more influential than their representatives. As a result they may be more influential when it comes to both the negotiation process and outcome.

---

[11]Faizullaev, A. (2014), Diplomatic Interaction and Negotiation, *Negotiation Journal*, Vol. 30(3), pp. 275–299.

5. Representatives' Behaviors and their Evaluation

Evaluation of the representatives' behaviors is somewhat problematic. It depends on the different points of view of the principals — whether individuals, groups or organization — on one hand, and the representatives' point of view, on the other. Principals convey their expectations to their representatives, who are expected to achieve these expectations. However, in order to achieve the maximum gains by employing representatives, principals often overstate their expectations and demands. Thus, the representatives are, in fact, supposed to achieve higher goals than that which their principals would have achieved were they to negotiate on their own.[12] Representatives are also required to achieve these goals as if they were their own. This makes sense because by maximizing their principals' gains, they may consequently maximize their own compensation. Furthermore, representatives are often also expected to achieve their principals' expectations and demands within the shortest possible timeframe, as there are high costs to the ongoing negotiation process. However, continuation of the process may be of interest to the representatives, especially if their remuneration is time-dependent. Representatives sometimes face a dilemma: If a minimally acceptable agreement could be achieved in a short period of time, their principals might be dissatisfied. On the other hand, would their principals be satisfied if they continued the negotiation with the intention of achieving a better agreement — albeit at a higher cost and with accompanying potential risks? And how would their principals react in this case if, in the end, they wound up achieving less than what was expected? By deciding to accept the minimal agreement, the representatives may feel their behavior is appropriate. Their principals, however, may have a different perception of their representatives' behavior. This is partly because principals have higher expectations of their representatives, and partly because principals are often detached from the process and unable to evaluate whether or not it is truly necessary to prolong the negotiation process. As a result, in both cases principals may harshly evaluate their representatives' decisions to either shorten or lengthen the negotiation time, and also their minimal (from the principals' point of view) achievements.

---

[12]Friedman, R. and Goates, N. (2012), The Matter of Constituents' Behavior When Negotiating Through Agents: An Empirical Investigation, *SSRN Working Paper Series*, November, 2012.

Moreover, in order to achieve an agreement, any agreement, representatives have to approach the opponents. The closer their contact with the opponents is, the higher the probability of achieving an agreement. Yet, the closer the representatives become to the opponents, the more the principals will suspect, even distrust their representatives' behavior. Thus, if representatives engage in essential and close contact with the other side in an attempt to reach an agreement, principals may tend to evaluate this behavior negatively. In addition, if the representatives are generally incompatible with their principals' predispositions, preferences and inordinately high expectations, even representatives' appropriate behavior and achievements may be perceived as dissatisfying and a failure by their principals. Moreover, principals who are emotionally involved in the negotiation — i.e. harbor negative emotions towards the other party — may, under the influence of such emotional stress, lose their ability to properly evaluate their representatives' behavior.[13] By and large, representatives may evaluate their behavior as appropriate and justify it — both for themselves and their principals. At the same time, principals may negatively evaluate their representatives' behavior, justifying their evaluation from their own point of view. Therefore, even negotiating in accordance with the principals' preferences may be risky for representatives. If the principals, for one reason or another, do not like the way the negotiation is conducted or dislike either the interim or final outcome, they may blame their representatives for what they subjectively perceive as a failure. On the part of the representatives, such blaming may lead to feelings of insult and frustration. Moreover, the representatives can only hope that if and when the decisions they make are found to be wrong in the eyes of one or all their principals, they will not be turned into scapegoats — their position and reputation irreparably damaged.

Practical Applications

- Employing representatives to negotiate on your behalf is problematic, both in terms of cost, erroneous decisions and communication problems. However, if you do not have essential knowledge of the negotiation's issues, are not an expert negotiator or need

---

[13]Fassina, N.E. (2004), Constraining a Principal's Choice Outcome versus Behavior Contingent on Representative Negotiations, *Negotiation Journal*, Vol. 20(3), pp. 435–459.

the representatives' connections and networking skills to promote your negotiation interests, the most reasonable decision is to try and employ the right representative. In addition, being highly emotionally involved in the negotiation is not good for either your health or the negotiation process and outcome. A representative can reduce such emotional involvement by distancing you and your opponents — both physically and mentally.

- Do not expect your representatives to always promote your interests in the negotiation. Your representatives have their own interests, as well as yours. In the case of conflicting interests, you can expect your representatives to first promote their own interests. In order to avoid such problems, you should be very careful in your choice of representatives and, afterwards, follow the negotiation process as closely as possible and try to control your representative.

- Giving ambiguous or no instructions may confuse your representatives. Try to make your instructions as clear as possible. Try to explain specifically what you expect from your representatives and, last but not least, demand a reliable and accurate report at each stage of the negotiation.

- Do not give full authority to your representatives at the beginning of the process, even if they are your best friends. Try to delegate authority in accordance with the negotiation process. A limited delegation of authority should be given at the beginning of the negotiation. Additional delegation of authority can be given if the negotiation process continues to your satisfaction .The authority to attain a final conclusion should be granted at the end of the negotiation if, and only if, you have first received a satisfactory report regarding the final agreement. However, take into consideration that delegating only very limited authority to your representatives may make them appear unreliable in the eyes of your opponents, causing them to reject your representatives' suggestions and demands.

- Consider your representatives' problems. In order to reach an agreement, your representatives must approach and even "draw closer" to your opponents. Do not be in a hurry to blame them for being disloyal or punish them. They might be doing their best to reach a good agreement on your behalf.

- Beware of revealing too much information to your representatives. Choose the information you reveal at each stage of the negotiation with caution. Some representatives tend to share information and may even do so with your opponents.

- Representatives can help you by using various tactics during the negotiation. They can help you stall for time and thus delay unwanted decisions. They can pass their delegated authority upwards, enabling you to reject what they believe are bad conclusions. They can also play the "bad guys", enabling you to be the "good guys".

- As a representative, it is highly important to ask for clear instructions. If you represent more than one principal, it is essential that a consensus is reached among the various groups/entities that constitute your principal. You should know specifically what is expected of you and how you are expected to behave during the negotiation. Take into consideration that if something goes wrong during the negotiation — because of ambiguous instructions or a misunderstanding — your principals may make you their scapegoat. To defend yourself against this possible eventuality, demand guarantees for your protection.

Chapter 14
Concluding Remarks

All good things come to an end, as has our short tour of the World of Negotiation. Of course, as with any tour, it is impossible to include everything. However, it IS possible to include the most important and essential "points of interest". So, let us now conclude our tour.

Negotiation is a way to manage and resolve conflicts. If there is no conflict, there is no need for negotiation. Negotiation is not a new phenomenon; it has been practiced since ancient times. Metaphorically, people have long been negotiating conflicts with others — and even with their God(s). So what, in fact, is new in the world of negotiation? The answer is: A growing body of ever-increasing knowledge about human behavior before, during and at the end of negotiation process. In recent decades, both practitioners and researchers have found certain consistencies in human behavior during negotiation situations. These findings have made it possible to study and approach negotiation systematically, with a great deal of newly acquired knowledge.

During our tour, this essential knowledge and the negotiation "basics" were presented. We discussed key theories, research findings and practical observations in a comprehensive and systematic way. Our approach to negotiation was interdisciplinary, discussing theories and research findings from a variety of disciplines, such as: Decision-Making, Conflict Resolution, Labor Relations, Economics, and Game Theory as well as Marketing, Psychology, Sociology, Organizational Behavior, Industrial Relations and Political Science. At times, there seems to be a gap between theory and practice. Some academicians are dedicated to the so-called "pure" theory, whereas other practitioners feel this approach is too abstract and irrelevant when it comes to real-life negotiations.[1] This book adopts Kurt Lewin's motto: "There is nothing more practical than a good theory". Accordingly, it seems that the perceived gap between negotiation theory and practice is, to a large extent, artificial. Negotiation theories and research findings significantly contribute to the practical negotiation aspect while, at the same time, practical experiences also contribute to the growing body of theoretical knowledge. Thus, although this book is not a "how-to" book, the theories and knowledge in this volume are, nevertheless, easily translated into practical applications.

Recall that some negotiation theories deal with competitive behaviors and their benefits, while others discuss cooperative behaviors and their advantages during negotiation. It is often assumed that cooperative behavior leads to a better process and negotiation outcome than competitive behavior. However, upon further examination, negotiators' behavior during the negotiation process often indicates a type of hybrid behavior — a combination of both cooperative and competitive behaviors. Thus, it is quite likely that it is this type of hybrid behavior that leads to improved negotiation processes and outcomes.

Generally, the negotiation process can be divided into five stages, which are not mutually exclusive: The pre-negotiation stage, the preparation stage, presenting the initial offers (the negotiators' objectives) stage, the "haggling" stage, and the final concluding stage.

The pre-negotiation stage. In this stage, disputants have to choose from among various conflict confrontation alternatives, carefully considering, their Best Alternatives to Negotiated Agreement (*BATNA*s) and Worst Alternative to Negotiated Agreement (*WATNA*s). The various available choices, as well the advantages and disadvantages of each choice, are discussed. The following stages are relevant only if negotiation is the disputants' preferred choice of conflict resolution.

The preparation stage. Gathering intelligence is the most important aspect of the preparation stage. However, negotiators encounter various problems

---

[1] See discussion in Avruch, K. and Nan, S.A. (2013), Practice in the Academy Introduction: The Constraints and Opportunities of Practicing Conflict Resolution from Academic Settings, *Negotiation Journal*, Vol. 29(2), pp. 205–212.

when attempting to gather intelligence, such as asymmetrical information, framing and humans' short memory capacity. Some insights into these problems are provided.

Choosing the negotiation location may also be problematic. Negotiators do not always take into consideration the advantages and disadvantages of each location, and also may disagree on the preferred location. The various possible decisions regarding the negotiation location are also discussed.

Finally, during the preparation stage, negotiators are often in need of external assistance. Such assistance can be in the form of human support, e-negotiation support or both. Both human and e-negotiation support are discussed.

Presenting the initial offers stage. Identifying the negotiators' highest objectives is the third stage. Proper presentation of the initial offers requires being well-acquainted with the negotiators' overt and covert interests, as well as the relations between interests and objectives. It also requires knowledge regarding the gap between intention and resistance points, and its implications for the initial presenting of the negotiators' objectives. Essential knowledge of these focal issues is provided, together with insights into their influence on the negotiation process and their impact on the negotiation outcome.

The "haggling" stage. During this stage, negotiators must be aware of all their power sources, as well as those of their opponents. Asymmetrical power has a significant impact on the negotiators' "haggling" potential. The negotiators must also be acquainted with all available strategies and tactics. Discussion and use of important strategies and tactics are also systematically presented.

The concluding stage. This stage can either end in an impasse or an agreement. There is always the question of which is better. Some advocate reaching an agreement, even at a heavy cost. Others argue that an impasse, or no agreement, is better than a bad agreement. Such arguments, as well as all the other negotiation stages, are influenced by values, cultures, ethics and issues related to trust, distrust and suspicion. These important issues all have a weighty impact on the negotiation process and outcome and are discussed in detail.

Globalization has changed, among others, many business and political procedures. But it has not done away with cultural values. Therefore, all the negotiation stages are influenced by the negotiators' values which are usually culturally dependant. Moreover, they are also influenced by relationships, trust, distrust and suspicion. The perception of ethical and unethical behaviors of all parties involved in the negotiation are also influential during all the negotiation stages.

Readers may also receive some insights into negotiators' diverse *perceptions*, which are extremely influential during negotiation. Negotiators do not always behave or make decisions based on objective truths, but rather act according to their own individual perceptions, i.e. their *subjective rationality*. This subjective rationality serves as the basis for many negotiators' decisions. The impacts of similarities, the Endowment Effect and emotions, are just a few examples of the negotiators' *subjective perceptions*. Both negotiators' *objective perceptions* and *subjective perceptions* are not always visible at the negotiation "table". Nevertheless, they both still have a great impact on the negotiation process and outcome. To a large extent, such negotiators' perceptions dictate the way in which they conduct the negotiation.

Sometimes negotiators chose, voluntarily or involuntarily, not to negotiate directly with their opponents, but to have a third-party intervention in the negotiation. Such a third-party intervention can be in the form of mediation or in the form of representatives. Obviously, third-party interventions have a significant influence on the negotiators' behaviors, the communication between the parties, the relationships between the negotiators and the third parties, as well as on the negotiation outcome and its short or long-term durability. The advantages and disadvantages of third-party interventions are debated.

Negotiating hostage-taking scenarios with terrorist groups is an extreme form of negotiation and a very risky one — as its outcome means life or death for the hostages. Unfortunately, it is a realistic illustration of problems typical to all negotiations conducted under high-pressure or crisis conditions.

Our world is always in flux and has continually experienced transitions, transformations and changes throughout history. These changes have led to new problems and raised new kinds of conflicts. The conflicts might change, and the problems may vary, but, human nature in negotiation situations has remained fairly constant. The continually expanding body of accumulated knowledge regarding conflicts and negotiation has been — and will continue to be — the best guide on our tour and understanding of the World of Negotiation.

Author Index

Subject Index

Printed in the United States
By Bookmasters